FOLLOW ME THROUGH

FOLLOW ME THROUGH

THE UPS AND DOWNS OF AN RAF FLYING INSTRUCTOR

MIKE BROOKE

The History Press

For my mum Lorna, my wife Linda and all our children and grandchildren

Front cover illustrations, from top: Chipmunks in close formation
(Gavin Mackay); Canberra T4 WE 192 (Author's collection).
Back cover illustration: The author (left) and fellow instructor Flt Lt
Hector Skinner. (Gavin Mackay)

First published 2013

The History Press
The Mill, Brimscombe Port
Stroud, Gloucestershire, GL5 2QG
www.thehistorypress.co.uk

British Library Cataloguing in Publication Data.
A catalogue record for this book is available from the British Library.

ISBN 978 0 7524 9701 3

Typesetting and origination by The History Press
Printed in Great Britain

CONTENTS

ACKNOWLEDGEMENTS

Writing an autobiographical book is an absorbing pastime. Like a good day's fishing it takes one away from the everyday cares of life. It also takes one back to the sunlit uplands of one's youth, where the ravages of time and old age are still far in the future. My wonderful wife Linda has already been through this process with me once during the three months that I was writing my first book: *A Bucket of Sunshine*. Then she would lose me to my study for hours on end, while I regressed to the years of my childhood and early twenties. Now I have repeated the exercise and, once more, she has been my proof-reader, editor and critic. After all, she did such a good job on my first volume, how could I refuse her the chance to do it again? And she did so with consummate skill, patience and alacrity. I cannot thank her enough. As always she is the wind beneath my wings.

Thanks must also go to Matt Savage of Mach One Manuals in Australia (www.mach-one-manuals.net) for letting me reproduce the cockpit photographs that appear in the Appendix. And to Ray Deacon for his permission to use the Canberra PR9 photographs that he provided; credits are given with the captions. I also sincerely thank all the folk at The History Press who have been brave enough to take me on again. I hope that you will agree with me that they have done another great job in the production of this book.

And last, but by no means least, I want to sincerely thank Air Vice Marshal Gavin Mackay for writing the Foreword to this book and providing so many great photographs of those far-off, fun-filled days in Glasgow, when we were both much younger!

FOREWORD

'Date: 5 January 1967. Aircraft: Chipmunk WG431. Captain: Sqn Ldr Etches. Pupil: Self. Exercises: Effects of Controls, Taxying, Straight & Level. Dual: 1 Hour.'

Even now, more than forty-six years later, seeing the logbook entry of my first sortie as a new and very excited cadet pilot on the Universities of Glasgow and Strathclyde Air Squadron (UGSAS) makes my heart beat that little bit faster and brings memories flooding back.

I was studying Civil Engineering at Glasgow University. My future lay in bridges, buildings, roads and dams, with McAlpine, Wimpey, Taylor Woodrow or the like. That plan did not long survive my encounter with UGSAS and its members, brought so vividly to life in this book about Mike Brooke's time as a Qualified Flying Instructor (QFI).

There was the CFI, George Etches, who always wore a multi-coloured 'terrorist-chic' balaclava under his bone-dome on test sorties, to disconcert the over-confident and divert the nervous; the fearsome Hamish Logan, whose leadership of late night sessions in the bar spawned the squadron catchphrase 'Logan Must Go!' (to bed earlier); Andy Bell, my primary instructor, who kept me spellbound with tales of Hunter ground attack ops in Aden, and whispered in my ear that (as the USAF so succinctly put it), 'If you ain't single seat – you ain't sh★t'; John Greenhill, the fatherly Boss; Heck Skinner, a couthie fellow Highlander; Colin Adams, the epitome of smooth; and Ian Montgomerie, the aesthete, who landed one hot day on Summer Camp to confide that opening the canopy and holding cupped hands aloft in the 100 knot breeze was 'just like fondling bosoms' – sparking a squadron scramble airborne to investigate the phenomenon. And then there was Mike Brooke himself: a cherubic dynamo of enthusiasm for all things related to flying and the RAF; a staunch champion of English (specifically Yorkshire) attitudes and values in a chauvinistically Scottish squadron; a talented artist, whose anthropomorphic cartoons of aeroplanes still hang in the CFS Elementary Squadron crew room; and a natural leader-astray of cadet pilots. Small wonder that I and several of my contemporaries were quickly seduced away from our intended 'respectable' civilian careers as engineers, lawyers, scientists or teachers. I never looked back, and I owe Mike and his colleagues a huge debt of gratitude for setting me on the path to becoming a fighter pilot.

Like its predecessor, *A Bucket of Sunshine*, this book covers a great deal more than Mike Brooke's progress through a particular phase in his RAF service. The reader will emerge with a working knowledge of how to fly a Chipmunk, including landing by night on a flare-illuminated grass strip, recovering from a spin, coping with the perils of carburettor icing, and the art and science of the eight-point roll (thanks Mike!). There are also some top tips on piloting the Jet Provost, the Gnat, the Meteor and, of course, the Canberra – including the dreaded simulated asymmetric approach, which probably claimed more lives than the real thing. More generally, you will find vignettes on the Smith-Barry method of flying instruction used by CFS, the different types of fog affecting aviation, wake turbulence, un-pressurised high flight and the 'bends', electronic counter-measures (ECM), and how to land safely – or not – at Gibraltar. Seasoned with some suitably disreputable jokes, it encapsulates just about everything one needed to know to be an RAF pilot in the '60s and 70s.

I am quite sure that you will enjoy this book as much as I did. For the military aviator, it will revive many memories of the 'I did that' variety. For the interested amateur, it will provide some fascinating insights into RAF life and flying operations of the time. For everyone, it promises to be a thoroughly good read, told at a cracking pace in a straightforward and engaging style, typical of the Mike Brooke I came to know as our paths crossed and re-crossed in the Service. Savour it best by transporting your imagination to a 'Black Flag' day, when the promised 10 o'clock weather clearance has failed (yet again) to materialise, but the Boss hasn't yet summoned up the nerve to call a squadron 'Stack' for the afternoon. Clear away the Uckers board, get one of the JPs (junior pilots) to make you a NATO standard coffee (or a 'Witch's Tit' if you prefer black, no sugar), sink into that battered armchair in the corner, and off you go, solo.

Air Vice Marshal Gavin Mackay CB, OBE, AFC, BSc, FRAeS, RAF (retd)

INTRODUCTION

Wing Commander Michael C. Brooke, AFC RAF (retd)

Mike Brooke was born in Bradford, West Yorkshire on 22 April 1944. After a grammar school education he joined the RAF in January 1962. Subsequent to passing through all-jet flying training as a pilot he was posted to No 16 Squadron in RAF Germany, where he flew the Canberra B(I)8 in the low-level, night interdictor, strike and attack roles.

On completion of this tour he was selected for the RAF Central Flying School course where he was trained as a Qualified Flying Instructor. Three flying instructional tours followed then, in 1975, Mike attended the Empire Test Pilot's School (ETPS) and graduated as a Fixed Wing Test Pilot. After graduation he spent five years as an experimental test pilot at the Royal Aerospace Establishments at Farnborough and Bedford, at the latter commanding the Radar Research Squadron. At the beginning of 1981 Mike returned to ETPS as a tutor, where he spent three years teaching pilots from all over the world to be test pilots. In 1984 Mike was awarded the Air Force Cross (AFC) for his work within the flight test community; HM Queen Elizabeth II presented the medal to him at Buckingham Palace in November that year.

After attending the RAF Staff College's Advanced Staff Course he spent six months at HQ Strike Command, where he was a member of the Command Briefing Team. In 1985 Mike was promoted to Wing Commander and given command of Flying Wing at RAE (Royal Aircraft Establishment) Farnborough. A wide variety of aircraft came his way, including helicopters such as the Gazelle, Wessex and Sea King. After three years at Farnborough, he returned once more to Boscombe Down, this time as Wing Commander Flying, in charge of all flying support activities and deputy to the chief test pilot.

In 1994, at the age of 50, Mike decided to take voluntary redundancy. He then spent five years in part-time aviation consultancy, working as a test pilot instructor with the International Test Pilots' School, Cranfield University and as a developmental test pilot for the Slingsby Aircraft Company.

In 1998, Mike moved to Texas to fly for a company called Grace Aire, who aimed to give flight test training in their ex-RAF Hunter jet trainers, gain

US Department of Defense flight test contracts and display the Hunter at air shows. Sadly, the company went into liquidation after two years so Mike returned to Europe, choosing to live in Northern France.

In January 2002, he returned to RAF service as a full-time reservist pilot, commanding one of the RAF's eleven Air Experience Flights, which give flying experience to members of the UK's Air Cadet Organisation. He finally retired from the RAF in April 2004, on his 60th birthday. Mike has flown over 7,500 hours (mostly one at a time) on over 130 aircraft types, was a member of the Royal Aeronautical Society, a Liveryman and a Master Pilot of the Guild of Air Pilots and Air Navigators, is a Freeman of the City of London and is a Fellow of the Society of Experimental Test Pilots. He also flew many historic and vintage aircraft with The Shuttleworth Collection, The Harvard Team and Jet Heritage.

This book is a mainly humorous insight into the life of an RAF Qualified Flying Instructor (QFI) at three levels: on a University Air Squadron, at the RAF's Central Flying School and with the Canberra Operational Conversion Unit. There are, literally, many ups and downs in this tale with both humour and fear on show. Student pilots will do the most unexpected things at times and Mike pulls no punches in telling his tale.

Mike is married to Linda, they have four children and seven grandchildren. They live in France where they have restored a 230-year-old Normandy farmhouse and created a garden from a field. Mike is a licensed lay minister in the local Anglican church, which he and Linda helped to found in 2003. Linda is following in his footsteps and training for the Lay Ministry in the same church.

PROLOGUE

It is the middle of June 1962. I am 18 years old. Instead of doing what many of my erstwhile teenage school friends are doing: hiking or rock-climbing in the Yorkshire Dales, motorcycling, fishing or just hanging out in a coffee bar, on the constant lookout for female companionship, I am sitting in the left-hand seat of a dual-controlled jet aeroplane over 2 miles above those self-same Yorkshire Dales. I am there because at the beginning of the year I joined the RAF and now I am training as a pilot.

My instructor is about to teach me my first aerobatic manoeuvre: a loop. He first demonstrates one. I sit still, all eyes and ears, with a *soupcon* of trepidation and a frisson of excitement disturbing the usually lifeless butterflies in the pit of my stomach. In the right-hand seat Flight Lieutenant Wally Norton, who I must address as 'Sir', dives the aircraft, a Jet Provost Mk 3, to over 200kts and then pulls it vertically upwards, imposing a load of three times the force of gravity on our bodies. The far horizon that I can see through the windscreen ahead of me disappears downwards. All I can see now is blue sky. A few seconds later the horizon reappears, but this time at the top of the windscreen. I look upwards and see downwards to the wide panorama of my native Yorkshire countryside, laid out a little disturbingly above my head. The G-force and airspeed have both reduced markedly, but the nose of the aircraft continues to rotate and we are soon headed vertically downwards. The speed is increasing and I am forced back down into my seat as Wally pulls out and the world is once more back where it belongs.

'Well, me lad, what did you think of that?'

A little breathlessly I say, 'Amazing, sir!'

'OK. It's time for you to have a go. Follow me through.'

I place my right hand on the control column; that's its formal name – real pilots call it 'the stick'. I put my left hand on the throttle. I push my feet forward and rest them lightly on the rudder pedals. Wally and all the other instructors that I will fly with over the next two years, and who will teach me to fly ever faster and bigger jets, use this well-established routine of demonstration, instruction and practice.

I will spend most of the next forty-two years flying aircraft of many different types, in many different places. I will even spend a good few years teaching others to fly and, in doing so, would find myself frequently saying, 'Follow me through.'

PART ONE

THE CENTRAL FLYING SCHOOL

He who can, does. He who cannot, teaches.
George Bernard Shaw, *Man and Superman* (1903),
'Maxims for Revolutionists'

1 CHIPMUNKS?!

After all my training was complete, in May 1964, I was posted to my first operational tour of duty with No 16 Squadron at RAF Laarbruch in West Germany. There I flew the Canberra B(I)8 in the low-level, day and night, nuclear strike and conventional attack roles. It was an exciting time.[1] The Cold War was at its height, I was on the RAF's front line operating a flying war machine, regularly at low-level, which meant at less than 100 metres from the ground, practising bombing and shooting and being ready to react to any Warsaw Pact aggression with a nuclear weapon-loaded aircraft. It was the best of times and it was the worst of times. And there were possibilities for even more stimulating times ahead for any young man who enjoyed that sort of flying.

After only six months on the squadron I was offered the exciting possibility of moving on, two or three years later, to the supersonic, low-level strike and reconnaissance aircraft known as the BAC TSR2. However, within another six months, that option became null and void when the Labour government cancelled the project. But all was not lost. To replace the annulled TSR2 option the government announced that it would purchase the American General Dynamics F-111 swing-wing bomber. I was told that my posting would then be extended so that I could go to the USA to train on that revolutionary aircraft. However, within another year both of these proposed replacements for the Canberra had been cancelled. Further cuts and changes of mind by the Ministry of Defence then put all the low-level, tactical strike/attack eggs

in the Blackburn Buccaneer basket; an aircraft originally built for the Royal
Navy's Fleet Air Arm. But that decision came too late for me.

By early 1967 I had instead been offered an accelerated captaincy on the
Vulcan bomber; but that did not attract me at all. I wanted to fly something
fast and exciting. So I decided instead to volunteer to attend the Central
Flying School (CFS), based at RAF Little Rissington, in Gloucestershire,
where I would be taught to be a flying instructor. In May 1963, at the end
of my basic flying training course, I missed the opportunity to join the
first advanced flying training course on the new Folland Gnat trainer. That
course had been shelved as the Gnat's introduction into service had been
delayed. Instead I had been sent to fly the almost obsolete, 1940s designed,
De Havilland Vampire. So, in early 1967, seeing another opportunity to fly the
Gnat, a diminutive but sharp-pointed, swept-winged aeroplane, I asked OC
No 16 Squadron to endorse my CFS application with a recommendation for
me to join the Gnat element of the course as a student flying instructor. This
he had done with both alacrity and a pen.

Before I left Germany a large packet of forms arrived in my mailbox.
It contained lots of information about the various CFS courses, plus an abun-
dance of forms to be completed and returned soonest. As I read them I found
that most were about University Air Squadrons (UASs) and the need for their
instructors to volunteer and, preferably, to have Permanent Commissions
(PC). Although I had one of those I wasn't the least bit interested in going
to some far-flung part of the UK and flying the slow, pint-sized, propeller-
driven De Havilland Chipmunk. So I diligently ignored all the UAS bumph
and filled out the other required forms.

Eventually I received a posting notice to attend No 239 CFS Fixed Wing
Qualified Flying Instructors' (QFI) Course starting on Tuesday 30 May 1967.
As my tour in Germany was due to finish on Friday 5 May I had over three
weeks leave coming. I had married my wife, Mo, in July 1965 and she and
I had lived in a rented flat close to the base in Germany. So it was first off
home to Yorkshire for a while to see our parents and then south to RAF
Little Rissington. At 750ft above sea level it was the RAF's highest UK air-
field, uphill from the well-known Cotswolds tourist trap of Bourton-on-the-
Water. I was going to become a teacher!

When I moved from Germany back to England, away from the front line,
the world was in the grip of the frosty geo-political climate that was the Cold
War. Nuclear-armed NATO, led by the USA, was deployed across Europe in
a Mexican stand-off with the USSR and its Warsaw Pact allies, also armed
with weapons of mass destruction and superior numbers of conventional
armed forces. The USSR was still suffering from the paranoia brought about
through the loss of more than 20 million of its citizens during the Second

World War, the conflict they called the Great Patriotic War. Much of that suspicion and mistrust was brought about by Hitler's treacherous reversal of his non-aggression pact with Stalin by the 'Operation Barbarossa' invasion of the Motherland in June 1941. In the Europe of the mid-1960s there was a line drawn in the sand of the continent across which neither side dared venture.

To counter many perceived threats of the time the RAF had over 140,000 personnel and was spread across much of the old British Empire. There were four functional operational commands based in the UK: Fighter, Bomber, Coastal and Transport. Overseas there were operational squadrons in four geographical commands: Near, Middle and Far East and RAF Germany. To supply a regular corps of fully trained aircrew for these operational units Training Command had flying training schools based at ten airfields in the UK. The approximate annual requirement for pilots of all disciplines was over 400. Therefore in order to train these pilots there was a need for about 120 flying instructors per year. The Central Flying School would train all of these.

The RAF's Central Flying School (CFS) is the oldest military flying training organisation in the world. It was founded in 1911 at Upavon on Salisbury Plain, in Wiltshire, training Army and Royal Navy pilots who would form the foundation of the Royal Flying Corps. The school's development over the following decades eventually led to it becoming the single tri-service and Commonwealth unit for the specific training of Qualified Flying Instructors (QFIs). From Upavon the school moved several times in various guises before, in May 1946, it reformed at RAF Little Rissington, near Bourton-on-the-Water in Gloucestershire. By the mid-1960s the CFS had outposts at RAF Kemble, also in Gloucestershire, for Gnat training, and RAF Shawbury, in Shropshire, for helicopter training. Air forces of many nations send pilots to the CFS to gain the prestigious 'QFI' (or 'QHI' for helicopter instructors) qualification. The school also has a standardisation team that operates worldwide: they are known as Examining Wing or, more colloquially as Exam Wing, or sometimes, even more colloquially and most frequently, as 'the Trappers'. Their role is to help standardise and, where necessary, improve flying instruction. The Trappers web extends even further into the RAF's operational world through the appointment of CFS Agents, whose role is to check and maintain flying standards on the operational squadrons.

My course's first day at CFS, towards the end of May 1967, was in keeping with the traditional RAF pattern. Go to the ground-school building, sit in a classroom and fill out a whole raft of forms; with, yet again, much repetition of name, rank and number. It was like being interrogated by paperwork! Then we were given various welcome chats by the Chief Ground Instructor (CGI), the Chief Flying Instructor (CFI) and finally the Commandant, a lofty, grey-haired and distinguished looking Air Commodore.

After being given a programme of ground studies for the next two weeks, we settled into the inevitable routine of classroom lessons on aerodynamics, meteorology, aero-medical sciences and all manner of things that we'd done before. The difference this time was that the subjects were dealt with much more rigorously. The reason given was that, as flying instructors, we were expected to know all this stuff in depth, as we would have to be able to explain any or all of it to our students.

We were a cosmopolitan bunch. There were guys from Australia, Canada, the Royal Navy and the Army on the course. Also among our number were three Arab pilots, but after a few days they disappeared. Saturday 5 June was the start of the Arab-Israeli Six-Day War. I've often wondered what happened to them.

Being under 25 years of age I wasn't allowed to occupy Officers' Married Quarters (OMQs) or a 'hiring',[2] so I was living in the Officers' Mess and planned to do so for a few weeks while I found somewhere suitable and affordable to rent privately. That helped me to gel more quickly with those course members who were in the same boat.

At the end of the first week the CGI came into the coffee bar at the mid-morning break and announced that there were two places for prospective University Air Squadron instructors that had not been taken up by volunteers. He then announced that student instructors Mathieson and Brooke would be allocated those places. I was so shocked that I chased him down the corridor as he headed back to the safety of his office and asked him if he was sure that he had got that right. He told me that indeed it was correct.

'But I'm going to Gnats!' I protested.

'No you're not, young fellah. The Gnat slots have all been filled. You are going to Chipmunks.'

I was astonished and my flabber was well and truly gasted. After lunch I went back to his office and in some trepidation, knocked lightly on his door. 'Enter!' he called out.

I then explained to him that I had applied to CFS specifically volunteering to fly the Gnat and that my application form contained a glowing endorsement from my squadron commander to that effect.

'Supply and demand, old boy. You and Mathieson have Permanent Commissions and that is highly desirable for UAS instructors. Sorry but that's the way it is.'

'Would it be possible to see if I could find someone else who has a PC who would like to swap?' I asked.

'Yes, I don't see why not. You obviously feel strongly about it, but I must know for sure before the end of next week.'

So I was now a man on a mission. I first talked to the Gnat candidates but, unsurprisingly, they were very happy bunnies and were not interested in my proposition. I then chatted with a couple of guys that I knew had PCs. They were on the Jet Provost course, but again I drew a blank. I went back to the CGI to tell him that I had failed in my quest and that I wanted to see whether I could be held over for the next course. He then surprised me by saying that he had spoken to the Commandant and that the great man was willing to listen to me. I rang his Aide de Camp and got an appointment for the next day.

I duly turned up at the Commandant's outer office, best hat on, trousers pressed and shoes shone for the occasion. I was ushered in and found that I was immediately invited to sit and tell my tale. The Commandant listened attentively and gave me occasional encouraging but benign smiles. At the end of my monologue, giving him all the background, he said that he would get his personnel staff officer to see what he could do and that the latter would be in touch with me before the week was out. I stood, put my hat back on, saluted smartly and left, wondering how long I might have to wait for an answer.

It wasn't long. By mid-afternoon I had been given the news that any pause in my training would not be looked upon kindly in the ivory towers, that is if it was even sanctioned, which I was told was most doubtful. I would most likely be given some menial ground post in some backwater, which wouldn't do my career much good. I considered all this for a few moments and realised that I would rather be flying anything than being the Families Officer in the Outer Hebrides for a year!

'OK,' I admitted, 'You win – I'll carry on with the Chipmunk course and hope that I get to an interesting UAS.'

Having hoped to be flying the small, modern and fast jet trainer known appropriately as the Gnat, I really had not wanted to fly something old, slow and propeller-driven; even if it, too, was small.

So at the end of the second week half a dozen others and I moved down the flight line to the hangar where D Flight of No 3 Squadron, CFS and their fleet of Chipmunks operated. We found that we were next door to E Flight, who operated the twin-piston engined Vickers Varsity, on which the multi-engined instructors of our band of brothers would be trained. The rest of the course, numbering about twelve, was at the other end of the flight line with one of the two Jet Provost squadrons.

Over coffee we met the staff instructors, a formidable band of folk, many of whom seemed easily old enough to be our fathers. One such officer, a silver haired, bluff northerner, Flight Lieutenant Jack Hindle, picked me out and announced that he would be my instructor. I noticed immediately that he was wearing a rather ornate No 16 Squadron badge.

'I've just come from 16 Squadron,' I said. 'What did you fly when you were on the squadron?'

With no hint of a smile, but a wicked twinkle in his eye he replied, 'Westland Wapitis.'[3] I thought that this was a curious answer because, as far as I knew, No 16 Squadron hadn't operated Wapitis and, anyway, he wasn't that old. However, I let it pass for the moment; it was just a taste of his wry northern humour. I discovered later that Jack had flown Hawker Tempests[4] with No 16 Squadron, after the war. His experience had, along with that of a couple of other D Flight staff instructors, landed him a role in the *Battle of Britain* film, which had only recently been completed. He told me that he had been too well built and the wrong age to do the action shots of running out to the aircraft. He had just flown the Spitfires or Hurricanes for the aerial shots. Lucky chap! Maybe something good could come out of flying these little tail-wheeled trainers, I wondered silently. Maybe, one day, experience of operating a Chipmunk might lead to offers of flying bigger 'tail-draggers'? But the next thing was more immediate: to start flying again and then learning to talk at the same time.

2 LEARNING TO FLY AGAIN

After a month or so I had found somewhere for Mo and I to live: a one-bedroom flat over an antiques shop on the edge of the market place in Stow-on-the-Wold. Our three rooms overlooked the local police station. I had also bought myself a 350cc BSA motorcycle for commuting the 5 miles to work, thus leaving our 1965 MG Midget for Mo to use. So, having unpacked the various boxes and cases that had arrived from Germany, we were soon settled into a new life as residents of a Cotswolds market town; a big change from my urban upbringing in West Yorkshire and our tiny flat in a small German village.

Back at work the course had now split into its separate specialist groups for even more classroom work. We Chipmunk operators were being acquainted with the mysteries of the Gipsy Major engine with its simple carburettor; valve lead, lag and overlap; twin magnetos and the four-stroke cycle, named after some chap called Otto — *vorsprung durch technik?!*[5] Not all this technical content was completely new to me as, in my youth, I had dismantled and re-mantled motorcycle engines many times — much to the despair of my father when he wanted to get the car into the garage. A new thing, to me at least, was the fact that the engine, tiny though it was, had three levers to control it! Jets had just one: the throttle. You got more or less thrust simply by moving the single lever forward and back; the throttle controlled how much fuel went into the engine to be burned. Simple! But in the Chipmunk we had the throttle to control the power, the mixture lever to make sure that the ratio of air and fuel going into the engine was correct and the carburettor heat control lever to make sure that the carburettor didn't ice up and restrict the amount of air going into the engine. As it happened we could almost forget this one as in RAF Chipmunks it was locked in the 'hot' position.

However, the way that a propeller works and mysterious associated terms like asymmetric blade effect, gyroscopic moment and blade slip were something totally new to me. I had gone through an all-jet-flying training system and had never laid hands on a piston-engined aircraft before. And this one had yet another new and probably challenging item – a tailwheel; all the jets I had flown had a wheel at the front – the nosewheel. I had heard that both take-off and landing in tailwheel-equipped aircraft were much more difficult tasks than in a nosewheel-equipped aeroplane. I wasn't entirely sure why – but I'd soon be finding out!

The Chipmunk was designed to replace the De Havilland (DH) Tiger Moth biplane trainer that had been widely used by the RAF during the Second World War. A man rejoicing in the name of Wsiewolod Jakimiuk, a Polish engineer living in Canada, created the Chipmunk as the first home-grown design at DH Canada Ltd. The Chipmunk is an all-metal, low wing, tandem two-place, single-engine aircraft with fixed tailwheel under-carriage and fabric-covered control surfaces. A framed and glazed canopy covers the pilot/student (front) and instructor/passenger (rear) positions; this slides back to give both occupants access to their cockpits. CF-DIO-X, the Chipmunk prototype, flew for the first time at Downsview, Toronto, Canada on 22 May 1946 with UK-based DH Test pilot Pat Fillingham at the controls. The production version of the Chipmunk was powered by a 145hp (108 kW) four-cylinder in-line, DH Gipsy Major 8 engine. In 1948 two of the Canadian-built, but British registered, Chipmunks were evaluated by test pilots at Boscombe Down. There were no major problems, although sensitivity to some spin recoveries was corrected by fixing two longitudi-nal strakes to the rear fuselage just ahead of the tailplane. As a result, the fully aerobatic Chipmunk was ordered as the *ab initio* trainer for the RAF. De Havilland (UK)'s factories at Hatfield and Chester eventually built 735 Chipmunk T Mk 10s and its overseas variants for fourteen international air forces. The differences from the Canadian model were the regrettable loss of the bubble canopy (shaped like that of the Sabre fighter), a modified version of the Gipsy engine and the use of an all-metal Fairey-Reed propeller.

The first seven RAF Chipmunks were delivered to Oxford UAS on 3 February 1950. All seventeen UASs would eventually receive the aircraft to replace their DH Tiger Moths and North American Harvards. The Chipmunk made its first appearance on the public stage through an unusual display at the 1950 SBAC (Society of British Aerospace Companies) Airshow at Farnborough. The aircraft was flown by two RAF instructors, Flt Lts Everson and Hough, in which both a range of smooth aerobatics and a hair-raising display of 'crazy flying' by the supposed student were flown. This innovative demonstration of the Chipmunk's flying characteristics led to many orders from overseas, including Portugal, Ireland and Denmark. In addition to equipping the UASs, the Chipmunk was selected as the elementary trainer for all National Service pilots and the then Reserve Flying Training Schools. Later it was the elementary trainer of choice for both the Army, at Middle Wallop, and the Royal Navy at Roeborough airfield near Plymouth. The Chipmunk also joined the elite ranks of the RAF College at Cranwell where it replaced the Percival Prentice in becoming the first aircraft that the cadets would fly. One Chipmunk, WP 912, became a temporary member of the Royal Flight, where it was used to teach HRH Prince Philip to fly; WP 912 now resides at the RAF Museum at Cosford.

The Chipmunk also had a couple of interesting 'war roles'. The first was a brief time with the re-formed No 114 Squadron, operating in the airborne spotter role from Nicosia in Cyprus during the anti-EOKA operations of the late 1950s. The second was in the 1980s when two Chipmunks were based at RAF Gatow, in Berlin, to exercise the rights of UK military aircraft to overfly the Russian Zone of the city. The aircraft also gathered much intelligence in support of the then secret operations 'NYLON' and 'SCHOONER'. From the 1950s onwards, the Chipmunk also became a popular civilian aircraft, being used for training, aerobatics and crop spraying. Most civilian aircraft were ex-military and many can still be found all over the world. There are two Chipmunks on the RAF books even today, one of which is a veteran of both Cyprus and Berlin: WG 486. These 60-year-old flying legends are with the RAF's Battle of Britain Memorial Flight at RAF Coningsby in Lincolnshire, where they give the flight's volunteer pilots their first lessons in flying a 'tail-dragger'.

I started flying the Chipmunk with Jack Hindle on Wednesday 14 June 1967. This would be my first flight for over six weeks. I had not previously experienced such a long time on the ground since I had started flying training over five years ago. It was also to be my first ever flight as a pilot in an aircraft with a piston engine, a propeller and a tailwheel. One immediate difference I noticed was that we did not wear an inflatable lifejacket (often referred to as a 'Mae West', in tribute to that rather well-built woman-shaped woman of the early cinema). Nor did we need to wear the funny straps that we used to put round our legs, called leg restraint garters, which helped to keep our legs from being damaged during ejection. At first I felt half naked without these encumbrances, but I soon got used to it and rather liked the feeling of freedom it gave me inside that tiny cockpit.

Looking around and getting aboard the Chipmunk was a whole new experience for me. It seemed very small and cramped after the Canberra. The wingspan was only 34ft, not much more than the span of the Canberra's tailplane and, at 25ft, the length of the fuselage was barely the same as the chord of the Canberra's wing! Once I had fired up the engine, whose starting system appeared to use 12-bore shotgun cartridges, I thought that the little machine would shake itself to bits before we got off the ground. It all seemed so crude and fragile.

Then, once the chocks were pulled away by the ground crew, who were well versed in avoiding that 'whirling metal on the nose', there was the complicated way of setting up the brakes to work differentially. I had to apply full rudder and pull the brake lever, which was like something from a 1930s motorcar, until I felt resistance. While doing this I had to lightly depress a collar around the top of the handle so that I could feel the small pall at the bottom of the lever clicking over a toothed ratchet. A couple of 'clicks' were then added, then the lever was released and that number of clicks was set from the off position. This meant that when I subsequently applied rudder I would get some differential brake to help me steer the little beast.

And steering accurately on the ground was vital, because with the aircraft sitting on its tail I couldn't see ahead because the Gipsy Major engine was in the way. I have a very short back, which didn't help either, even though I was using an extra cushion! So the first lesson was in weaving; not as in cloth, but as in moving the nose continuously from side-to-side, so that I could make sure that there was nothing in front of us that I might run into and chew up with the prop.

By the time we got to a position near the end of the runway I was getting a bit apprehensive. I wasn't sure I could keep this diminutive but lively aeroplane straight on the runway. Even though the wind wasn't strong I could feel its effect on us as we moved along the taxiway, and Jack had reminded me to keep the stick back to prevent the tail from coming up inadvertently. In my previous jet flying the wind had to be blowing a near gale before you really noticed its effect on the aircraft. But before take-off there was something else new. We had to run the engine up to check that both magnetos were working properly and that the oil pressure and temperature were acceptable for us to commit aviation. With jet engines, if they start – generally speaking – you can use them without further ado!

After carrying out this noisy procedure it was time to ask Air Traffic Control (ATC) for permission to take off, then line up on the runway and go. As I opened the throttle smoothly and progressively to full power I had to dance on the rudder bar to keep straight and then move the stick forward to lower the nose and get the wings to the correct angle to start producing lift. As the nose went down there was a definite directional lurch – so that's what 'gyroscopic moment' does![6] Despite being subject to the pulling force of only 145 horses, it all seemed to happen very quickly and we were airborne. I accelerated (if that's the right word) to 70kts and raised the nose to climb at that speed. In the Canberra the airspeed indicator had only just started to read at 70kts!

To say that the rate of climb was sedate would be an understatement; it was around 700ft per minute (fpm). I was used to at least 3,500fpm after take-off! It was noisy, there was constant vibration and the view wasn't great. The cockpit canopy, which I had shut firmly before we took off, was close to my helmet in all directions so I felt that I could barely move my head sideways. The instrument panel, which was very uncomplicated, seemed very close. As I looked around I could see the wings sticking out (not that far) on each side and, with a great deal of effort, I could twist around and just make out the tail. It was then that I remembered that the fuel gauges were not in the cock-pit with me, but outside on the top of the two fuel tanks in the root of each wing. I could only just make out what they were indicating! But, I told myself that, like all things unfamiliar and new, I would soon get used to it.

Once we had climbed to 6,000ft, which had taken about ten minutes, I was encouraged by Jack to get more of a feel for my 'steed'. First of all we stalled the aircraft in straight and level flight with the flaps up and then down. The minimum stalling speed was about 40kts: ridiculous! Then Jack took control and said, 'Follow me through.' So I put my hands and feet lightly on the con-trols and he showed me how to get the Chipmunk into a spin. I hadn't done this for over four years, so I was a bit apprehensive. After closing the throttle, the application of 'full rudder' and 'full back stick' made the little machine flip over on its back, drop its nose and start rotating at what felt like a very rapid rate. It was actually taking only a couple of seconds to do one rotation.

Just as I was starting to get dizzy, Jack applied the recovery drill and the Chipmunk stopped spinning as quickly as it had started. He then let me have a go. The tedious bit was climbing up again to a safe height to start all over again. We needed to have recovered at a minimum height of 3,000ft above ground level (agl). This reminded me again that there was no ejection seat, something I had not flown without since my Air Training Corps gliding days. If the aircraft did not recover by that height, we would have to open the canopy, undo our seat harnesses, stand up, hurl ourselves over the side and pull the ripcord of the parachutes that we were wearing. It was all so differ-ent! Like going back to the so-called halcyon days of aviation, but at least we didn't have an open cockpit.

However, for the first time in well over three years I could easily, with very little physical effort, manoeuvre an aircraft in a really spirited manner.

It was great to be doing this again! Having tried steep turns, which needed full power to retain a reasonable speed, I progressed back into the world of aerobatics.

A loop from a dive to gain about 130kts seemed to be over before it had started and only took up about 600ft of sky! Barrel rolls were similar, but when I tried a slow roll the engine very disconcertingly coughed and spluttered as we reached the inverted position. It did a similar thing as we cartwheeled round the top of a stall turn. I also discovered that it was easier to complete that manoeuvre one way than the other, which, I was told, was all to do with the engine torque and propeller slipstream effects. After a few more manoeuvres Jack realised that I was enjoying myself far too much so he told me to close the throttle and glide to earth to make an approach to a suitable field, going around at not below 100ft. This exercise would become very familiar to me; it was called a Practice Forced Landing or PFL for short. And we were going to find a farmer's field to land in!

If the engine had stopped in my Jet Provost or Vampire and I had not been able to make it to an airfield with a proper runway, the drill was to make an emergency call and then pull the black-and-yellow exit handle. Mr Martin Baker's excellent seat would then get me out of the aircraft in seconds and I would catch up with events hanging on the parachute. The rest was up to gravity and luck.

During the descent for our Practice Forced Landing, I was taught that it was essential to open the throttle at regular intervals to ensure that the engine would respond properly when we needed it at the bottom. Apparently, prolonged time with the throttle closed might oil up the spark plugs and cause the engine to misfire badly or even stop. No wonder everyone was so pleased when Frank Whittle invented the jet engine!

During this part of the exercise I was taught how to tell where the wind was coming from and how to choose a suitable field. Then how to fly a spiral pattern in the sky to make sure that I would end up pointing both into the wind and into my chosen field at the same time. Once I'd got a basic handle on this we returned to Little Rissington for a few circuits and landings.

Jack demonstrated a normal, powered approach and landing to me first. Initially I thought that he was a long way out from the runway until he explained that we were going to land on the grass runway, which was halfway between us and tarmac one. Another new experience! We flew downwind at 90kts and did the pre-landing checks; these had a mnemonic that could be remembered easily by recalling the phrase '**My Friend Fred Has Hairy Balls**'![7] At the end of the downwind leg the speed was reduced to 70kts and the first of two stages of flap was selected using a large lever on the right-hand side of the cockpit.

The final approach was initially flown at 70kts, then full flap was selected, the speed reduced to 65kts and, when we were close to the ground, the throttle was pulled smoothly back as far as it would go. Then the idea was to fly level at a few inches above the ground until the nose reached what is known as the '3-point attitude'. This position of the nose above the horizon had to be learnt. At that stage one had to stop moving the stick back and, in theory at least, the little machine would flutter the last few inches smoothly to earth and touchdown with all three wheels at the same time. This was known as a 'three point landing' or 'three-pointer' and was a highly desirable outcome.

Well, the practice was very different. I tended to produce at least three landings from each approach, none of which were three-pointers! Jack was chuckling away in the back seat and giving occasional hints and tips. After what seemed to be an age of flying around the circuit, bouncing on the grass and spending a lot of time skittering sideways he said: 'Right, lad, that's enough of that. Let's stop next time and go 'ave a coffee.' None too soon for me, I mused. I was beginning to get despondent – would I ever get the hang of flying this funny little flying machine?

It turned out that what Jack had really meant was that we would stop next time and he would get out and 'go 'ave a coffee'. As he dismounted he leaned over and said: 'Just go and enjoy yourself for half an hour. I'll see you later.'

I couldn't believe his confidence! By the time he had climbed out of the back and his straps there had secured so that they wouldn't interfere with the controls, I was seriously wondering if he had sound judgement. I had not really felt comfortable anywhere near the ground in the 'Chippy' and I just hoped that enough basic instinct would get me back safely. Half an hour wasn't long, so I took-off and climbed up high enough to do some more of those delightful aerobatics and then returned to do a few circuits. The landings weren't much better than before, but they weren't any worse; so if they were good enough for Jack they were good enough for me. Actually from my third approach I actually touched down only once, so I decided that was sufficient and taxied back for my cup of coffee.

So that was the fourth aircraft type in my Log Book. Now all I had to do was learn to fly it well enough to have the spare capacity to talk to a student at the same time. But I wouldn't start learning how to do that for another couple of weeks. Thankfully there were about another dozen flying hours to be devoted to honing up various skills and gaining an instrument rating (IR).

When the day came to do that, I had to fit the usual blind to my helmet visor; this was designed to stop me from looking outside while still allowing me to see the instruments. However, the cover that was used over the artificial horizon (AH) in the other trainers I had flown could not be used because we were sitting in different cockpits. So when it came to the part of the test when reference to the AH was *verboten*, known as 'limited panel instrument flying' and much trickier, then the AH had to be put out of action. This was relatively easy in the Chipmunk because its rather basic design meant that the slightest attempt at an aerobatic manoeuvre frightened the AH so much that it refused to work properly until one had flown straight and level for five minutes. So the 'limited panel' part of the trip was done towards the end of the sortie and was initiated by the examiner carrying out a loop or a barrel roll before handing the aircraft back in some ridiculous attitude. Then one had to recover back to straight and level flight using the remaining over-sensitive instruments, all of which had a variety of errors and lags. Instrument flying had never been my strong suit so I found trying to fly this flighty little bird accurately, without reference to the outside world, extremely challenging. But somehow I succeeded and gained a new IR, albeit coloured white again instead of the green one I had on the Canberra.[8] However, I had the feeling that clouds and poor visibility would be things that would be seriously avoided in the Chipmunk.

We also did some night flying, but only about four hours in all; perhaps another thing to be avoided. I soon discovered why. The Chipmunk's electrical system was very basic; something like a 1940s motor car: it had a single engine-driven dynamo and a 12-volt battery. The only things that used this meagre electrical power were the heater coil embedded in the airspeed measuring pitot-static probe on the left wing, the three red, green and white navigation lights, the radio and intercom and the taxi lamp, which was like a small car headlight let into the top of the left undercarriage leg. There was also a minimal set of internal cockpit lights, selectable and dimmable by a couple of rotating dimmer switches. When I first walked out in the gathering darkness I remembered that my last night flight was also my final flight in the Canberra B(I)8 on No 16 Squadron and that had been on 20 April. It was now 4 September.

I had always enjoyed flying at night so I was looking forward to this. Thankfully the airfield lighting at Little Rissington was good, so finding my way to the end of the runway and getting safely airborne was not spiced with too much drama. Once up and away it was delightful to be flying over the dark expanses of the Cotswolds, decorated by the lights of the villages and towns. The first task was to get my navigational bearings, so a very pleasant quarter of an hour was spent just stooging around at 3,000ft picking out the salient features floating by below. After a few non-aerobatic manoeuvres (aerobatics were not allowed in the dark) we headed our way back to the airfield where we made some approaches to the grass runways, delineated by a single line of 'gooseneck' flares, which acquired their name from their shape. They were metal containers that looked like the large old-fashioned oilcans that railway engineers used on the wheel bearings of their steam trains. The goosenecks contained paraffin and a large cloth wick; once lit they gave off a good yellow light for several hours.

The trick of landing on grass in the dark with only one line of lights was not easy to pick up. It was all down to getting a feel for when the groundwas only a few inches away, even though I couldn't really see it. The trick I had to learn was to look well ahead as I tried to level off a few inches above the ground and use my peripheral vision to give me the feeling that the near horizon was coming up around my elbows. It seemed strange at first, but it was a good guide to getting the aircraft down, usually on three points, without too much drama. The worst thing one could do was to look downwards for the ground in the gloaming.

Once we had landed, on the left-hand side of the goosenecks, we had to smartly move to the other side to allow other Chipmunks to use the grass now behind us. Once we had crossed the line of flares we had to stop and carry out the 'After Landing Checks'. As I sat there I just hoped that none of the other guys were ambidextrously dyslexic and might land on the right-hand side of the goosenecks. I was also reminded to move well beyond the line of flares before stopping. Apparently some cove had once stopped with his starboard wing over the flares, which had then caught fire while he was doing his checks. Apparently he then panicked and jumped out, leaving his little mount to the mercies of the firemen, who arrived just in time to stop the fuel tank from exploding! Oh, the joys of retro aviation!

3 LEARNING TO TALK AGAIN

When people first started to teach others to fly, the machines and the teaching methods that they used were both rudimentary and unpredictable. Although CFS had started up in 1911, it was not until the middle of the First World War that thoughts of standardising the teaching seemed to come into anyone's consciousness. A man who is still revered as god-like at CFS – Lt Robert Smith-Barry – took the first steps in this direction. His portrait is still prominently displayed in the hallowed halls of the Central Flying School.

In 1915 Smith-Barry introduced a curriculum of classroom lessons and a progressive syllabus of flying lessons to teach new instructors the most effective way to impart the knowledge and skills required to fly an aircraft, both efficiently and safely. He was also instrumental in standardising the words and actions to be used, the former becoming henceforth known by all instructors as 'the patter'. Smith-Barry also changed the approach to the riskier elements of flying, such as stalling and spinning, by getting instructors to demonstrate them to their students rather than just avoiding these flight regimes, as had been the case beforehand.

He also invented a communication device for those early two-seat flying machines, such as the Avro 504 biplane, where it was usual for the instructor to sit in a separate cockpit, either ahead of or behind his pupil. This device was a simple tube with a horn-like end, somewhat similar to the speaking tubes found on board ships of the day. These were first introduced in 1916 at the RNAS (Royal Naval Air Service) Flying School at Gosport, where Smith-Barry was serving at the time. Ever since then the device has been known as the 'Gosport Tube', which was not a proposed underground replacement for the Portsmouth Harbour ferry of the same name.

The teaching pattern that was established by the great S-B and his colleagues has been followed ever since; only the specifics change with the aircraft type and stage of flying training. The first element is the verbal briefing. This tells the student what he is going to be taught in the air. The briefing is done on a board or screen, with diagrams if needed, and should take no more than fifteen minutes. Then, in flight, are the next two elements: demonstration by the instructor and practice by the pupil. Usually there will be the need for correction and further practice until the instructor is satisfied. After flight there will be a debrief, again ideally no more than fifteen minutes in length. At this the instructor will use praise and/or constructive criticism as required by the student's performance. This debrief should include any items that need to be studied before the next sortie. All of this flying instruction is based on a progressive understanding of the theoretical subjects behind the art and science of aviation. Hence the ground school.

In concert with teaching the mechanics of flying an aeroplane the instructor has to teach and engender something called 'airmanship'. This is the aviator's equivalent to the sailor's 'seamanship'. The basics of this subject are taught from the very outset of flying training, but need much repetition because it takes time and experience for good airmanship to mature. Airmanship includes many things but could possibly be best summed up in the phrase 'situational awareness'. A pilot who understands clearly what is happening all around him at all times is less likely to get himself into situations from which his ability and judgement might fail to rescue him.

The flying training syllabus consists of twenty-two separate elements, each of which is numbered for ease of reference. For instance, 'Exercise 4' is learning how to fly in straight, level and balanced flight and 'Exercise 17' is learning how to make a successful forced landing without the use of engine power. Not surprisingly the lessons are taught in numerical order and all the basic elements, such as straight and level flight, turning, climbing and descending, are all 'joined up' in Exercises 12 and 13 – take-off and landing. Those two exercises are the beginning and end portions of what is known as a visual circuit. For that the aircraft climbs after take-off, turns 90°(usually left), levels off at the circuit height (usually 1,000ft), turns through a further 90° and flies straight and level parallel with the runway on what is known as the down-wind leg. It is there that a call is made to the air traffic controller telling him one's intentions (usually honourable) and the pre-landing checks are completed. Then another 90° turn is made onto what is called the crosswind leg. Now the speed is more often than not reduced and a descent initiated (usually with some flap selected). When just about in line with the runway the final turn is made, speed may be reduced further and full flap selected. The aircraft is now on 'finals'. Now comes the tricky bit; the angle of descent has to be held at about 3°, the speed gradually reduced to achieve a set speed as the aircraft crosses the beginning of the runway (known as the threshold) and finally makes a smooth landing not too far down the runway.

What I have described is the first kind of circuit taught and, not surpris-ingly with four 90° corners, it is known as a square circuit. Later in training, particularly on higher performance aircraft, students are taught to turn and level off, or turn and descend at the same time so that the circuit becomes an oval shape. Everything else stays the same, it is only the speeds and flap settings that vary. Also, in everything military except the very basic trainers, one has to remember to retract and extend the wheels at the right times. Forgetting the latter is a great embarrassment, expensive and every pilot's nightmare scenario. But still it happens!

Over the fifty years between Smith-Barry's time at CFS and my arrival there, the principles of instructing had remained the same. Military and civil flying schools around the world now copied the teaching methods of the RAF's school. So I was entering a system that was well-proven and held in high esteem. And who was I to argue with that? In fact, I had no intention of arguing! I would be far too busy learning 'the patter' and trying to synchro-nise my control of the aeroplane to the stream of words leaving my mouth.

The teaching pattern I would soon get used to was that Jack Hindle would give a blackboard briefing while I sat watching, listening and frantically making notes. Then we would fly that sortie, with me acting as the student while Jack sat in the back teaching me whatever aspect of the syllabus we were tackling that day. Then it was my job, with the aid of my notes and the Chipmunk Instructors' Handbook, to prepare as near a copy of what Jack had so impeccably taught me.

After that I would fly with a fellow student instructor, each of us in turn giving the other the thirty or so minutes of the lesson. This led to many hilar-ious episodes when the words came out in the wrong order and the 'student', always known as 'Bloggs', would do exactly as he was told, even if it meant that the end result was nothing like that which was intended.

The summer of 1967 literally flew by! I would often fly twice a day so we were ploughing through the exercises at a rapid rate. There was also continuing ground-school work and occasional tests and exams to be taken, but on the whole I was enjoying myself even if in a slightly masochistic way. However, one day I was brought up a bit short: Jack told me that I was under review. I was a bit miffed at this as I felt that I was picking things up reasonably well and I was certainly not slacking in my application to the course. The problem, he explained, was that my fairly soft voice became almost inaudible when I was concentrating on getting the words right. As is usual at this point, I would now have to fly with someone else for a second opinion. A day later a rather tall, craggy faced and greying staff instructor appeared at the Chipmunk Flight; he was someone I hadn't seen before. I asked a staff instructor who the new man was and he said, with a definite air of reverence and awe: 'That's John Winterbourne. He's from Exam Wing and you don't want to get on the wrong side of him.'

Having made a mental note of that and assuming that I would not be likely to go anywhere near this living resurrection of Smith-Barry, I went to the crew room to get myself a coffee. I had barely boiled the kettle when the said Flt Lt Winterbourne appeared in the doorway and inquired as to whether I was Flying Officer Brooke. I assured him that I was and he said: 'Right, mine's a Standard NATO.[9] Brief me on Exercise 9 in fifteen minutes then we'll go flying together.' Good grief – no pressure then!

I had survived one review sortie during my basic flying training so I was determined not to fall at this fence. I don't remember much about this sortie except that I felt that I was shouting at my rather large and taciturn 'student'. I tried hard to make sure that I used the right words and co-ordinated what I was saying with my actions. John was not a man of many words, so as we taxied back to the squadron dispersal area I had no idea whether I would soon be seeking other employment.

After making coffee for us both and Jack Hindle, the three of us went into a briefing cubicle to listen to the great man's assessment of my performance. It was a huge surprise to me that he was actually quite gentle and complimentary. My 'shouting' had paid off. Jack seemed pleased, but I knew that from now on I had to keep my voice levels up. I decided to pretend, for a while at least, that all my 'students' were hard of hearing. As John Winterbourne left the crew room to stroll back to the rarefied environs of Exam Wing, Jack patted me on the back and came out with a piece of old aviator's philosophy: 'Onwards and upwards then, lad.'

As the course progressed I started to become quite fond of this odd little flying machine and I began to be able to do more with it. I explored some of the more esoteric aerobatics, such as the 'Porteous Loop',[10] the 'Salmon Leap' and 'Reverse Stall Turn', all of which relied on a brief application of pro-spin controls to create a more rapid roll rate, known as a 'Flick Roll'. That type of roll was very easy to start but much more difficult to stop exactly when you wanted. These tumbling interludes in the inexorable sequences of patter, usually in bright, blue Cotswold skies, made it all worthwhile!

4 A COUNTRY LIFE

Living off-base in Stow-on-the-Wold made for a bit of an isolated social life. But I had to work for at least a couple of hours in the evenings, just to make sure that I kept ahead of the game. Nevertheless, when we did socialise, there was a good rapport among many of us on the course. The other 'volunteer' for the Chipmunk course, 'Mat' Mathieson, an ex-Hastings co-pilot, and I had become close friends; Mat was quite content with being on the Chipmunk course. We didn't know it at the time but our friendship was due to last for a very long time. Few of the course members had children yet and lots of us lived in privately rented flats or cottages, scattered all over the Cotswolds. I had bought a dog, a golden retriever/yellow labrador cross bitch, whom we had christened Shandy. The story of her acquisition was quite amusing.

I had discovered her whereabouts from a handwritten advert in the newsagents in Stow-on-the-Wold and Mo and I decided that we would go to take a look at her on the following weekend. As it happened, Don Etteridge, a single Australian Army Air Corps Lieutenant on the Chipmunk course, was spending the day with us. As he had a four-seat car, a Mini, the three of us set off in that on our search for the puppy. The advert had given the seller's address in the village of Fifield, which was not far away. We drove into the village and spotted the local shop and post office. Don pulled up outside the door and rolled down the window to ask directions of someone coming out of the shop. However, before he could utter a word, a huge golden retriever came down the post office steps, lowered his great head, stuck it through the open window and licked Don's face in an extremely friendly way.

The dog was eventually persuaded to desist by its owner, the Postmistress, and having dried his face Don asked the way to the house we were seeking. When we arrived there and, after a pretty yellow labrador dog and its owner had welcomed us, we were taken to see the puppies. There were two males and one bitch left so we opted for the little girl. I asked if the price reflected that there was no Kennel Club registration to go with her, which the lady confirmed. She told us that the mother had a pedigree and gave us a copy of it, but sadly the father didn't. When she said that he was a golden retriever the penny dropped.

'Not the Post Office dog?!' I asked.

'Yes,' she said. 'How do you know?'

I then related Don's rather damp encounter with the aforesaid dog. The lady laughed.

'Well, at least she'll be friendly, but she won't be petite like her mum!' was her rejoinder. That did turn out to be true. In fact, a couple of weeks later, when she was allowed out, and I was standing outside a local shop with her a passing male pedestrian stopped and looked at her and then said to me, 'Aahrr, that'll be a bid dawg when it grows up.'

'How do you know?' I responded.

'Well – just look at the soize of 'er feet,' came the Gloucestershire-dialect reply. 'I bet 'er dad is the Fifield Post Office dawg.'

Indeed, Shandy was quite large for a female and lived to the age of thirteen. She was always friendly, calm and tolerant as well as being a great companion and conscientious nanny to the children that would eventually come our way. Perhaps her only failing, if it was one, was that she would retrieve anyone who stopped to pet her when she was sitting outside our house. She would do so by grasping them gently, but firmly, around the wrist with her mouth and then drag them, oh so carefully, to our front door! Her favourite people always seemed to be old ladies.

We often went for long walks in the beautiful, Cotswold countryside in summer, accompanied by our happy, hairy and frequently wet and muddy four-legged companion. Stops at various 'watering holes' for ploughman's lunches, washed down by a glass or two of golden 'scrumpy' was usually part of the plan. Visits to the many charming villages and market towns led to the acquisition of a few extra, and probably unnecessary, household items.

But living there wasn't all rural innocence and charm. One morning I went out of the door of our flat to mount my BSA and go off to work only to find that it wasn't there! And the place I always parked it was in direct view of the police station! So, I walked across the road and reported the absence of my red-and-silver pride and joy. I then took the MG Midget from the garage and departed. That afternoon the BSA was found, not far away, and had been recovered by our local Bobbies. It wasn't damaged but, for reasons unfathomable, the felon had taken the battery. Actually I had the last laugh because I knew that the old one was just about clapped out and I had been intending to replace it very soon!

One highlight of our course was that we were there for the annual Summer Ball. In the usual RAF Officers' Mess fashion each unit on the station was allocated a room to decorate. No 239 course was given the Main Bar to 'do'. By a process approaching consultation, we decided to decorate it in the style of a First World War squadron headquarters. Tents were borrowed from the RAF Regiment[11] folks and they were erected inside the bar, with suitable gaps for access and egress. We constructed various simulated bits of German aircraft out of wooden batons and paper and then painted and pierced them to represent 'trophies'. A blackboard was erected with pilots' names and aircraft allocated for battle. The entries on the board were embellished with sarcastic comments against the pilots' names because they were all various members of the CFS staff. The *pièce de résistance* was a large, sepia-tinted photograph of a group of pilots posing in various First World War uniforms. Walking sticks, dogs, wing collars and even an oilcan and a bicycle were in evidence. It was entitled No 239 Squadron, RFC, St Amiens July 1915.

The photograph was actually of most of the members of our course. I was annoyed to have missed the opportunity to be in it; but as would become the pattern for much of my career, I was flying. In fact, I remember seeing the guys setting up for the spoof photograph as I taxied out. The end product, tinted, mounted and framed was outstanding and many people looked at it asking how we had found such a wonderful piece of First World War memorabilia!

The Summer Ball was a great success with an amazing selection of food and drink available in wonderfully decorated surroundings. A good time was had by all – some more than others judging by the hangovers endured during the weekend afterwards.

Meanwhile the course went on and the synchronisation of 'patter' and flying became a little easier. With a couple of weeks to go I really felt I was, at last, getting on top of the job. 'Uncle' Jack was happier, although sometimes it was difficult to tell, and I was looking forward to graduating and going somewhere to use all this new-found skill.

5 SPECTATOR SPORTS

Summer also brought other diversions. At that time CFS had three formation display teams. They were: 'The Red Arrows' flying nine all-red Folland Gnats, 'The Red Pelicans' flying six Jet Provosts and 'The Skylarks' with four Chipmunks. All these teams had to have time to practise over the airfield, either at Little Rissington, Kemble or at Aston Down. Eventually they each had to gain the Commander-in-Chief's approval to 'go public'. Most of the practices would take place after normal flying hours, in the late afternoon or early evening, but the final approvals were flown at Little Rissington during normal hours.

One fine day we were all told to be on the ground by a certain time as the teams were going to be viewed by the great and the good and, hopefully, be given clearance to go to the many airshows across the nation that year. The Skylarks were on first. So we all stood outside to cheer our local heroes on. The team was made up of four staff instructors, led by Flt Lt John Merry, the Chipmunks' Squadron's spitting image of the comedian Kenneth Williams – although he was a much more accomplished aviator. The team arrived from the rear of the crowd in line abreast and carried out a loop, but at the top they split into two pairs and then would carry out opposition aerobatic manoeuvres, initially, in pairs, and then singly. It was an impressive show because the wind affected the team's efforts to keep the display at the central datum. Also the Chipmunk easily lost height during aerobatics and careful handling had to be used by the pilots to make sure that the altitude didn't reach zero before the end of the ten-minute display slot! Most of the aerobatic manoeuvres were recognisable with the exception of a vertical pull-up at display datum by the opposing pairs, from which the outer aircraft would stall-turn away from the inner pair and they would then fall nose down into a co-ordinated vertical dive. This manoeuvre was known as 'the Gruntfuttock', a name derived from the then popular radio programme *Round the Horne*, with a motley crew of actors, led by Kenneth Horne and featuring the aforementioned other Kenneth – Williams.

Once the Skylarks had landed and cleared the runway, to thunderous applause, the Red Pelicans were next. A very tidy close formation show ensued with many changes of formation and several difficult manoeuvres for the 'Constant Thrust, Variable Noise' Jet Provost. However, the JP's size and relatively low speed made for a close-in and tight display, which stayed right in front of the crowd. Well done lads!

Then the moment we had all been waiting for. The nine Red Arrows (known in those days as 'the Arrows' – whereas today they are known by aficionados as 'the Reds') taxied out for their twenty-minute slot. They were then the only full-time RAF formation display team and had only been flying as a nine-ship for one year. Their leader was Sqn Ldr Ray Hanna and he had eight skilled chaps hanging onto his wings and his every word. Their Gnats were equipped with smoke generators made by injecting diesel fuel into the hot exhaust gas at the exit of the engine's jet pipe. The natural white could be coloured red or blue with dyes. The Arrows' full show started with all nine jets sweeping by, looping and rolling in tight formation. We watched wonderful manoeuvres such as 'the Twizzle Rolls', which used the Gnat's rapid rate of roll to its best, and 'the Caterpillar', where a game of follow-my-leader with different coloured smoke left a wonderful pattern in the sky. The team then split and the Synchro Pair would carry out exciting opposition manoeuvres while the rest of the team positioned for alternative passes with such things as 'the Rollbacks' and a slow formation pass with the undercarriages all down.

As the show came towards its climax the team had to rejoin for the final downward 'Bomb-burst'. This meant that the Synchro Pair had to catch up with the team who were to rejoin formation from a pull-up that started over the crowd-line heading towards the centre of the airfield. Throughout this wonderful spectacle I was standing near the gap between two of the hangars and, as the team swept overhead and pulled up, the Synchro Pair came through the gap going like bats out of hell. Amongst all the noise of jet exhaust and that peculiar rushing sound as the air folds itself back into place there was a CRACK! Then I noticed that there was something trailing from the tail end of the second of the Synchro Pair. He climbed with the rest and joined formation by the apex of the half loop – 'All Aboard!' was his radio call. Then on the way down all nine broke away to every point of the compass, smoking and dropping down the sides of the hill on which Little Rissington stood. Eventually they reappeared and carried out their co-ordinated break and landed in a neat stream.

We soon found out that the telephone line between hangars 3 and 4 had disappeared. Red 7 had 'borrowed' it. I believe that this incident was the birth of the phrase 'To wire' somewhere, meaning to fly over it extremely fast and extremely low.

Another interruption to a normal working day came later when the annual competition for the Brabyn Trophy came along. This was a competition to find the best solo aerobatic pilot from the staff at CFS. On 30 May 1967 Flt Lt Roy Cope-Lewis, a Gnat instructor from No 4 Squadron, was practising for his slot in the Brabyn competition at Kemble. A crowd of the guys were gathered outside to watch him. He arrived over the airfield at high speed and pulled up for a vertical roll. But what everyone saw was that once Roy had checked the Gnat in the vertical it continued to pitch over forward and head towards the ground. Just after the apex and under some considerable negative G-force, there was a puff of smoke and Roy came into view sitting on his ejection seat. His parachute soon opened and he fluttered to the ground, arriving long after his jet had impressively exploded on impact. There was, of course, a stunned silence – but only for a few seconds – until some wag watching started a round of applause and yelled: 'Great stuff, Roy. Give him another jet and let him do it again!' Such is aircrew humour. Poor old Roy broke his ankle landing on rough ground.[12]

The fault was in the hydraulically powered and rather complex tailplane control system of the Gnat. A mechanism known as the Hobson Unit, presumably named after a Mr Hobson somewhere, was prone on occasions to running to full travel for no real reason but with predictably catastrophic results. It wasn't the first time that this had happened and it probably wasn't the last. But the big difference was that it happened during a low-level, high-speed flying display. Thankfully not at an airshow with thousands of the great unwashed watching! I had flown as the Canberra display pilot in RAF Germany for one season, and although I didn't know it, I would do much more display flying in the years to come. But even then I knew how rapidly things can go so wrong and how quickly a decision to leave that small, warm cockpit has to be made. Well done, Roy.

Another Gnat tale that came my way from one of the guys on the Jet Provost (JP) part of our course went as follows. Three JPs, with the usual crews of two student instructors each, were doing a tailchase during their formation phase. As they pulled out of a looping manoeuvre a voice came over the ether on the CFS 'Quiet Frequency',[13] saying: 'Come on number three, get a grip and close up. You could get a Gnat between you and the number two.' Suddenly the crew of the third aircraft in the tailchase was looking right up the jet pipe of an all red Gnat. After a couple of minutes, and with a long squirt of white smoke, the Gnat pulled out and disappeared. It later transpired that the guilty party was another Roy: Roy Booth of the Red Arrows.

6 GRADUATION

Back at work the course progressed steadily through a wonderful English summer of scintillatingly blue skies. I was flying over a beautiful part of England and gaining confidence in this new role. I was actually beginning to enjoy myself again. Regretful thoughts of not flying a high performance aircraft, especially at low-level, were still there but receding.

We were due to finish the course by the end of September so, as the fields turned to yellow ochre and then the harvest was brought in, our collective thoughts turned to which of the seventeen UASs we might be posted. We had all flown with each other at least once and our instructors were pressing us on towards our final handling tests, which would mimic a full instructional sortie with at least two lessons to be taught. There would also be a full assessment of our ability to fly the aircraft accurately throughout its flight envelope, as well as of our handling of a minimum of two practice emergencies. This final assessment would last half a day, with a pre-flight briefing, a flight of at least ninety minutes and a detailed post-flight debriefing.

Those of us who had volunteered to enter the competition for the Chipmunk Trophy, a prize for the best aerobatic display of our tiny steed, were also allowed three additional sorties to practice and refine our aerobatic sequences. I was one of those volunteers, but I had to be careful that I didn't spend too much time doing aerobatics instead of polishing my 'patter' and my flying technique.

Another thing that came our way was the opportunity to fly one trip in the other aircraft that members of our course were learning to instruct on. At last, I thought, I could get my hands on a Gnat. However, the Gnat Squadron, which was based about 20 miles south of Little Rissington at RAF Kemble, was too busy to take any 'extras'. Foiled again! But I did get to fly the Varsity and Jet Provost, which was a bonus. I had trained on the 'JP' so it wasn't something new, but it was fun to climb above 10,000ft and fly faster than 130kts again. I had only flown the Varsity a few times, but as a fairly non-participatory co-pilot and checklist reader. So it was great to have a go at actually flying this large, twin-engined beast from the 1950s; it was a noisy, lumbering thing compared with the JP and the Chippy.

By mid-September Jack Hindle reckoned that I was ready to take my final test. I flew a couple of revision sorties with two other staff instructors, who were both very helpfully critical and, on 21 September, another member of Examining Wing arrived to put me through my paces. I had to teach him one full exercise and then bits of other exercises, as well as coping with a couple of simulated emergencies and flying a selection of circuits. I do remember that my last landing, on the runway in a crosswind, was particularly smooth and, pleasingly, on three points! Through the medium of teaching the techniques of landing I had actually also taught myself to do it! Anyway, the upshot was that I passed. The good squadron leader gave me a few pointers to try to improve on, but he was happy to release me to torment real university students for the next three years. I was both relieved and pleased. Jack was pleased too, and probably glad to see the back of me!

A week later I flew my low-level aerobatic sequence over the airfield for the gaggle of experts who were gathered on the control tower balcony to judge our efforts. I came second, Mike McKinley was the winner; I didn't really mind, but he was really a helicopter pilot, which made it a bit hard to take! Later the great John Winterbourne said that he thought that my aerobatic sequence and the manoeuvres themselves were actually the best, but that I had lost a few crucial marks because I had not positioned myself in the best place to be seen easily by the judges. Another lesson learned that would turn out to be very useful many years in the future.

By now our postings had come through. I was going to Scotland to join the Universities of Glasgow and Strathclyde Air Squadron, known by its rather prosaic acronym of 'UGSAS'. The other press-ganged member of the

Chipmunk mob, Mat Mathieson, was also going north of the border. Even further north than me, to Aberdeen UAS, based at Dyce Airport.

University Air Squadrons are training units of the RAF Volunteer Reserve (RAFVR) that provide basic flying training, force development and adventurous training to undergraduate students at British universities. These units exist to provide a taste of life in the RAF and give experience and opportunity to their members who might wish to take up a career as an officer in one of the RAF's many branches. In 1967 the primary aim of the UAS was not to recruit but rather to instill 'air mindedness' in the future captains of industry and the people with the potential for high-level influence inside and outside government.

UAS members are expected to attend training nights, usually on a weekly basis, as well as regularly attending to fly and going to annual training camps. The flying syllabus at that time followed a pattern similar to Elementary Flying Training (EFT) and allowed a student to do approximately twenty flying hours per year. This was supplemented with ground training and adventurous training, both in this country and abroad.

Most students hold the rank of Officer Cadet, which has the status and privileges – but not the rank – of an officer. Some may obtain commissions in the RAFVR, in the rank of Acting Pilot Officer. Others were given acting commissions under a scholarship scheme for medical and engineering undergraduates.

Historically the UASs were first formed in 1925, at Cambridge and Oxford universities. The scheme was subsequently expanded until there were seventeen UASs throughout the British Isles. Just prior to the Second World War the UASs were an important source of pilots for the RAF. During the Battle of Britain UAS cadets, who were already members of the RAFVR, were called up for active service in the middle of studying for their degrees. Many of the top-scoring fighter pilots of the Battle of Britain were members of the RAFVR.

But I wasn't there yet. The time for our Course Graduation Dinner was soon upon us at which we were all presented with our certificates as Qualified Flying Instructors and the swots were given their prizes. Although glad to receive the certificates we had to remember that we were now on the bottom rung of this particular career specialisation. The QFI cachet has four levels of professional competence in ascending order of merit: B2, B1, A2 and A1. We were now B2s, but we were expected to upgrade to B1 within six months. Our powers of flight authorisation would be limited and we would be under the close supervision of our future Chief Flying Instructors until we had clawed our way up to B1.

The course finished the next day, so we packed up our goods and chattels into another pile of boxes and labelled them up to be taken by the RAF to our new unit beyond Hadrian's Wall. 'I'll tak the high road and you tak the low road ...'

PART TWO

GLASGOW & STRATHCLYDE UNIVERSITY AIR SQUADRON

7 AND I'LL BE IN SCOTLAND AFORE YE

The art of teaching is the art of assisting discovery.

Mark Van Doren

My wife and I now had two weeks to get ourselves organised to go north and settle in before I started work on 15 October 1967. The first thing that I had discovered was that, despite still being under the qualifying age of 25, I would be allocated an Officers' Married Quarter (OMQ): No 25 Woollcombe Square, New Scone. It was one of a dozen or so that were built primarily for army occupation on the edge of the village of New Scone, near Perth, in south-east Scotland. When we heard the news it seemed strange that we would be living about 70 miles from Glasgow. I soon found out that this was because the squadron flew from the airfield at Scone, which was operated by the Airworks Company and whose main task was to operate a large civilian flying school; the support of the UAS was just an adjunct to that. Our ground crew would all be civilians and we would use the civilian Air Traffic Control and meteorological services already in place.

The journey to Scotland from Pudsey, near Leeds in Yorkshire, started on a bright October day, me on my 350cc BSA and my wife, accompanied by a large yellow dog, in our British Racing Green 1965 MG Midget. The journey took us most of the day, driving up the Great North Road (A1) until we reached Darlington, where we chose to take the High Road, more correctly known as the A68, over the Cheviot Hills towards Edinburgh. It was exciting and not a bit worrying driving through a large, unfamiliar city, but we found our way out with moderate ease as we followed all signs to the 'new' Forth Road Bridge and Perth. Once over the bridge the 'Low Road' took us directly, via Kinross, to Perth and on to New Scone. It was then just a matter of locating the married quarters. A quick call into the local Spar shop put us right and we arrived in the late afternoon. Our next-door neighbours, fellow UAS instructor Flt Lt Andrew Bell, and his wife Vicky, had kindly bought us a pack of essentials, so a long overdue cup of tea was soon on the go.

We had arrived on a Thursday and I was told to report for my first day's work on the Saturday. This was to be another novelty of UAS life: for most of the year I would be working a Wednesday to Sunday week. Our new 'weekends' would be Monday and Tuesday. Friday was spent shopping in Perth, where we had to get used to the fact that absolutely everybody spoke with a Scottish accent. It perhaps seems odd that we would find it strange, but at the beginning of our life in Scotland it was. In those days the spread of regional accents was still limited; unlike today they were not so often heard outside their native regions. It was going to be almost like another overseas tour.

At that time OMQ were furnished with absolutely everything, so the fact that we didn't yet have our own bits and pieces was not a drama. On the other hand, the houses were not centrally heated. There was a coal-burning fireplace in the living room, an anthracite stove in the kitchen, which also heated the hot water, and a wall-mounted gas fire in the dining room. The main bedroom had a four-bar electric heater and that was it. Having got used to the excellent central heating of our flat in Germany, where our landlord was the chief heating engineer for the whole of RAF Laarbruch, I could already sense that getting through Scottish winters was going to be a bit of an endurance test!

Most of the instructors lived on the Scone 'married patch', where we were mixed in with various army officers who worked in the local area. Opposite our house was the home of the UAS Chief Flying Instructor (CFI), a short, puckish looking squadron leader by the name of George Etches. He owned one of those Messerschmitt bubble cars, which he used on his daily commute 5 miles up the road to the airfield. It had a distinctive loud exhaust noise when it started up and, as he backed it out, it always seemed to stall before he set off to work. When I asked him about this he told me that it wasn't stalling. He had to stop the engine because reverse wasn't selected by the gearbox but by the engine running backwards. Once he was in position out of his gate he had to stop the engine and restart it to run in the opposite direction. *Vorsprung durch technik* again – cunning German engineering!

On my first day at work on this new and rather odd little unit I drove up the road to the airfield. I found the ex-wartime wooden huts that served as the UAS flying headquarters and stepped through the door directly into the main operations and planning room. Everyone looked round as I entered and those instructors I had not yet met came over and introduced themselves. After a short time the CFI appeared from his office holding a sheaf of papers. Students were summoned from the crew room and the daily briefing began. I tagged myself onto the end of the line of instructors and listened patiently. Many years later I was told by one of the officer cadets that they all thought that I was a new 'holding' student.[14] My younger-than-23 looks, coupled with my flying officer's single rank stripe, had convinced them that I was only there while I awaited some other course at the start of my flying career. But by then I had logged almost 1,200 flying hours and was actually their new instructor. When, at the end of the briefing, George Etches announced this there were several gaping mouths. I didn't catch on at the time.

The next task was to read my way into all the appropriate documentation and sign lots of times to prove that I had done so. I was beginning to despair at the mountain of books and paper in front of me, which had barely seemed to diminish, when the CFI appeared in his flying kit and invited me to attire myself similarly and join him for an official acceptance check flight. We then committed aviation together for about an hour during which the good squadron leader showed me the ropes of flying at Scone. At the time the airfield had three grass runways laid out in a triangle and indicated by red and white marker boards. The grass was very rough and patchy and there were lots of soft areas, also marked out for avoidance. The place was very busy with a mixture of single-engined and twin-engined Cessnas coming and going on their civilian pilot-training sorties.

The visual circuit pattern, flown at the usual 1,000ft but over some 500ft-high hills to the south-east, was always very busy. It was not unusual to be told that there were six aircraft ahead and that you were the seventh in line to land on the runway. The RAF usually limited the visual circuit to a maximum of four or, at most, five aircraft. With a lot of *ab initio* students,[15] the size and regularity of their circuit patterns often varied wildly. This all made the radio traffic levels high and getting a word in edgeways was almost impossible at times. The runways were very rough and the soft areas on the airfield, often exacerbated by the frequently intemperate Scottish weather, added to the challenges.

However, the CFI seemed happy with the check flight. The debrief was not lengthy and I was looking forward, with no little trepidation, to making my first ever instructional flight with a real student pilot. But before that the CFI had to go and collect an aircraft from Edinburgh Turnhouse Airport, the home of Edinburgh UAS (EUAS). He took me with him in order to show me the route and procedures involved, to introduce me to some of our fellow instructors at EUAS and, of course, to fly our aircraft back to Scone.

The route was very picturesque. We flew south over the River Tay and on past the town of Kinross and the beautiful Loch Leven with its prominent island. The castle on the island was where, in June 1567, Mary Queen of Scots had been imprisoned for nearly a year. That was after an uprising by the nobles of Scotland against her and her new husband James Hepburn, the 4th Earl of Bothwell. In May 1568 she escaped and went, via Dumfries, to England. She fared no better there, as she was seen as a threat to the throne of her cousin, Good Queen Bess, and the poor wee lady spent most of the rest of her life detained at the Queen's pleasure in a series of manor houses and castles throughout the realm. After nineteen years of this incarceration she was executed for her alleged part in a plot to overthrow Elizabeth and seize the English throne.

Once we were south of the loch there were more urban and industrial areas. As we approached Dunfermline, still at our cruising altitude of 2,000ft, the two bridges across the mouth of the River Forth were looming ahead. The road bridge was still quite shiny, having been open just three years, but the mighty rail bridge, which made its road traffic sister look flimsy beside it, was still in full, sturdy stride across the river. And, sure enough, there was a gang of men about one-third of the way across from the north bank painting it. The colour they were applying was a rusty brick red; I mused that it might be so that the actual rusty bits still awaiting the gang's ministrations didn't look too bad by comparison.

By now we were talking to the Edinburgh Approach controller on the radio and had received permission to enter the control zone 'via the bridges'. In compliance with the rules of the air we were observing the 'right-hand rule' by keeping this particular line feature on our left. George soon told them that we had the airfield in sight and we were cleared to make our visual approach to the southerly runway. It was nice to see tarmac again and George pointed out salient features around Turnhouse airfield. The last part of the final approach was very interesting as we descended parallel with the gradient of a grassy hill, which was part of a golf course, only a couple of hundred feet below us.[16] Then we crossed the main Edinburgh to Glasgow railway line and, soon afterwards, the airfield boundary to touch down on the beginning of the runway. This was not the main runway as it was not long enough for airliners; but it was plenty long enough for little 'puddle jumpers'[17] like the Chipmunk and the Edinburgh Flying Club aircraft.

After landing we taxied into the EUAS parking area, shut down and went across to find a coffee in the crew room. Here I was introduced to several of the instructors and some of the students. After coffee I mounted my small but perfectly formed steed and headed back to Scone via a practice approach or two at RAF Leuchars, home to two squadrons of Lightnings and the East Lowlands UAS. The former held two armed aircraft on continuous Quick Reaction Alert (QRA) ready to intercept any potentially hostile aircraft coming across the North Sea. In the late 1960s these aircraft and the other six fighters held on QRA nationally were quite busy as the USSR often sent their bombers to probe UK airspace. I'd done my share of waiting for action in QRA so, even though these guys were flying a fighter, I was pleased not to be doing it again.

George had by now taken over the Chipmunk destined for UGSAS (Universities of Glasgow and Strathclyde Air Squadron) and was flying it directly back to Scone; after all he was a busy man. My route towards Leuchars took me out of the Edinburgh control zone via the bridges, again obeying the right-hand rule, and then more or less along the coast from Kirkcaldy to St Andrews, over the ancient kingdom of Fife. About halfway there I was passed on to Leuchars Approach Control and made my way, via a radar-controlled approach, into the visual circuit at Leuchars. Now I was using a 7,500ft-long runway – something I hadn't done since leaving Laarbruch five months previously. The runway at Little Rissington was only 6,000ft long and we Chipmunk folk used the grass there much more than the tarmac. The downwind leg, flown parallel with the runway, seemed to take ages at 90kts, less than half the speed I used to fly it in my Canberra! I carried out a few touch-and-go landings, known as 'rollers', before taking my leave and heading due west back to base.

As I crossed the mighty, silvery River Tay, south of Dundee, I could see the modern rail bridge and beside it the stumps that are all that remain of the old rail bridge destroyed on 28 December 1879 in a storm, and forever commemorated in the poem of Mr William Topaz McGonagall. Alongside the 'new' Tay rail bridge, opened on 13 July 1887, was the even newer road bridge, which had been in use for just one year.

When I got back to Scone I found that none of my batch of students, whose names I had been given that morning, were actually there. So I took the opportunity to read my way further into how the UAS operated. It was so different to the self-contained and heavily supported operational squadron environment from which I had come. There we had a whole station of several thousand people all dedicated, well at least employed there, to make sure that the operational squadrons had all they needed to function efficiently. Here we had three folk in the Administrative 'Town' HQ in Glasgow and for everything else we had to rely on RAF Turnhouse and RAF Pitreavie, both nearer Edinburgh than either Perth or Glasgow.

The next day was a Thursday and I was told that we would be leaving after lunch to go to Glasgow for the weekly ground-school sessions with the students at the Town HQ. This resided in a four-storey house in the grand Regency sweep of Park Circus, close to Kelvingrove Park on the western side of the city centre. This weekly migration was going to be another odd thing I would have to get used to. One of the other instructors, Bob Hutcheson, would drive us down in his car with me, Andrew Bell and Bob Trowern in the other seats. There we would meet up with George Etches, Flt Lt Hamish Logan and the CO, Wing Commander Dunn, who lived in Dunblane, which was about halfway between the two elements of his empire. I had yet to meet Hamish and the Boss. The former had a reputation for brusqueness that went before him, but I was beginning to suspect that the others had been winding me up a little with tales of his fearsome bearing and temperament.

We arrived at about teatime and I was taken on a tour of the rather tall and imposing building. The ground floor had the classrooms and up a graceful curving flight of stairs were the bar, the stock room, the toilets and a large and very comfortably furnished anteroom. On the third floor were offices for the Boss and for administration plus a small dining room. Right at the top of the building, in the roof space, was a large bedroom and a bathroom. After I had met the Wing Commander and the tall and rather daunting Hamish, there were yet more people to meet. The most important one of these was the Squadron Secretary, Miss Margaret Sinclair, MBE. She was a sweet and efficient Scottish lady who was undoubtedly the glue that held the whole organisation together. Margaret was devoted to the UAS and all 'her boys', cadets and instructors alike. She kept a record of them all and stayed in touch with many throughout the rest of her life. In the back office there was the tall, bespectacled and rather cadaverous Mr Munro; he reminded me of 'Chalky', the schoolmaster from the Giles cartoons. He was the Squadron Clerical Officer and his *raison d'être* was to deal with the post, file the files and guard with his very life the contents of the stationery cupboard. I would soon learn that extracting anything, from a pencil to a new Flying Log Book, from 'Mr Munro's Cupboard' was an operation that required every bit of craft, tact and guile that one possessed.

I had yet to be given a ground-school topic on which to lecture, so I sat in on a couple of classes and then joined everyone in the bar for a few for the road, that is for all of us except our driver. When time was called we remounted Bob's red Morris 1100 and set off back to Scone, ninety minutes away. We got home at around midnight having stopped at a fish-and-chip shop, known to the others as 'Nessie's', which was the name of the large lady who ran it (unless it was an unkind sobriquet that likened her to the supposedly large and monstrous occupant of Loch Ness!). There I learned to ask for my victuals not in the Yorkshire fashion of 'a fish and a portion', but rather in the Scottish style of 'a fish supperrr'. In fact there was an enormous variety of strange fare on offer: white pudding, black pudding, fruit pudding, fishcakes and scraps. There was, however, no evidence of deep-fried Mars bars. After the consumption of said fish supper in the cold October night air, it was off back to home and bed. My next challenge would be to fly with a real, live student.

8 THE REAL THING

On Friday 20 October 1967 I finally got my hands on my first real, live student. He was a tall, well-built and muscular looking chap called David Chinn. I had also been issued with my own aircraft, upon which my name had been painted, another first; it was Chipmunk Mk 10 serial number WP 967. I would fly this particular airframe for almost all the three years I would spend on the staff of UGSAS.

Young Officer Cadet Chinn was not a real beginner; he had flown solo and our job today was to carry out some post-solo consolidation flying, involving stalling, spinning, aerobatics and circuits and landings.

I briefed him, probably a bit too thoroughly, and as we strode out to the aircraft together, I was not sure who was the most nervous. I watched him do the external checks and then we strapped on our parachutes and climbed aboard. As he was calling out his internal, pre-start checks I noticed how high he appeared to be in the cockpit in front of me. Good grief, I thought, I'm going to be able to see even less forward than I usually can, and that was precious little! However, he seemed to know what he was up to and I of course, keen as mustard and fresh from CFS, was watching and listening like a hawk for any mistakes or omissions. By the time we had taxied out, got airborne and climbed to 6,000ft I was beginning to relax – but only a smidgen. After a couple of stalls and one spin I had come to the conclusion that David Chinn was quite competent and I imagined that he had been allocated to me as my first student by the kindly CFI to help ease me into this new life.

However, his head and shoulders were still occupying most of my limited forward view, so I was particularly strong on emphasising one of the QFI's favourite mantras: 'LOOKOUT! – all around and not just in front!' The apparent inability of students to move their heads and eyes around was the first difference I noticed between the real 'Bloggs' (the name we used for students) and the pretend ones we had all role-played at CFS. Looking out a lot, and in all directions, was so ingrained in qualified pilots that we never thought to stop doing it.

After a suitable time, during which Chinn attempted an assortment of basic aerobatics with variable success, we set off back to Scone to do some circuits. It was now that I could start to make some critical inputs as he struggled a bit with achieving smooth approaches and the three-point attitude at touchdown. After a demonstration by me with the inevitable instruction to 'Follow me through' and then another two or three attempts of his own he seemed to have remembered how to do it properly. As we taxied back in I gave a silent sigh of relief. So far this wasn't as difficult as I had expected.

Over the next few days I flew with students at a similar stage of their course. I was flying four sorties each day, all of around one hour's duration, as well as trying to brief and debrief each one sufficiently. Then I had to write up a summary of their individual progress on each trip in their RAF Form 5060 Record of Training books. All that added up to more hours than were available in the nine-hour working day. That was another thing that they didn't tell us at CFS – or give us practice at. I had to take some books home and write them up during the evening. Moreover, I rapidly discovered that if I didn't make notes after each flight they all blurred into one and it was difficult to recall who had done what.

Over the next few weeks I settled in, but I was still finding my instructional feet at times. Unsurprisingly, not all my students were of the same ability as Dave Chinn. I was also now learning how to deal with different temperaments and attitudes; another issue that passed us by at CFS. Some students were as keen as mustard and others made me speculate as to why they had opted to join the UAS at all. Some, but sadly only a few, had a natural affinity with aviation and a good level of aptitude and ability in flying an aircraft. On the other hand, some students lacked any detectable psychomotor skills and one wondered how they rode their bikes safely! Thankfully, most had abilities and intellects that lay somewhere between the two extremes.

One day, early in my time at the UAS, I found that I was slated to fly with Officer Cadet Crawford. I had not met him before and when I did I thought that he looked a bit old to be still at university. When I asked him about his studies and how much flying he had done I discovered that he was doing a doctorate. In fact he was older than me and had more hours on the Chipmunk than I did! Although he was no shining star as a pilot it was quite a relaxed trip for me; so much so that I made a gross error of judgement. I finished the sortie with a low flypast over the UAS huts and pulled up steeply and carried out a slow, climbing roll. It was the sort of thing that we had done occasionally on my squadron in Germany. After I had landed, the CFI made it abundantly clear that it was not the done thing here! I never did it again.

A problem that reared its head occasionally with the students was that of communication. Partly down to the Chipmunk's barely adequate intercommunication system (intercom), but mainly because of the varying Scottish accents and phraseology that my young charges would use. It wasn't long before I was starting to detect different regional accents and tying them in with the points of origin of the students. The hardest to understand were the Glaswegians and the easiest were those from Inverness and north of the Great Glen.

And it wasn't long before I came to expect the unexpected, which reinforced the teaching I had received on using the correct words and unambiguous phrases. The first time this happened was when I was flying with one of my less gifted pupils, a lad by the name of Burnett. He was small and reminded me of a nervous water vole. He always seemed to be on the edge of terror when we flew together. I was sure that it wasn't me; I was always gentle with the lad, just because he seemed so tense. Even in the depth of winter, when the cockpit temperature was well below zero, he wore little extra clothing under his flying suit and yet still sweated like a small Tamworth piglet in the front cockpit. It also took me ages to get him to look outside, an essential practice when flying around in the sky where, in the regime in which we operated, there was no radar to look after us. I finally got Burnett to move his head left and right by reaching forward and grasping the communication cable that came out of the back of his helmet and used that to keep his head moving from side to side. After a while he started doing it on his own – although I'm not sure that he was actually seeing much.

One day we were flying together to do what is known as General Handling; that comprises of all those up and away exercises, such as stalling, aerobatics, steep turns and spinning. On this occasion I had asked young Burnett to climb to 6,000ft and enter a spin to the left and recover after three turns. Well, much to my surprise, that is exactly what he did. He levelled off at 6,000ft and accelerated to the usual cruising speed of 90kts and then, with no preamble or semblance of preparative lookout or pre-spinning checks, he just booted on full rudder and pulled the stick fully back.

The result was a very rapid flick roll and a loud remonstration from the occupant of the back seat. I took over control, closed the throttle and carried out the normal spin recovery actions of using rudder to oppose the yaw and moving the stick forward until the spin stopped. After our recovery to straight and level flight there ensued a very one-sided conversation between me and young Burnett. By this stage the poor wee chap was speechlessly terrified and the only course of action was to take him home and have a good conversation about his future on the UAS. By the end of the following month he had decided that flying was not for him and I never saw him again.

Flying over Perthshire, with any standard of student, was a joy. The scenery was magnificent, with hills, glens, lakes (sorry – lochs) and forests. We tended to operate to the north and west of Perth, so heading towards the foothills of the Cairngorms and the Central Highlands. However, we could not fly when the weather was bad. That really meant when the cloud base came below about 800ft above the ground, as we had no way of finding our way back to Scone other than navigating visually. However, one consistent factor that affected our operations was the wind. When it blew it really blew. Sometimes the turbulence from the mountains became a significant problem that brought with it an increase in the number of students being airsick.

One day we were over the hills, some way from base, when the dreaded words, 'Sirrr, I think I'm going to be sick,' came through the intercom.

'OK. I have control, get out your sick bag and TURN YOUR MICROPHONE OFF!'

I would then fly the aircraft as smoothly as I could while nature took its course three feet in front of me. That was usually, but not always, the end of any useful training for that flight. One of the problems was that although all the students carried sick bags, just like the ones that are found in airliners (without the commercial branding), there was nowhere to easily stow the now sloppy bag of bits. Because of this I once made a big mistake.

About five minutes after young Stewart had emptied his stomach of its breakfast I heard, 'Sirrr, the wee bag's startin' tae leak!'

We were still at least fifteen minutes from landing, so I asked, 'How badly?'

'Och, it's terrible, sirr, it's drippin' all down ma flyin' suit.'

We were over one of the many unoccupied bits of Scottish moorland so I said, 'Right, I'm going to slide the canopy back and slow right down. When I tell you, and NOT BEFORE, drop it out of the left-hand side.'

I duly decelerated to about 50kts and slid the canopy back sufficiently for him to carefully extend his hand and arm, grasping the, by now, soggy bag and let it go. However, the airflow ripped the squelchy bag open and most of its contents flew back into the cockpit whereupon the airflow headed it straight at me. Fortunately I had the visor on my helmet down and I instinctively ducked. Suffice to say that the journey back to base was flown as fast as the little aeroplane would go, with the canopy still partly open to give maximum air conditioning. When we finally got home, before I went to shower and change, I had to apologise profusely to the ground crew for the mess inside the rear cockpit. Young Stewart was then equipped with rags and a bucket of hot water and despatched to WP 967 to do the necessary!

It is strictly against the Air Navigation Order[18] to drop things from aeroplanes (with certain exceptions – fully charged sick bags not being one of them) so I suppose that there was a sort of poetic justice in the incident. I knew that I would never try that again.

On another windy day, of which there were lots, I was flying with a student who was just starting on the basic exercises and I was teaching climbing and descending. As we passed about 3,000ft, with him trying to hold the correct nose-up attitude to give the recommended climbing speed of 70kts, I noticed that the speed kept increasing, although the attitude looked just right. I took over from him and raised the nose until the speed settled at 70kts again. The nose was way too high and instead of the rate of climb being 500fpm it was about three times that. I then realised that we were in something called a mountain wave. The air blowing from the north over the Cairngorms was being lifted over the mountains like a wave over a boulder in a river. And just like in a river there was a pattern of rising and falling waves downstream. We were climbing in a rising bit. I decided that today was not going to be the right day to teach this exercise so I told young McBloggs to relax. I then reverted to my gliding days and explored the air to find where the best lifting effect of the wave was. In a few minutes we were climbing at nearly 2,000fpm. As we passed 10,000ft I asked my student to let me know if he started to feel at all short of breath. He said he was fine and was really enjoying the experience. It was a virtually cloudless day and I continued our climb to 12,000ft; I hadn't been this high myself for ages! We could see right across Scotland from the Kyles of Bute to the Firth of Tay. After a few minutes I set off downhill, which was no mean feat to start with. But I knew that if I headed downwind, to the south, we would fly out of the up-wave into the descending air. Sure enough after a few more minutes we were descending like a lead balloon and were back at Scone in no time at all. Before we landed I got McBloggs to swear on all that he held dear to say that we had not gone above 10,000ft, the maximum allowed without oxygen equipment.

The Scottish wind was also responsible for another rather less pleasant incident. I was flying with another student and he had performed reasonably well. It was December 1967 and there had been a lot of rain, so the airfield was very soggy. The bigger twin-engined types from the civilian school had chewed up a lot of the taxying surfaces, so one had to be really careful moving around on the ground.

We had landed and the student was taxying the aircraft back to our dispersal area. Again there was a very strong northerly wind blowing and as we turned to go downwind, towards the aircraft parking area, the left wheel went into a deep rut. This caused the student to involuntarily pull the stick back, just as a gust of wind lifted our tail up. In a second or so I was looking at the ground over the student's head as the propeller dug into the soft turf and the engine stopped. My first thought was, 'They're going to need a ladder to get me out of here.' I was about 10ft up in the air! I then thought more rationally and made sure that the student had turned off the magneto switches and the fuel selector cock and then told Air Traffic Control that we were stuck. Just as I did so the wind must have abated a little and the aircraft started to fall back onto its tail again. It came down with a bit of a thump, but at least we could both get out. A tractor turned up eventually and a muddy-legged Chipmunk was extricated and towed back, to be fully checked over. It needed a new engine.

The winter continued long in Scotland, the wind blew and the rain poured. But there were days of pure blue and frosty clarity to be had in Perthshire. As the winds veered more northerly the mountains extracted all the moisture from the air before it arrived at Scone. With direct northerlies, coming from the Arctic, the air crackled with icy overtones and the skies stayed cloudless all the short day. We were issued with sets of fluffy, white, two-piece underwear, like long johns on steroids, to wear under our flying suits. The temperatures at 5,000ft were now getting down to those that could be found inside the average domestic freezer and there was nothing between us and the air outside except a layer of 12-gauge aluminium. Moreover, even with the canopy closed a draft still blew in from the back, straight onto my neck. December 1967 was a month in which the good flying weather came our way more often than the bad. I flew an average of three instructional sorties on virtually every working day.

By that December, Squadron Leader George Etches had departed on posting and had been replaced as CFI by Squadron Leader Arthur Pullen. He was a fairly large gentleman who cast his shadow much further than George over the UAS. He was much more aware of his status than his predecessor, haughty to a degree and did not engender the same level of fellow feeling with us junior officers. His sometimes overbearing manner meant that it would be a while before we got used to the change in atmosphere emanating from the CFI's office at Scone. We all agreed that Arthur must have been born middle-aged.

After the Christmas and New Year leave period, which Mo and I spent with our parents back in West Yorkshire, we returned to snow on the ground and sub-zero temperatures. But by the first day of work we were able to fly. The usually soggy airfield was now frozen solid so the chances of nosing over into the mud again were much reduced. However, the now unyielding, rutted surface made travelling over it, especially during take-off, a real bone-shaking experience. Even worse was the 'tramline' effect of getting the small Chipmunk wheels locked in a rut and being unable to steer the aircraft where you really wanted it to go.

The New Year brought us about fifteen new students. All *ab initio* ones, most of whom had never flown before in anything. I was allocated three of this new wide-eyed bunch: Cadet Pilots Craig, McRitchie and Parker. This meant that I now had to dig out my instructor's handbook, turn to the front-end pages and start refreshing myself on those early instructional exercises that I had last done at CFS and hadn't looked at again for at least three months.

So, as 1968 progressed apace, so did we. I was still flying three of four sorties per day and sometimes five or six; it was no longer just a flying job like it had been on my first tour. Now it was a flying, talking and writing one.

The New Year also brought us a new boss in Wing Commander John Greenhill. He was a Scot and had taken up residence in Glasgow. We also received a new QFI, fresh from CFS: Flt Lt Colin Adams, who replaced Bob Trowern. Bob had gone back to his roots in RAF Coastal Command and would be flying the mighty Avro Shackleton again. So, I was now no longer the junior instructor, although I was still the only flying officer on the unit. But there were two challenges coming up to change things for me. One was that I would have to re-grade my B2 Instructional Category to B1 by the end of March. The other was that I was now eligible to take the promotion exam for upgrade to Flight Lieutenant.[19] The former would happen soon via a test taken with our new CFI. The latter would be achieved through sitting the examination at RAF Leuchars, but only when I could be released from UAS duty. I was now spending much time studying in the evenings for both events, as well as trying to keep up with the pace of life that my students were putting me through. Suffice it to say that I passed the B1 flight test on 10 March 1968 and was promoted to Flight Lieutenant just a month later. So I was now able to authorise students to fly, except for their first solos, and I could hold my head a little higher in the staff room. However, the constant demands of ploughing through the syllabus kept my feet (not literally of course) on the ground.

I was now teaching meteorology and piston aero engine technology in the ground school at Park Circus, as well as holding the secondary duty of deputy Bar Officer. Hamish Logan was the Wines Member (aka Bar Officer) and so it was through that I got to know him better. Hamish was a larger-than-life character whose gruff manner was mostly a front. He was a big chap, but he was great fun at times and taught me how to run the bar and do the weekly stock checks. One day I was doing half of the job and he was doing the other. We were both doing mental arithmetic but I was counting under my breath. Suddenly he said, in his grumpy mode, 'For heaven's sake! Can't you do that inside?' For a second I wondered what he was talking about, then I realised it was his way of asking me to add up silently. When Hamish left and I took over as Wines Member I was glad of his crusty guidance; he had taught me enough to run a pub, let alone the bar at 12 Park Circus.

So life was busy, interesting and I was finding that imparting my own love of flying and helping students to discover that they could do more than they thought possible a very satisfying outcome. The next event that was heading rapidly towards us was to be my first experience of a summer camp.

9 SUMMER CAMPS

Every year, during the summer holiday period, each UAS left home to spend six weeks based at an RAF airfield. This was done to give us the chance to do some concentrated and uninterrupted training during the summer holidays. Students came in batches for two weeks at a time. These 'camps' also fulfilled the RAFVR charter of cadets spending at least two weeks per year on continuous training. This was a mandatory requirement of their service and the monetary allowance that went with this added to the otherwise meagre recompense that they received.[20] The notification of which UAS went to where usually came out from the particular ivory tower that dealt with such things by Easter. My very first summer camp with UGSAS was going to be held at RAF Bicester, in Oxfordshire, normally the home of Oxford UAS, whose accommodation we would be taking over. It seemed sad to me that we would not be going to a more operational station, which would give our students a wider view of real RAF life. RAF Bicester was the home of the RAF Gliding and Soaring Association's (RAFGSA) HQ and, of course, Oxford UAS, but not to any other flying units.

We instructors were due to depart south in our aircraft on Wednesday 12 June, so we were given the Sunday off and thus had three days to prepare. The other logistics were complicated by the need to transport by road our administrative support, our ground crew, their tools and spares, as well as a couple of dozen students. The unit had one permanent RAF driver, Corporal Jim Stephenson, and the airwork ground crew had two civilian drivers. There were two twelve-seater minivans for the people and a truck for the heavy stuff.

I must admit that I wasn't overly interested in the logistics; I would be flying my own aircraft to Bicester in company with the other six instructors in their aircraft. The control sticks would be removed from the rear cockpits so that we could stow our baggage there. By now another instructor, fresh out of CFS, had joined us: Flt Lt Ian Montgomerie. He was a tall and rather willowy individual who seemed to have arrived at an RAF career from the opposite side of the circle to me. He had lived in Edinburgh and his late father was a renowned Scottish poet. Ian was married to a good-looking and outgoing lady called Emily and they occupied a flat in Perth. Ian always wore his hair that bit longer than usual and I thought I recognised in him some artistic style that was slightly at odds with the military ethos. However, he was a good guy to have around, although at times he and I didn't naturally and easily hit it off. However, we soon found common cause, along with Colin Adams, in our subterfuges against the occasional additional and unnecessary obligations imposed on us by our dear CFI, who was fond of coming up with last-minute trivial problems to be solved or memos to be written. I was also grateful to Ian for the occasional more esoteric classical education event, such as a visit to a Glasgow theatre to watch Samuel Beckett's *Waiting for Godot* and the airing of classical music or poetry on his portable radio. It was good for me because, compared with Ian, I was a bit of a Philistine!

The morning of 12 June arrived with a bright day forecast and our aircraft neatly lined up ready for loading. The Boss would lead the formation of seven and I was allocated the number two slot on the right of the lead ship in the arrow formation we were briefed to use. We got airborne at about 10 o'clock with the prospect of a two-hour flight to RAF Church Fenton in the Vale of York, where we were due to refuel the aircraft and ourselves. All went well and the Boss led us up to 5,500ft to fly south. However, as we got nearer to our destination the cloud filled in below us, obscuring the ground, and we had to climb higher to keep each other in sight.

The sky over the Vale of York is always a very busy parcel of airspace with several training bases, all flying at maximum rates with their Jet Provosts and Chipmunks. We managed to get a radar service to see us through the busiest bits, but it did mean that we were often turned off our track and so we started using more fuel than had been planned. While we were still some way from Church Fenton several of us had called our 'bingo' fuel state,[21] indicating that we were getting low on go-juice. It was too late to change plans so we ploughed on. Eventually we were able to descend through gaps in the cloud and the airfield at Church Fenton hove into view. We organised ourselves into two sections for the break and joined the circuit with some haste. When my aircraft was refuelled they had been able to put in just half a gallon less than the tanks actually held! Time for lunch.

After our stomachs had been replenished at the aircrew feeder, always known as 'the Greasy Spoon', we returned to our small steeds, started up, taxied out and took off in neat formation – the Red Sparrows? The next leg to Bicester was due to be about one-and-a-half hours, so I was feeling much more relaxed about the fuel state. We arrived for a massive run-in-and-break[22] over the grass runway at Bicester. The airfield was split in half with the gliders using one side and powered aircraft the other. This operating environment was going to be a new challenge for our students.

But they were not due to be with us for another four days, so we instructors had a bit of time to organise our offices and set ourselves up with all the essentials. After a couple of days the place was how we wanted it and we could look forward to starting work proper on the Monday, when the Scottish hordes would invade our peaceful reverie. In the meantime it was the weekend. I was wondering what to do with the time when we were approached by the CFI of the gliding school who was trying to find out whether any of our aircraft had the glider towing bits attached. We had one such, WK 803, so the supplementary question was asked: 'Would any of you guys like to help us out with some aero-towing this weekend?'

Always ready for any new aviation experience I put my hand up. No one else seemed bothered so we made arrangements for the following day. I had been aero-towed many times during my own gliding days, consequently I knew what was wanted. It was just a matter of going up to the gliding school for them to tell me what they wanted in terms of speeds on tow for the various types of gliders that they had. I was also briefed on the way to land safely with the tow rope still attached, making the interval between launches much more acceptable, and how and where to drop the rope at the end of a batch of launches. The tow-rope-attached approach and landing was very entertaining. One had to make the approach higher than normal but at a slower speed with full flap down, then once safely across the airfield boundary, close the throttle and dive off the excess height and then level off rapidly to touch down not too far down the runway. It was fun and challenging.

I think that the towing went well enough. However I do recall that, after pulling a couple of slick sailplanes up to 2,500ft, they hooked on a Kirby Sedbergh two-seater. I had flown the Sedbergh at gliding school with the Air Training Corps, where it was universally known as 'the Barge'. Sure enough nothing had changed. Once I had taxied forward to take up the slack in the rope and received the green light to get going I opened the throttle as far as it would go and nothing much happened. Eventually the 145hp up front started to win over the inertia behind and we started moving forward. Once the Sedbergh was off the ground, about ten seconds before I was, things got a little better. However, when we were both airborne I had the added task of climbing! The Chipmunk's Gipsy Major motor was thrashing the air with all that its propeller could muster and I was seeing about 2–300fpm on the rate-of-climb indicator; less than half the usual value. I left the flaps at their take-off position and held about 55kts and just sat there, nose high, but barely gaining height. I started to watch the oil temperature and pressure carefully and was very relieved when, at 2,000ft, the pilot of 'the Barge' decided that he had also had enough and I shot forward and upwards as he pulled his release knob and the load came off. I closed the throttle and put the aircraft into a steady glide at 70kts to help the poor little motor recover from its exertions. I really did not want another tow like that – thankfully there was only one Sedbergh and that was now airborne. I also managed to get a couple of flights in sailplanes that day. It just made me nostalgic for the gliding club back at RAF Laarbruch.

When the students arrived we hit the ground running and I flew an average of four sorties per working day for the rest of the six weeks of the camp.

The first summer camp was a great, if exhausting experience and it was very satisfying to see 'my boys' making good progress. Several did their first solo flights and the more senior students were making great strides with the more advanced aspects of the syllabus, such as navigation, low-level flying and instrument flying.

Moreover, I managed to escape for a weekend up in Yorkshire, where my wife was visiting the parents. Officer Cadet Greg Marshall was due a navigation exercise to land at another airfield. His parents lived near the airfield at RAF Finningley, not far from Doncaster in Yorkshire; in fact they ran a local fish-and-chip shop. So I gained permission from the CFI to take my aircraft to RAF Church Fenton, near Tadcaster, dropping young Marshall off at Finningley on the way. I would then collect him the following Monday morning and return to Bicester.

So Greg planned the two navigation exercises, to and from Finningley, and I contacted my wife to ask her to collect me from Church Fenton. The following day we set off for our weekend at our respective parents' homes. Everything went well on the way to Yorkshire. We didn't get lost and Cadet Pilot Marshall learned a bit more about speaking to RAF radar units. We landed safely on what now seemed to be the enormously long 9,000ft runway at Finningley and, after dropping my young companion off, I was soon on my way further north to Church Fenton. Needless to say I spent a very enjoyable weekend away from the frantic atmosphere of summer camp; the only snag was that we had to rise very early on the Monday morning so that I could leave Church Fenton at a decent hour to collect Greg from Finningley.

The weather on the Monday was fine but very hazy; it was like being back in the North German Plain's 'goldfish bowl'! Nevertheless, I could see just about enough to navigate safely and I set off towards Finningley, about fifteen minutes' flying time away. The haze got even thicker around Doncaster and when I was given instructions to land I wasn't exactly sure where I was. As I got closer to Finningley I could see that the airfield was out to my left and, as I had been given clearance to make a direct approach, I turned left onto the centreline of the runway and started to descend. I called the nice lady in the control tower to tell her that I was at about 2 miles out on the final approach and wanted to land.

'Whisky 05 you are cleared to land,' was the sweet reply. But then, 'Hang on a minute – where are you?'

I was about to say something to help when she said, 'Ah, there you are! You are still cleared to land, but you are headed to the wrong runway!'

'Sorry,' was the best I could do. In my eagerness to get down I had forgotten that the controller had told me to use the south-westerly runway and here I was approaching the north-easterly one. It just goes to prove that, in the flying game, you cannot relax too much or allow things to distract you, whatever your experience.

I had another trip away the following Friday, but this time not far. Just down the A34 from Bicester to RAF Abingdon where Aberdeen UAS were holding their summer camp. I had been invited by my CFS course-mate Mat Mathieson, now an Aberdeen UAS staff member. They were having a party with all the folk at Abingdon that had helped them. It was a good do and it was great to be mixing with the guys from the UK's most northerly UAS again.

I had promised the CFI that I would be back in time to start work at 08.30 the next morning – we were working Saturdays during the camp. But when I opened my bedroom curtains there was thick fog outside. I had a good breakfast and headed off to find my aeroplane. It was all neat and tidy, ready for me. I had rung the Met Office to ask when they thought that the fog would clear. I should have known better by now because the answer to that question is always the same: 'About 10 o'clock.' They must learn that at Weather College!

I called Bicester to find that there was no fog there; in fact the CFI sounded like he thought that I was malingering. So I next called Air Traffic Control to see if they had any reports of just how deep the fog was. They told me that several aircraft had passed over and they reckoned that the top of the fog was at less than 500ft and that the sky was clear above that. I told ATC that I would depart in twenty minutes' time and went out in the thick white vapour to try to find my steed. It was still there dripping with dew, but looking as ready as I was to give it a go. I had never before taken off in such low visibility, but we practiced it during our annual Instrument Rating Tests. I started up and taxied out, which wasn't that easy, and eventually found the beginning of the runway. It was about 8 a.m. so the fog wasn't thinning much yet. When I had been cleared to go I lined up on the northerly runway. The lights at the sides of the strip were on full illumination and I could see three sets of them ahead so that was enough to keep straight. So, judiciously applying full power, I set off into the milky atmosphere ahead.

The Chipmunk gets airborne relatively quickly so I transferred all my attention to the instruments as soon as I could and climbed to 100ft and accelerated to 70kts. I was concentrating hard, but the training was paying off and just as I started to feel comfortable the world turned bright blue. The top of the fog was at 300ft. So I gave this news to Abingdon ATC and continued my climb to a couple of thousand feet and turned right towards Bicester. As I levelled off I could see that the fog was dispersing ahead of me and by the time I had passed abeam Weston-on-the-Green there was none at all. It was going to be a lovely sunny summer's day again.

And that was what most days at summer camps were like. Sometimes I began to wish that the weather would have a small tantrum of thunderstorms or high winds, just to give us a break from the workload of flying four or five instructional sorties per day. But then I would see the way that my guys were progressing and enjoying the experience. Especially when they first went off on their own: a very special occasion for me too. Although one of them did let me, and himself, down, by doing a rapid 360° flat turn, called a 'ground loop', after touching down from his first solo circuit. It surprised both him and me, as I watched from the control tower, but no damage was done to him or the aircraft; except to his pride of course.

It had been a tremendous introduction to the big event of the UAS year. We had flown hard and played hard. Our final aircrew/ground crew party at the Bridge Inn in Abingdon exemplified very well the latter, when many of us rounded off the evening swimming in the Thames. As we readied ourselves for the return to Scone at the end of July I noticed that I had flown almost sixty hours in the previous twenty-eight days, which was the maximum allowed by the regulations at the time. Because I still had to fly my Chipmunk back home I would then exceed this maximum. Discretion being the better part of valour, I told the Boss. He gave me a wry smile and said that he hadn't heard what I had said. 'Fair enough,' I thought, 'but I'd better get home without incident or there'll be hell to pay!'

I went on two other summer camps before I left UGSAS in August 1970. In 1969 we were allocated to Oxfordshire again, but this time to RAF Abingdon, the home of the relatively new Andover medium transport wing and the Parachute Training School. The Blackburn Beverleys that had been there for many years had been retired. Indeed, some of them were parked at RAF Bicester when we had been there on camp the previous year. Our six weeks at Abingdon very much followed the pattern of the previous year, lots and lots of flying with students at three levels of experience and myriad levels of ability. Some would do their first solo trips, some would learn some of the more advanced exercises and some would go home by train to hand in their uniforms.

On one 'day off' we instructors made a visit to the Shuttleworth Collection at Old Warden in Bedfordshire. We arrived in a neat 'Five Arrow' and landed before the afternoon's flying display of old and venerable aviation machinery started. We parked our Chipmunks with the other visiting aircraft and we walked across the grass runways to the public enclosure. No sooner had we arrived there than we were greeted by a bunch of chaps who turned out to be RAF test pilots from the nearby Royal Aircraft Establishment airfield at Thurleigh. Among them was Flt Lt Ron Ledwidge, who had been on the same course as me at No 231 Operational Conversion Unit, learning to fly the Canberra.[23] Ron had been in Germany on No 3 Squadron at RAF

Geilenkirchen, while I was at RAF Laarbruch on No 16 Squadron. We were both flying the Canberra B(I)8.

The last I had heard of Ron was his award of the Air Force Cross for saving both his own and his navigator's (nav's) life when there was a failure of the roll control system. Ron's Canberra had refused to stop rolling when he had started a turn at low level. When he reached the inverted position he had pushed very hard to get the nose above the horizon and stop the aeroplane descending into the ground. He then continued alternately pulling and pushing until he had managed to climb, still rolling, to a safe height for his navigator to escape; there was no ejection seat for the navs in the B(I)8. Once he was sure that his nav was safely away Ron cut the engines and ejected. He thoroughly deserved his medal; I hope that the Queen gave him tea and biccies as well. Ron had since passed through the Empire Test Pilots' School (ETPS) and was now on the Aerodynamics Test Flight at Thurleigh. It was great to see him again and we enjoyed watching the flying display together. Little did I realise then that I would, in a few years' time, follow in Ron's considerable footsteps by attending ETPS and, later still, operating from Thurleigh. Eventually, I would also become one of the pilots for the Shuttleworth Collection. But all that was in a still unknowable future – even QFIs don't get issued with crystal balls!

The flying display was well worth watching and I marvelled at the slow and graceful flight of the older machines; even the Chipmunk could overtake some of them. We flew back in formation and spent the rest of the camp back in the frenzied activity of a flying training unit at full operating speed. By the end of that camp I had flown over fifty hours in six weeks.

For the 1970 Summer Camp, just by way of a change, we went north instead of south, to RAF Kinloss on the Moray Firth. Kinloss was much more truly 'operational' than either Bicester or Abingdon. It was the home of two maritime reconnaissance squadrons, one still operating the Mk3 (Phase 3) Avro Shackleton, but the other squadron and the Operational Conversion Unit were changing over to the then brand new Nimrod; the Mighty Hunter converted from the De Havilland Comet. We arrived at Kinloss on 5 June 1970 after a one hour and fifteen minute flight from Glasgow, over the magnificent scenery of the Western Highlands and the Great Glen with its string of shining lochs; I looked, but Nessie was nowhere to be seen.

At our welcome party I discovered with great pleasure that the Station Commander was Group Captain 'Crash' Amos, who, as a Flight Lieutenant, had been my flight commander at RAF South Cerney, the Initial Officer Training School in early 1962. The usual settling in period of a couple of days was followed by the arrival of the first batch of cadets. The newer guys were in much need of circuit training, so I spent most of the first week droning round the landing pattern. I reckon I got to know every farm and hedgerow in the countryside below me. There was one farm that had the biggest tyre-covered pile of silage that I'd ever seen! Things went generally well, but there were two incidents I remember vividly.

The first happened to me. I was flying with Cadet Pilot Mattick, wittily christened 'Otto' by us all, and we had just got airborne. At about 200ft there was a loud bang from the front end and the engine lost some power, the speed reduced and there was a definite new vibration, larger than the usual ones. I took control from the now frozen Otto, rapidly lowered the nose to regain speed, closed the throttle and turned off the magneto switches while making a hasty 'Mayday' emergency call. In very short order we were back on the runway – at 8,000ft long there was plenty of it left for us. The tower had already alerted the fire section and they arrived as Otto and I were dismounting. I persuaded these keen chaps that they didn't need to encase the little flying machine in their sticky white foam or actually do anything else. I took a look under the cowling and there was definitely something amiss, there was a smell of burnt oil, but beyond that I couldn't see anything obvious.

Eventually the ground crew turned up with a tractor and towed WZ 861 back to our hangar. It turned out that one spark plug was missing, not as in misfiring, but as in not there. That and a chunk of the cylinder head around the plug had parted company with the rest of the engine so we were flying on only three cylinders. The bits were found on the runway and the cylinder was replaced with a new one. I did the engine air test just to prove that it wasn't my fault. Everything was fine.

The other incident, actually an accident, did not turn out quite so well. Officer Cadet Norrie Beasant, who was halfway through his second year, went off solo to do some general handling, during the course of which his engine quit. He made a creditable attempt at a forced landing in a field but sadly a stone wall got the better of him. The aircraft was written off and Norrie ended up in Elgin hospital for a few days. The lad recovered and after graduation he joined the RAF where I believe he ended up flying Tornadoes.

The social life, when there was time for it, was good and the lads arranged a Midsummer's Night beach barbecue that went on into the gloaming that passes for night that far north on 21 June. Also, I hired a static caravan on a site nearby for a week and Mo came to stay with two-month-old Sonia, who had been born in Glasgow.

The last thing I remember from our stay at Kinloss had to do with the aircraft wash bay. Installed on a turn-off taxiway was a large square area, which had a whole array of spray nozzles and drainage culverts. This was for washing the precious new Nimrod jets when they came back from flying for hours through the salt-laden air over the North Sea or the Atlantic. The old 'Shacklebombers' weren't treated so well, but they were about to retire.

One day ATC warned everyone that the aircraft wash bay was going to be tested, for the first time, with a real, live Nimrod passing through it. When the moment finally arrived, those of us who were not actually airborne went out to watch.

The Mighty Hunter landed and turned off the runway into the bay. Nothing happened. It was supposed to go through at about walking pace and about halfway across it slowed down even more. Still nothing happened. Then the Nimrod decided that it wasn't going to have a shower that morning and taxied out of the bay. An RAF Mini car, occupied by not one but two Wing Commanders, OC Operations Wing and OC Technical Wing, was following the Nimrod, no doubt to make sure that the device worked properly. As the Mini entered the bay it disappeared in a veritable deluge of water, which kept going for about three or four minutes. I don't know to this day whether they had their windows open on that warm June morning, but I like to think that they did.

10 REORGANISING AND REMOVING

The *raison d'etre* for the UAS presence within the RAF, and therefore under the auspices and budget of the Ministry of Defence, has been examined and re-examined over the years. In the 1960s there was a body of opinion, usually clothed in red or pink, that felt that the publicly-funded UAS system was too elitist. Possibly because there was the potential for undergraduates to save hundreds, if not thousands, of pounds by giving them the opportunity to spend three years qualifying for the Preliminary Flying Badge, which in turn allowed them to apply for a civilian private pilot's licence.

Some of these critical folk also held the opinion that better value for money might be achieved if the UASs' primary aim became one of recruitment and the preliminary training of aircrew, in lieu of the rather vague objective of instilling air-mindedness into undergraduates and thus, in time, the captains of industry, commerce and politics. In the mid-1960s this recruitment aspiration tied in with government proposals for the early advancement in rank for RAF officers who were university graduates. Moreover, the Wilson-led Labour government was wielding a huge financial axe at the defence tree. It had already cancelled several advanced projects for the RAF, including the TSR2, and by 1968 was overseeing the withdrawal of forces from bases to the east of the Suez Canal. Anything in the defence budget that was not seen to be of a supreme cost-benefit was being cut.

In early 1968 the results of the latest study into the future of the UASs was released by the MOD. The refocusing of the squadrons' function on recruitment was now clearly stated as the primary objective and we were told to encourage the best cadets to apply for RAF Scholarships, so committing them to a period of full-time RAF service of not less than eight years. The other outcome of the study was that the national UAS cadre would be cut by a quarter. Some UASs were to be combined and co-located and others, including Glasgow and Strathclyde, were to be reduced in size. The only UAS that would then retain a Wing Commander as Officer Commanding and an establishment of seven aircraft would be London; all the other UASs would be commanded by a squadron leader and hold an establishment of four or five aircraft.

As fate would have it, this edict from on high coincided with the increasing need for us to move out of Scone airfield, whose surface was becoming rapidly unusable for Chipmunks and, anyway, was earmarked for extensive work to put down at least one hard runway. That and the reduced number of staff led to the only sensible conclusion: we needed to move closer to Glasgow. However, there were no suitable military airfields available so negotiations started with the management at Glasgow International Airport for us to be allocated office, hangar and parking space there.

Scotsman Flt Lt Hector Skinner had replaced Bob Hutcheson after the Summer Camp at Abingdon; it was a fair swap – one Scotsman for another! Bob had been posted to the staff at CFS to teach others to be Chipmunk QFIs. Hector had come from an exchange tour in Ghana, flying Chipmunks with their military flying training school and he became our new CFI. He and the Boss became rapidly and deeply involved in the arrangements for our move to Glasgow.

Another staff change was the arrival of Flt Lt Andrew Jamieson from CFS; or 'Jamie', as I had known him when we had served together in No 16 Squadron, in Germany. He soon got us calling him by his preferred sobriquet of 'Drew' instead of Jamie. He had replaced Colin Adams who had gone off to be the ADC to the Commandant of the RAF Staff College: a good career move.

At the end of October 1968 we moved the flying element of the UAS, lock, stock and several barrels, to Glasgow Airport. The allocated office block north-east of the terminal was adequate if somewhat spartan, but we soon knocked it into shape. The aircraft parking area was not far from there, but the hangar was about a mile away, at the south-western corner of the technical site. The ground crew now had to start their day with lots of towing, but with five instead of seven aeroplanes to haul. Once we had settled in we started flying and had to carve out a flying area, outside the Glasgow Control Zone, but not so far away that we would lose too much productive training time. In conjunction with the local Senior Air Traffic Controller (SATCO) we worked out an exit and entry route by following the River Clyde to Dumbarton and then making a right turn to fly north to an area that was essentially over the whole of Loch Lomond and a good portion of the surrounding countryside.

On good weather days the flight up the Clyde was fascinating and scenic, all the time under the beady eye of Glasgow Approach Radar until we reached the prominent, plum-duff shape of Dumbarton Rock. There we made the almost 90° right turn to follow the River Leven, past Alexandria, to the southern end of Loch Lomond. That marked the point where we could climb above 2,000ft and head north or north-east into our own picturesque play area. Sometimes it was hard to concentrate on the job in hand because the magnificent scenery drew your eyes naturally into searching for even better vistas. To the north-east of the Loch stands Ben Lomond, one of the 283 Scottish mountains whose summits exceed 3,000ft above mean sea level. These peaks are known by those who like climbing them as 'the Munros'; they are named after Baronet Sir Hugh Munro who first catalogued all such Scottish peaks at the end of the nineteenth century. Ben Lomond is the most southerly of all the Munros and its location close to Glasgow makes it one of the most popular to 'bag' first; for climbers and not flyers, that is! As far as we were concerned it was going to be best to stay south of Big Ben Lomond and stay over the Loch or the lower plain of land to its east. That would give us the maximum vertical distance between terra firma and ourselves.

So the first challenge for our boys was to learn the route outbound and inbound as well as all the radio procedures that went with it. The second challenge for us all was to learn about flying in the controlled airspace around the airport, which was often occupied by airliners. Although they nearly always made straight-in approaches we still had to keep our ears and eyes well open for these much larger and higher priority airborne brethren.

The biggest danger to us would come from something called 'Wake Turbulence'. This phenomenon arises from the fact that a spiralling vortex of air is shed from each wingtip on every aircraft in flight. The size and strength of that pair of mini-tornados streaming behind the wings is directly proportional to the aeroplane's weight. In humid weather these vortices can clearly be seen; the bigger the jet, the bigger the vortices. These horizontal whirlwinds can persist for several miles after the aircraft has passed, especially behind big jets like the Boeing 747. So our tiny little flying machines had to stay well behind any airliners landing or taking off and the ATC controllers helped us using their radar. They would update us on the position of commercial traffic and we taught the students how best to interpret and use that information. I was really surprised how most of them picked up this very important bit of airmanship so quickly. Mind you we had scared them enough with some films about Wake Turbulence that had some graphic crash scenes in them!

So it wasn't long before we had settled in to our new environment and had not made ourselves too unpopular with the natives. However, one day my student did try his best to upset that happy status quo. I cannot tell a lie, it was 'Otto' Mattick who did it, sir. The time had come when I had to let young Otto do his first take-off without assistance from me. We lined up on the north-easterly runway and Otto started to open the throttle. As the speed increased he was veering to the right a little and then he pushed the stick forward – too far and too fast. I told him to ease back a bit and get the aircraft going down the runway, not across it. At this point he froze, still holding the controls in his iron grip! I shouted, 'I HAVE CONTROL!' at which point he was supposed to release all the controls. He released the stick but was still holding the rudder pedals off-centre. Otto was a strong lad, a potential rugby prop forward, and I pushed hard with my left foot, but I could not move the rudder pedals. I shouted at him to relax his feet just as we reached the edge of the runway. Thankfully I felt the rudder pedals come back under my control. But we barely had flying speed, nevertheless I eased the stick back as far as I dared to get some airspace between us and the grass that we were about to run across. As I felt the aircraft starting to lift there was an enormous BANG from behind me.

'We must have hit one of the runway side lights,' I thought. The impact had slowed us down a little, but we were still scraping along a foot or two in the air. I just hung on and, as carefully as I could, I flew level to get the aircraft to accelerate. I looked out ahead and the control tower was appearing around each side of Otto's helmet. The top of it was still a considerable height above us. I decided to turn, rather than waiting for climbing speed to arrive on the airspeed indicator.

As we went past the glazed upper floor of the tower, where the local controller and his assistants sat, I saw someone wave; I think that their fist was clenched. I climbed to circuit height, made sure that Otto was not in too bad a state of shock and asked Ian Montgomorie, who was doing circuits with his student, to come and have a look at our back end. Within a short order of time he had slotted into line astern and said, 'The tailwheel is at 90° to the fuselage, to the right, and there's a bit of damage to the tailcone, otherwise you're fine.'

I decided that the best thing to do would be to land towards the right-hand side of the runway, hold the tail up as long as I could and then be prepared for a big swing to the left when the tailwheel finally touched down. In fact that's exactly what happened but we stayed on the runway and we had to shut down and then get towed back. The following week the Boss received a bill for a new runway light! Otto got it right at the next attempt. He went on to do quite well and I met him several years later when he was flying Tridents for BEA.

Not long after we had moved to Glasgow Wg Cdr John Greenhill was posted out and a new Boss arrived. He was Sqn Ldr Barry Dale, an ex-Jet Provost QFI who had converted to the Chipmunk at CFS. He soon settled in, aided greatly by the wonderful Margaret Sinclair, and he started flying as soon as he could find the time. The formidable Arthur Pullen had left by now and the new CFI was to be 'Uncle' Hector Skinner. The new arrangement felt much more cosy and friendly than the previous one. I for one enjoyed the slightly smaller unit greatly. The new Boss became popular with the students and staff alike and he did everything that he could to be as much of an instructor as the rest of us, while still learning his way round the university and his duties as OC.

Flying continued when it could and the year went on. Another joy of flying a light aeroplane is that you notice even the subtle changes of the seasons as they go by. In winter, when there is no snow, the countryside floating by below is very brown. All the trees are leafless and many of the fields are ploughed and are that rich burnt umber of freshly turned loam. Then in April a green blush starts on the copses and the hedgerows, winter-sown cereal crops start to shoot and blossoms start to decorate some of the trees in pink or white. Soon the green takes over completely, except for large squares of bright lemon yellow where the oilseed rape is flowering. There is also the occasional patch of the blue of linseed. The gorse blossoms yellow on the hills and the sheep stand out like so many white maggots scouring the heather-clad slopes. Soon enough that flowers too, royal purple, and the woods and copses turn a darker hue of green. The cereal fields turn to yellow ochre and the harvest starts. Back then the farmers were allowed to burn their surplus straw, so September days were often made hazy blue by the slate coloured smoke rising into the atmosphere. In our little flying machines it was a good idea to avoid the pillars of acrid grey, as they tended to have a lot of turbulence in them, they smelled awful and made your eyes stream with tears. In October the browns returned, but through a patchwork of reds, oranges and yellows as the cold air switched off the leaves' production of chlorophyll. Then one day there would be white shadows along the hedgerows; the frost not yet melted by the sun. Then there would be other days when the snow came and magically bleached the world white.

One night it was perishing cold. The dawn temperature at the airport was reported as −18°C! The sky was a crackling blue, so when we got to work we started flying as soon as we could. My student and I were the first out over Loch Lomond and we were climbing up to 6,000ft to do some stalling and spinning. As he levelled off the engine started to run roughly. I took over and tried varying the power and turning off the magneto switches in turn, all to no effect. I was beginning to think about positioning myself for a forced landing when I remembered to try turning the carburettor heat off. A lever on the right-hand side of the cockpit operated this and was wire locked into the ON position. I told my student to operate the lever and within a couple of minutes after varying the power the rough running had ceased. I passed this information back to base and asked for the temperature at 6,000ft. 'Minus 25 degrees,' I was told. That explained the problem. The carburettor heating system warmed the air entering the throat of the carburettor by about 15°C so avoiding the usual range of +20°C to −10°C (dependent on humidity) in which ice may form inside the air intake. That increased the mixture strength and caused rough running. If the ice continues to form unchecked it will eventually cause the engine to stop altogether.

With these exceptionally cold temperatures the carburettor heating was warming the air up sufficient to put it back into the middle of the icing range. We put this problem up the line and received permission to turn the carburettor heat off if the surface temperature at take-off was below −10C°. Actually with these sorts of temperatures we would rather have not flown at all because, even with our 'Bunny Suits' and extra socks on it was not possible to fly for much more than forty-five minutes without a serious risk of hypothermia.

In the winter of 1968 the Wilson government decided that the UK would remain on what they called British Standard Time, effectively Greenwich Mean Time plus one hour. The effect in Scotland was that it stayed dark well into the morning hours. By the beginning of December, and through January, we were able to log the first flight of the working day as Night Flying! It was useful as we instructors had a requirement to stay current at night flying throughout the winter season. The rest of Scotland wasn't too happy with the arrangement though and British Standard Time was scrapped in 1971.

Winter brought the winds as well as the snow. Sometimes so much so that we could not fly, either because the crosswind component of the wind was stronger than our limit of 15kts or because the turbulence was just too much for most of our students to cope with. However, I did go flying on one windy day, when the direction of the west-south-westerly wind was reasonably coincident with the direction of the runway. At height there were very strong winds, starting from 50kts at 2,000ft and rising to over 80kts at 8,000ft. I was hoping that we could do something useful as this particular student was getting well behind his fellow squadron members in his training. A combination of bad luck with weather and the demands of his university course had meant that he had not been airborne for over a month.

When we arrived over Loch Lomond it was very rough, but he was not feeling airsick and he was coping reasonably well. As we climbed higher we had to do so on a westerly heading because we would otherwise have drifted east at a rapid rate of knots. We managed to do a stall at 6,000ft and a loop and then we were at the eastern limit of our area. Beating our way back into wind to give us some free airspace took ages. When we got there a couple of turns to look all around us, and one more aerobatic manoeuvre, had us back at square one. I told him that we were losing the battle and encouraged him to stick the nose down, leave max rpm on the engine and descend at 140kts to 2,000ft. We flew almost sideways down to Dumbarton Rock and then I had an idea for a bit of a 'wheeze'.

'I have control, you relax for a while,' I said. I then turned right instead of left, pointing down the Clyde towards Helensburgh instead of up the river towards Glasgow. I selected full flap and slowed down to 45kts and looked over the side. Sure enough we were making slow progress backwards over the centre of the river! The radar controller called on the radio to ask my position; he said that we seemed to have disappeared from his display. I told him where we were, but he said that he couldn't see us. At this very slow rearwards speed we probably looked like one of the many ships coming upriver to Glasgow. I kept up this jape for about five more minutes and then I thought that I would let the controller off the hook. I increased power, raised the flap and turned downwind and up-river.

'Ah, there you are!' I heard. I told him that I had the airfield in sight and he told me to call the local controller. We landed without further incident but the landing run was less than 100ft.

A final memory from Glasgow was when we taxied out behind a rather old and tired looking Scandinavian Air Services Boeing 727. The pilot lined up on the runway and applied power for departure. At that juncture huge volumes of black smoke started issuing from the three engines. It was a calm day so the noxious vapours just hung in the air behind the aged jet as it struggled into the air. I was cleared to line up and, as a bit of a joke, I asked for an IFR[24] departure. The controller saw the joke and ignored me. However, a heavily Scandinavian accented voice came over the ether: 'When you are as old as this jet, you will be allowed to smoke as well.'

There was great satisfaction in teaching lads at this very basic level to fly. Many of them had no prior knowledge of aviation or the military. These students were always the most challenging. Very basic things such as how to read a compass, or whether the rudder pedals worked like bicycle handlebars or a boat's rudder, were necessary teaching points. Although these guys were undergraduates, it was amazing how few of them could work out in their heads the simplest calculations. Things like how much safe flying time was left with the amount of fuel in the tanks. Or how long it will take the aircraft to get to the next turning point or destination at the present speed.

A favourite tease of mine involved the 'pitot head'. This is a little tube that protrudes below the left wing. It has a hole in the front down which the air blows and the air pressure is displayed as the speed on the airspeed indicator: where else? But static pressure is also needed for measuring the height, shown on the altimeter. So this is done by a series of slots around the outside of the pitot head. These slots are offset in a regular pattern around the circumference of the tube. When showing the students round the aircraft during the pre-flight external inspection, I would point out the pitot head because the cover that went over it, to prevent anything, such as insects, blocking the hole, had to be removed before flight and stowed in the cockpit. So, when they took the cover off I would ask, 'Why are the slots all round the tube offset from each other like that?' They would ponder long and hard to come up with some scientific explanation. When they finally gave up I would say, 'Well, if they were all lined up with each other the end would fall off!' This was usually received with a groan; but at this stage of their training, a respectful groan.

When we had our annual visit from CFS Examining Wing, about a year after we had moved to Glasgow Airport, the report included some very complimentary remarks about the high sense of awareness of our students in and around the airport. This was very rewarding as the thought of some of our wee chappies being within 10 miles of an airliner full of fare-paying, talking ballast had given some of us nightmares. I think that our fears obliged us to make sure that the level of situational awareness was driven to its highest possible level. Flying at Glasgow Airport and in our nearby allocated airspace was never dull, always challenging and very enjoyable; well, most of the time.

11 LIVING IN GLASGOW

The weather in the west of Scotland is much more dynamic than it is in the east, so we lost more flying time due to low cloud and rain than we had at Perth. On some days, when we couldn't fly, I would go to some of the lectures that our students attended at the universities or visit them in their labs. Andy Crawford showed me the university's first electronic computer: it was the size of a large room. However, in the lights and whistles department it didn't disappoint. Later I was taken into a lab where I first saw a laser light firing. Mike Bell introduced me to one of his aerodynamics professors, one Dr Babbister who had authored at least one seminal tome on aerodynamics that was well known by most of the world's English speaking aerodynamicists. He was known as Professor B-b-b-babbister because he had a dreadful stammer. I also sat in on several lectures, most of which I cannot now remember, with the exception of one. That was by a prominent social scientist on the subject of dealing with change. His main thrust was that things were changing in virtually every aspect of life at an exponential rate and that the human psyche was on the threshold of not being able to keep up and adapt. I had empathy with his argument because my world was in the throes of change. We had moved to Glasgow halfway through my tour of duty and that had been fraught with problems.

Initially I had been told that there might not be any OMQ for us to move into, so my wife and I talked about the possibility of buying or renting somewhere. We needed to start searching so I asked some of the students where we might look and where we might stay overnight to give ourselves two days hunting. Alex Cargill and his bunch of mates had a flat in the city and they offered to put us up. Footsore from our perambulations we arrived to take up their offer. Apart from a couple of nights on the winter survival course in Bavaria I have never spent such a cold night trying to get some sleep. It was winter and perishing cold and the place had no heating! I was suddenly glad that I had not gone to 'uni'!

In the end the Army, bless 'em, came up with a married quarter for us in the leafy Glasgow suburb of Thornliebank. It was not far from a large open area of parkland known as Rouken Glen Park. This was a super place to walk our labrador, Shandy. The park had a stream, more correctly known as a 'burrrn', flowing through the eponymous glen and a large lake. One icy winter's day Shandy suddenly took off after some ducks across the frozen lake until she reached an area of ice that could not support her considerable weight. She went in with a large splash and then, of course, she couldn't get out. Every attempt she made just broke the edge of the ice. There was an island in the middle of the lake and she swam to that and stood on the shore barking. We had no idea what to do until some kind soul liberated a rowing boat and pushed it across the ice until it too broke into the water and then the rescue was made. We took a very cold dog home after giving grateful thanks to our helpers.

My daily commute to the airport was very much like any of those made by many civilians in their everyday lives; but it was all new to me. Since leaving home six years earlier, I had not lived in an urban area and had rarely commuted any meaningful distance to work. However, I soon got used to the traffic, although I thought that the way that the average Scottish motorists drove they must have some Italian or French blood: everything was done so competitively and at great speed. I got rear-ended at a roundabout and the only thing that my assailant said was, 'Och, ye could hae got oot three times overrr! Why didn't ye go?' The fact that a stream of Glaswegian Formula 1 racing drivers were coming at me round the island at high speed didn't seem to count.

Glasgow was a place that still had its dark side. My commute into the city for work at the town HQ took me through the notorious Gorbals area. The tall, dark tenement buildings shut out what little sun or light that there was, although some of them were in the process of being demolished. We once went to an evening show at a cinema on the edge of the Gorbals. I parked the car on the street and was immediately approached by a wee lad, who appeared to be about 10 years old.

'Gie us a bob[25] an' I'll watch over yer carr, mister,' he said. The protection racket had obviously filtered down to the kids.

'I'll give you sixpence now and the rest when I come out and find my car untouched,' I offered. This seemed to impress on the small entrepreneur that he was entering a proper business deal, albeit with a Sassenach, so he accepted. My wife was more sceptical, saying, 'Perhaps we'll find the car damaged and the lad gone.'

'We'll see,' I replied with as much optimism for human nature as I could muster. In the event the wee gangster was there, the car was untouched and he went away a whole shilling better off.

Often, on my way home from the city centre, I saw men who were obviously deeply inebriated and either leaning on or relieving themselves against walls or, as on at least one occasion in Paisley, literally lying in the gutter. However, the commercial part of the city centre was vibrant and always busy. One evening a few of us staff members went to a pub where we had been told there was a good comedian. Sure enough he was a very funny, if occasionally rude, lad. He had a mop of frizzy black hair and a beard. One of his cleaner jokes was:

'There were two ducks on a tandem cycling down Sauchiehall Street. The one on the back went "Quack! Quack!" The one on the front said, "Ah cannae go any quacker!"'

Another:

'I was walking down the street and I saw a sign which said "Glasgow School For The Blind". Why was it there?'

Then:

'There was a well known prostitute in the city centre known as Hairy Mary. One night a young policeman came around a dark corner to find Mary standing there with her skirts hitched up, holding a bag of chips in the same hand and eating them with the other. "Now then Mary," said the policeman, "Ye cannae stand there exposing yerself like that." "Oh," says Mary, "Has that wee sailor gone?"'

I told you he was a bit rude and that wasn't the worst. However, he was hilarious and his delivery was superb. He even got some of the locals laughing. I don't remember his name, but some years later when I first saw Billy Connolly on the TV he was indeed an older version of that hairy young man.

Another thing that I experienced for the first time in Glasgow was Indian food. As a youth my parents had taken me to Chinese restaurants on many occasions, but that was before the other Asian immigration wave had started. It's hard to believe now, but such cuisine was unknown before the 1960s. My colleagues advised me to start with a Biryani, as that was not too spicy and it came as a complete meal; so I did. However, it wasn't long before I was trying other dishes and calibrating my taste buds' capacity to accept hotter spices. I stopped at Madras and have retained my love for Asian food ever since.

But, without doubt, the highlight of this part of our time in Scotland was the birth, on 18 May 1970, of our first child. We gave her the names Sonia Caroline, the former being after the wife of my navigator in Germany.[26] Sonia was born in the maternity part of the Glasgow Royal Infirmary and was a 'bonnie wee bairn'. She was a very special gift because we had suffered the tragedy of a miscarriage during our time in Perthshire. Sonia has always been proud of her Scottish naissance and invariably supports the national team during the annual Rugby Internationals.

The arrival of a baby in anyone's life brings changes totally out of proportion to the size of this new person. I had to sell my beloved MG Midget and BSA motorbike and invest in something that had more carrying capacity. Much to the horror of my colleagues I actually purchased a Ford Anglia van. It might not have been very pretty but it had lots of room, only the two seats that we needed and did not attract unwanted attention in downtown Glasgow. However, I was told that, as it was painted green, I should not park it in the Ibrox area. My blank look gained the explanation that green was the colour of Celtic Football Club and hence represented the Roman Catholic Glaswegian population and Ibrox was where Rangers Football Club played and was the epicentre of the Protestants, who didn't like anything green; perhaps with the exception of the grass on football fields.

Living in and around the great, raw and always exciting city of Glasgow was an experience that I could not have predicted when I left Germany. Sometimes one experienced its darker sides, like having to lock the car doors when stopped at the traffic lights or never venturing down Sauchiehall or Bath Streets late on Friday or Saturday nights. That was when two things happened: the inevitable rowdy disturbances and the Scottish Regiments out on their recruiting campaigns. Until then I thought that press gangs were a thing of the past. But overall, there were more good things than bad.

Many years later, when Glasgow was a European City of Culture, I returned. The place had changed in many ways out of all recognition. But the under-current of humour, strength and individuality was still there. It's a proud boast to sing 'I belong tae Glasgow, dear old Glasgow Toon.'

12 JOURNEYS SOUTH

CFS graduates are graded by their ability, ascertained during a rigorous examination of their knowledge and skill. In the spring of 1968 I had gained a B1 (Average) category. This category had been confirmed during a flight with Sqn Ldr Hines of CFS Exam Wing during our Summer Camp at RAF Bicester in July 1968.

When I got back from a long camping holiday round western Scotland during the summer leave period of that year, I was summoned to the Boss's office. He told me that he and the CFI had agreed that I should have a go at upgrading my category to A2 (Above Average). Hector Skinner had already booked me a short 'crammer' course with the Standards Flight at RAF Church Fenton, which was the home of the Preliminary Flying School, which also flew Chipmunks.

So, on Tuesday 9 September I went to work with my bag packed and set off for Church Fenton in Chipmunk WG 431. The weather was forecast to be cloudy all the way and I was going to have to climb above the lowest layers to remain above Safety Altitude.[27] All went well until about one hour into the flight. It was then that I noticed that the button on the Direction Indicator (DI) had been pushed in. The DI is a gyro that can be rotated to match the reading of the magnetic compass, which was on the floor between my feet: the only place the makers could find for it! The button on the DI can be pushed in when the DI, which can wander a bit, needs realigning or during aerobatics and spinning. When the button is pushed in the DI does not move with the aircraft. I must have touched it with my map and not noticed. As the cloud-covered world below me looked like the top of an enormous cauli-flower I could not confirm visually where I was. I knew where I should have been by now, but I had no idea just how long I had been following a rigid and useless DI. I soon realigned it and it wasn't that far out, so perhaps I might not be too far from my estimated position, which was 10 miles west of Newcastle.

The RAF's Distress and Emergency unit operated a service called a Training Fix, as much for their benefit as for the user. So I changed to their frequency and called them for this facility. The transmitting aircraft's position is found by the intersection of several bearings from their radio receivers projected onto a map.

'Quebec 06, you are 10 miles east of Newcastle,' the controller told me. I acknowledged in a slightly higher voice than normal. I didn't want to be over the North Sea, thank you! I was just calculating the change of heading to take me to Church Fenton when he called me again.

'Quebec 06, transmit again to check your position,' he instructed. I did so.

'Oops, sorry old boy, I should have said that you are 10 miles WEST of Newcastle.'

I thanked him politely; it's not kosher to be rude over the air. Thankfully I was almost on my planned track; it was not a good idea to be over the North Sea in a single-engined aeroplane in the middle of winter. As I got further south the cloud broke up and Leeming Radar saw me down into the Vale of York. I landed at Church Fenton after two hours and fifteen minutes airborne.

I spent the next three days under the ministrations of Flt Lt John Carr, a large, amiable and very able chap who gave me lots of tips to improve my instructional technique. I flew with him and his boss, Sqn Ldr Johnston. By the end of my short detachment I was crammed with information and helpful advice. With grateful thanks I set off back to Scotland feeling much better prepared to put my head in the Examining Wing lion's mouth. The weather for the return flight was outstanding and I booked into the UK Low Flying System and flew virtually the whole way at 250ft above the ground (well officially), over the heather-covered moors and hills up the spine of England into the Scottish Lowlands.

However, I had to wait until the end of October for my visit to CFS. I decided to take some leave and drive down to Yorkshire and then on to Little Rissington, leaving my wife at her parents' place. I arrived at CFS on 27 October and settled into the Mess. The following morning, having spent the evening abstemiously with my books, I reported to Exam Wing HQ with my flying kit. Flt Lt Gordon Webb was awaiting me with an open smile; what did he have up his sleeve, I wondered? We had a coffee while he explained what we would be doing. A briefing on a specified exercise, a flight during which I would first teach him the briefed exercise, and then he would throw in a couple of no-notice exercises. There would also be a period of general handling, at least one major emergency and one of each type of visual circuit.

I went away to prepare the briefing and so started one of the longest and hardest days in my flying career thus far. Gordon was very fair and his soft south-western burr made him easy to listen to; except that it was me who had to do all the talking. After one hour and twenty minutes we were back on the ground and he sent me off to lunch. I felt that I had not made any major errors and that I had handled the practice forced landing quite well; but there was much more to come.

We reconvened after lunch and Gordon began grilling me on all manner of rules and regulations, technical things and was posing situations to check my airmanship. By now I had a huge headache and asked if I could have a coffee. At which point Gordon said, kindly, 'I was just going to suggest that myself. While you are having your coffee, I'll debrief you and then we'll go see the Boss.'

Suffice it to say that when I did go to see the officer commanding Examining Wing he greeted me with a smile and shook my hand. 'Congratulations, Mike,' he said. 'You are now an A2 QFI, well done.' I thanked him and Gordon and then made a decently hasty exit to go and lie down in a darkened room for a while. After dinner I partook of a few celebratory drinks and then, the next morning, wended my way back to Yorkshire.

Another trip south started on Wednesday 4 February 1970. Apparently we had a Chipmunk equipped with a hook-and-release mechanism for glider-towing, WB 581, which was needed down south. It was arranged that I would fly it to RAF Newton, the home of Nottingham UAS, where I would exchange it for a machine not so equipped that was coming to Newton from Hamble, on the south coast near Southampton. The Boss, Sqn Ldr Barry Dale, wanted to go to RAF Ouston, not far from Newcastle and the operating base of Northumbrian UAS, so he asked me to drop him off on the way. He was quite content to sit in the back seat nursing his overnight bag; mine was in the small luggage locker behind his shoulders. We arrived at Ouston after just over an hour but we couldn't raise anyone on any of their VHF radio frequencies. So we carried out the radio failure drill of flying past the control tower rocking our wings; they gave us a green light to land. After Barry had extricated himself from the back seat a radio technician came out and fiddled with the radio. Whatever magic he performed on it worked and I appeared now to have a fully serviceable communications system, so off I went further south. I was aiming for Church Fenton but the forecast had been a little downbeat with the threat of snow.

As I flew further south I ran into cloud and went down to keep clear of it. It then started to snow, lightly at first, but as I flew further into the Vale of York it got heavier. I called RAF Leeming and they told me that the snow was falling steadily there, so I asked for a radar approach to their southerly runway. All the way down the glide slope I could still see the land below me, but only just, and when I landed the ground was starting to turn white. As I turned off the runway I could see through the white murk an enormous USAF C-141 Starlifter transport aircraft, with its rear ramp down and doors wide open. The thought that I could just about taxi straight into its well-lit and warm looking freight bay passed naughtily across my mind. However, I was directed to the Visiting Aircraft Flight where they promised that they would refuel and look after my miniscule steed for the night.

The next day the weather had cleared and only forty-five minutes after leaving Leeming I was landing on Newton's grass runway. I had hoped that the Chipmunk I was due to pick up was ready to go and that I would make it back to Church Fenton before dark. However, it had not arrived so I would have to wait. In fact, by the time it turned up it was too late, so I stayed overnight in the Officers' Mess at Newton. The following morning I set off north again, via Church Fenton to top up the fuel tanks to ensure that I would get to Glasgow with enough fuel to divert, if necessary, to Prestwick. The homeward trip was reasonably uneventful if a bit long and very cold. Whoever dreamt up the idea of swapping over two Chipmunks from opposite ends of the country in the middle of winter?

13 FLYING COPPERS, FLYING TROPHIES AND MOVING ON

Twice during my tour in Scotland I was, along with everyone else on the unit, involved in practising our war role. Yes, the RAF's Chipmunk force had its own special job in wartime. It was called 'Aid to the Civil Power' and that role could also be generated in peacetime for a variety of other purposes if the government so decreed. For the purposes of the war role the three-day exercise took the form of flying police officers to various locations to discover a multitude of things, all of which were invented for the task. The scenario was of a world after a nuclear attack.

The first such exercise was flown in mid-September 1968, while we were still at Scone, under the title of Exercise MAIGRET – lots of points for originality by the folks who choose these names (*Maigret* was the title of a then-popular TV detective series with a French protagonist)! There were five policemen and we were each allocated one to fly with; mine was Sergeant Lake. We had to introduce them to map reading their way around and get them used to being thrown about a bit; however, most of them had done it all before. They also had to be proficient at using the radio to report what they had seen; no problem there either. All the flights required a lot of low-altitude work to identify things on the ground and it was all great fun, even if the real thing would be deadly serious. Following roads, twisting and turning through steep-sided glens up into the hills was the best part. However, an eye had to be kept out for the incline of the hills being steeper than our poor little flying machine could cope with! It all went off well and not too many constables were airsick. The only issue that we raised in the exercise wash-up was the lack of any simulated decontamination facilities and we considered that we would all be getting radiation sickness after a few days. The final evening was spent together in a local hostelry and we went our separate ways all a bit wiser.

The second such exercise was held from Glasgow Airport in September 1969; this time it was Exercise Z-CARS (again, the title of a then-popular TV series about police)! The aims were the same and the low-flying fun was even better. The officers of the law seemed to throw themselves fully into the various exercises and the three days of flying were very packed. Due to airsickness, the odd policeman's breakfast or lunch was 'eaten' twice, but no serious injuries ensued! It was great, even for a short time, to be doing something quite different with another adult on board.

Each year the squadron was involved in an inter-UAS flying competition for the Scone Trophy. The Scone Trophy was the regional competition for UASs based in Scotland and Northern Ireland. There were other regional competitions and it was the winners of each region that then went forward to compete for the national Hack Trophy. There were two categories in which we could enter a student pilot. One was Spot Landing, where the nearest three-point landing to a marked spot got the highest marks; just to make it a real competitive event the engine had to be at idle throughout the approach from 1,500ft. The other category was a five-minute aerobatic sequence. This was judged from the ground and for safety the students were not allowed to come below 1,000ft; plus there was an instructor in the back seat just in case! The latter was, of course, from another UAS.

In May 1969 the Scone Trophy was held at Scone and our entrant was Acting Pilot Officer Gavin Mackay; he had to fly a short aerobatic sequence and do a Spot Landing. Just before the competition I flew with Gavin Mackay to help him learn some more advanced aerobatics and to help him get his sequence polished. He was actually quite good so I thought that I would show him an 8-point roll. This is not so easy because when the Chipmunk's engine is upside down it stops.

The main requirement for an 8-point roll is to get up plenty of speed, at least 130kts, then raise the nose quite a bit above the horizon and immediately initiate a rapid roll. No sooner has this got going that you have to use lots of opposite stick to stop the roll, for just a second, at 45° angle of bank.

Then that exercise is repeated, as rapidly as possible, to go to 90° angle of bank; and so on another six times to regain upright flight. Careful co-ordination of rudder and stick is required to keep the nose going where you want it, straight ahead, and not to lose any altitude. The repetition of the full aileron in the desired direction of roll and then the opposite to momentarily stop the roll at each 45° point has to be quite harsh. Anyway, I demonstrated it to Gavin, having naturally asked him to 'Follow me through'. After we had got back to the upright position and straight and level flight I asked him to try it. There followed a mighty thrashing of the control column left and right as he counted off the eight points. Sadly he got to eight well before we had come upright again. I got the impression that he'd got his head down and wasn't really watching what the aeroplane was doing. But, after a couple more demonstrations and practices he had got it sorted out.

The day of the Scone Trophy arrived and I was on supervisory duties in the back seat of a Chipmunk, flying with the aerobatic entry from Aberdeen UAS. From there I could see that it was not as good as Gavin Mackay's. Gavin touched down right on the money and sure enough, at the end of the day, his combined scores were sufficient to win us the Scone Trophy. A good time was had by all that evening and I flew carefully back to Glasgow the next day.

But winning the Scone meant that we were now entered for the Hack Trophy, which was going to be competed for at RAF Ternhill in Shropshire on 12 July. So we arranged that our Summer Camp at RAF Abingdon would end on 11 July. From there most of the cadets set off by road and we QFIs followed by air the next day; our potential star act, Gavin Mackay, was flying with Ian Montgomerie. It was a fine but windy day and as we flew north in our five-ship formation, I noticed that much of the traffic on the M6 was faster than we were. Nevertheless, we arrived in time to take our places in the viewing area.

As far as I could tell Gavin's landing was very near the spot and his aerobatics looked both smooth and lively; his 8-point roll was immaculate! We then had to wait while the judges added up all the scores. Then to our delight the winners were ... 'The Universities of Glasgow and Strathclyde Air Squadron!' Another celebratory evening followed, only tempered by the knowledge that I had to fly my small but perfectly formed WP 967 home the next day. It was a good note on which to go off and wind down after a very busy summer camp.

Gavin Mackay was an outstanding student and eventually joined the RAF where he became a fellow course-member with the Prince of Wales while he was at the RAF College at Cranwell. On graduation from there Gavin became a QFI, later he flew the Harrier and eventually rose to air rank.

During the Summer Camp of 1970, at RAF Kinloss, I was 'dined out' by the squadron. I had, for over six months, been pushing hard to get a posting onto some jet that was more sharply pointed than the Canberra and much, much faster than a Chipmunk. I had even volunteered for the Red Arrows, although I didn't really expect that to go far. I received a very nice reply from the leader, Sqn Ldr Ray Hanna, telling me that my background experience was not what they were looking for. In the 'Preferences for Next Posting' part of my annual personal report I had made it fairly clear that I wanted to go back to the front line in the low-level attack role. At that time the RAF was getting the Blackburn Buccaneer Mk 2 and the McDonnell F4 Phantom for these roles and I was hoping that I would be able to head in their direction.

As another possible string to my bow I was thinking of the possibility of becoming a test pilot. This thought had been stimulated at that same Summer Camp at Kinloss. There I had met a Nimrod pilot, who was actually involved in setting up the Nimrod simulator. His name was Jock Wingate and I discovered that he had been through test pilot training. I casually said to him, over a beer one night, that I would like to become a test pilot, but that I thought that my basic academic background would be an obstacle. Jock was very encouraging and told me that the academic side, while needing some application, was not the stopper that I might think. He encouraged me to apply in March the following year, when the applications were sought. I put that into my future possible plans file.

Despite all these plans my destiny had been sealed. One day the Boss called me into his office and said, 'You must have impressed them a bit down at CFS. I've just had a call from the postings folk that told me that you have been requested by CFS to go back to the Chipmunk Squadron as a staff QFI.' They say that flattery will get you anywhere but it's not true; I was gutted. The Boss could see that I was not best pleased and asked me if there was anything he could do. I asked him if they could be persuaded differently as I really wanted to get onto 'fast jets'. He said that he would call them back.

However, the upshot was that it was a done deal and that I should accept it like a man! So after my summer leave it was going to be back to the Cotswolds. On the move again: such is the military life.

14 IN RETROSPECT

Our three-year tour of duty in Scotland was as close to an overseas tour as you can get without actually crossing any sea. The culture and language were different enough as to be noticeable, the latter especially as we had to learn all sorts of new uses for old words. For instance, you don't go shopping in Scotland, you 'do your messages', and you don't live somewhere, you 'stay' there. Things are 'bonnie', 'wee' and 'grand'. Children are 'bairns', streams are 'burns' and lakes are, of course, 'lochs'. In the pub, usually called a bar, you ask for a pint of 'heavy' or a 'haf an' a haf', which is a beer with a whisky chaser. Culturally the English are universally despised and the French are admired.

Even then, in the late 1960s, the aspiration of Scottish independence lay not far below the surface and Scottish men loved wearing skirts called kilts, purses called sporrans and, most disturbingly of all, knives in their socks.

In 1967 the Scottish National Party had gained 28 per cent of the vote in Pollock, near Glasgow, and later that year a redoubtable SNP lady, by the name of Winnie Ewing, had won the parliamentary seat of Hamilton (where the Academicals football team play). However, Scotland was still a long way from gaining full autonomy. Nevertheless, it often seemed that BBC Scotland had a great deal of independence from 'Auntie' down in London. A very annoying aspect of TV viewing was that just after a good programme or football match had been announced the dreaded words: 'But, for our viewers in Scotland …' would be heard. The programme that we so wanted to watch would be ousted from the tartan airwaves by such items as *An Evening With Kenneth McKellar* or *To the Ceilidh,*[28] with *Jimmy Shand and his Band*. It was a very annoying aspect of Scottish life. I never did get used to the music – especially the bagpipes played anywhere other than on a distant heather-clad hillside; the more distant the better!

Then there are the varying Scottish accents and dialects. Over in Perthshire the wee man who did the grounds maintenance around the married quarters might as well have been speaking Dutch or Icelandic for all that we could understand of what he said. But just down the road in Perth there were folk who spoke with a clarity that was enviable, despite their very evident accents. Over in Glasgow the general accent was much more harsh and phrases and words often ran together into an unintelligible jumble. Most Glaswegian men seemed to like talking out of the sides of their mouths. At the time the Scottish comedian and comic actor, Stanley Baxter, started a TV show in which he had a section called 'Parliamo Glasgow'. It was hilarious and yet, to us, very helpful. Of course there were parts of the cities and the country where the accents became totally different. In Glasgow it was Kelvinside and in Edinburgh it was Morningside. They were the 'posh' parts of the two cities and a joke that applied to folk from both areas was: 'What is the definition of sex in Kelvinside/Morningside?' Answer: 'It's what the coal's delivered in.' In the far north, around Inverness and the Black Isle, a very pure and lightly accented version of English could be heard; this was the most comprehensible of all Scottish accents.

While we were North of the Border we travelled and hiked as much as we could and saw sights that were truly awesome. At many a waterfall at the right season of the year we watched the salmons' exhausting efforts to reach their spawning grounds in the shallow gravel beds on the moors. On one occasion we walked down to a pool below the Sma' Glen and you could have walked across the water on the backs of the salmon waiting there to carry on their journey. I have never seen so many big fish crammed into such a small space. When I could I would go fishing. I caught only one salmon, but I caught several sea trout. On one occasion, fishing the River Earne south of Perth, a huge salmon jumped right out of the water not two feet away from me. The splash it made sounded like the body of a grown man falling into the water.

There were so many wonderful scenic places to visit: the Trossachs, an area of forests and lochs, surrounded by mountains; Loch Tay and the falls of Killin; the Western Highlands and Islands and the Kyles of Bute and the Isle of Arran. We tried our best not to waste the opportunity to travel. If the weather is good in Scotland then it is a beautiful place to be, but if it is raining then, like a lady on the Black Isle said, 'It sometimes forgets to stop.' The other saying that we came across was: 'If ye cannae see the mountain, then it's raining. If ye can see it, then it's about tae rain.'

As I've already alluded to, another benefit of this tour was the opportunity to see undergraduate life and share a little of it. As a grammar school lad, with no A-levels, it was a privilege to do that. I flew with about seventy-five different students, all individuals with different abilities, motivations and capacities. There were some I will never forget, for both good and bad reasons, and some whose names no longer ring many bells: but I am getting on a bit now and sometimes have trouble with the names of my grandkids! There were those who needed a lot of application to teach and those who took to flying like the proverbial duck to water. Many went on to flying careers, both civil and military, and some went on to pursue their chosen specialisation with success. The main thing that I drew from the experience was that teaching is not a one-way street. Your students teach you almost as much as you teach them, about life as well as esoteric occupations like being a pilot.

The whole experience wasn't without its tragedies. Early in my tour Flt Lt Rob Melville had come to us on a holding posting, before he went off to CFS to learn to be a QFI. He was a native of the Perthshire town of Crieff and was fully expecting to rejoin us as an instructor after he had graduated. I think that it was in early 1968 when we heard that Rob had been flying with the CFS Chipmunk Flight Commander, Flt Lt Owens, when the aircraft had gone out of control and either spun or stalled into the ground. Flt Lt Owens, who was occupying the front seat, was killed on impact and Rob was severely injured. He had multiple internal injuries and was in intensive care for quite a time. After several months he was released from hospital and he returned to us to act as our adjutant, working in the HQ in Glasgow with Margaret Sinclair. Rob never returned to flying.

Another sad and tragic thing that some of us witnessed was the near destruction by fire of the new Sports and Culture Centre being constructed in Perth. We were all flying on a fine and breezy day when one of our company noticed a pillar of black smoke rising above the city centre. He went across to look and noticed that the dome of the round building, which was almost finished, was well ablaze. He told the rest of us and, of course, we all flew over to see. It was quite a sight. There were several fire engines there, with at least one long, extendable ladder erected, dousing the flames with huge quantities of water and several other hoses playing on other lower parts of the building. In the end the majority of the structure was saved but the roof was totally destroyed.

We left Scotland better in many ways than when we arrived. We were richer for the experience of being with undergraduates and 'staying' in such a great and beautiful country. We left Scotland with more than we arrived because we now had our daughter, Sonia Caroline. So now it was onwards into the future and over new horizons as a family unit. On the road again, all the way south to Gloucestershire and back to the highest RAF airfield in the UK: Little Rissington. Hardly pastures new but certainly a different job of work.

PART THREE

CFS (AGAIN!)

15 PRETENDING TO BE BLOGGS

After leaving Scotland in July, I had the luxury of a whole month's leave to wind things up and get us to Little Rissington by 18 August 1970. However, there was not going to be an OMQ available, even though I was now over the age of 25; on the other hand, I was told that I would be allocated a 'hiring' in the beautiful village of Bourton-on-the-Water. When we arrived there it turned out to be an attractive bungalow in imitation Cotswold stone, on a corner plot, with a large expanse of open grass at the front and a small garden at the rear. It was fully furnished and, after our crate of possessions had arrived via the storage unit at RAF Quedgeley, also in Gloucestershire, we soon had our own goods and chattels, meagre as they were, installed.

Living in a tourist trap had its good and bad sides. Bourton-on-the-Water is a very popular tourist attraction and used to get absolutely overrun with 'grockles' (non locals) in the holidays and that made shopping a real trial, especially with baby Sonia in her pushchair. However, we soon learnt that we could use the many alleyways that ran between the houses and gardens to escape the crowds. It was amusing to watch the visitors looking up these winding pathways between stone walls wondering where they went, but not daring to explore.

A good thing about living there was that there were plenty of things for our own visitors to do, right on our doorstep. Bourton had a plethora of things to amuse and divert: Birdland, the Model Village, a Motor Museum, a Model Railway Centre as well as lots of interesting shops, several pubs, restaurants, tea rooms and hotels. On balance it was a good place to set up a family home.

From there it was a three-mile commute up the hill to the main gate at RAF Little Rissington. As I drove in through that gate on that first day back it was as if the past three years had barely happened; little, if anything, had changed. I called into Station HQ to get all the arrival paperwork and then took the familiar road to the hangar from where D Flt of No 3 Squadron CFS operated their Chipmunks. As I walked into the crew room I was greeted by a familiar Scottish burr. 'Och, they'll send just about anyone tae the staff at CFS these days!' It was Bob Hutcheson, my fellow UGSAS instructor and erstwhile neighbour with whom I had worked at Scone. Bob was the Flight Commander.

Amazingly two of the staff instructors who had been there three years ago, when I had passed through, were still giving out the collective CFS wisdom. One was my old mentor, Jack Hindle, now proudly wearing squadron leader's rank tape; he was one of the first of a new breed of officer – Specialist Aircrew. The RAF had decided that they needed to motivate the guys who reached their first optional exit point at age 38 to stay. The solution was to offer them a new pay scale, remaining as flight lieutenants and flying, with the possibility of promotion to squadron leader in their later years; all that and no more desk jobs either. A lot of the older staff at CFS had taken up this generous offer. As I heard Gordon Webb say one day: 'All this extra money for no extra responsibility – how could I refuse?'

Jack Hindle and I had a bit of a reunion and reminisced for a while before he had to go off to produce yet another QFI for the RAF. The other staff member who was still there from my previous time was Flt Lt John Snell. He had not moved away in the intervening years and was still there smoking his pipe and plying his trade as a staff QFI. John cut a spry figure for his age, probably around fifty-five then. He was known as 'Mr Bo Jangles' because of his light footed agility and ready wit. I was given a coffee and then pointed in the direction of the CO's office. However the man himself emerged before I got there so my arrival interview was conducted in a very friendly manner in a corner of the coffee bar.

The Boss was Sqn Ldr Jack Sprackling, a tall, blond, rather debonair chap who seemed welcoming and put me at my ease. When we'd done the round of the usual background questions he urged me to get on with my arrival procedures and bureaucracy. I had quite forgotten what it was to be like to be on a proper RAF station. When you arrive you are given a card and, in a bizarre version of autograph hunting, you have to visit all sorts of people and places, in a certain order and get them to sign the card. From this exercise you usually were given even more forms to complete and sign. Nevertheless, it is an excellent, if slightly barmy, method of finding your way about a new station.

Once that was done, it was back to my desk to read all the various tomes that would regulate my flying for the next couple of years. Then, once they were read and understood, if not totally remembered, more signatures were required. You do get used to it eventually, but I always felt that the expectation that one would have future perfect recall of that huge volume of words was totally unrealistic. It was really an exercise in authority covering its backside and being able to hand the blame downwards when things went awry.

During those few days of relative inactivity, that is no flying activity, I met the other staff instructors. There was an irrepressible Irishman called Paddy Cullen; a man much like Paddy McCormack, who had helped to teach me to fly the Canberra six years beforehand. This Paddy also had a great sense of humour, leprechaun-like build and an impish glint in his eye; he was even shorter than me. Later on, one Friday afternoon, Paddy and I had finished flying and we had repaired to the bar together for the traditional Happy Hour. I bought the first two pints and we chatted as we drank. Paddy was obviously much thirstier than me, so by the time he was ready for his second I was still only halfway down mine. So I told him that I would just have the top half; I had to drive down the hill later, he had only to stagger a few hundred yards to his married quarter. Paddy duly ordered the pint and a half and handed over the glasses. When they came back he asked the bar steward, quite seriously, but with a typical Irish blarney:

'Excuse me, but which one of these two pints is the half?'

Then there was Mike Telford, a tall, well-built man with a rather booming voice and a ready, if sometimes peculiar, sense of humour. Mike had flown Strikemasters, which were like Jet Provosts on steroids, in the Sultan of Oman's Air Force. He also lived in Bourton-on-the-Water, in his own house, and we were destined to often commute together up and down the hill in each other's cars. Another staff QFI was Don Merriman who, like me, had flown the Canberra B(I)8 in RAF Germany, but on No 3 Squadron at RAF Geilenkirchen. Tony Harrison was, I think, another ex-Canberra man, and the unit's Instrument Rating Examiner (IRE). Tony was a tall, dark and fairly handsome chap with an easy manner who was good to have around.

I started flying on 24 August 1970, doing my acceptance check flight with the Boss. I then flew a few extra-curricular sorties, transporting people about visiting Woodvale in Lancashire, West Malling in Kent and Upper Heyford, just up the road in Oxfordshire. It was a very gentle and enjoyable way to get back into 'the game' after six weeks away from it. But that all changed with the arrival of September. First, I had to fly a couple of sorties with someone from the Standards Flight, who were there, as the unit's name suggests, to keep the flying and instructional standards up to scratch. They were a sort of mini-Exam Wing, but just operated at Little Rissington. I flew with Flt Lt Dick Snell who checked that I was putting out the approved 'patter' and helped me brush up on some of the flying exercises. Dick was no relation to John Snell, but often jokingly called him 'Dad'!

Among the first batch of trainees I had been allocated were Flt Lts Jackson, Woollacott and Eastwood, but as on other training units occasionally I would fly with other staff's students. It was great to be flying with grown-ups again and when I was playing the part of the student (Bloggs) I quickly learned to inject a bit of fun into the lessons. Of course, I now had nearly three years' experience of real students to draw upon. It was all aimed at making sure that the guys in the back, acting as instructors, chose the correct words and phrases to get over their meaning concisely and correctly. At the end of courses I was often accused of taking it too far, but I always told my graduating students that they would be amazed at what university undergraduates might do in and to an aeroplane. During the last part of my CFS tour I met a few of these early student instructors of mine and they invariably told me hilarious stories about what their students had done to them. 'I told you so,' was my usual reply.

One day when I was well into my role as a particularly thick 'Bloggs', the man in the back asked me what the fuel gauges were reading (good airmanship teaching) so I replied:

'I've no idea, sir. *Alice in Wonderland*? – *Tinker Tailor Soldier Spy*?'

'No, Bloggs, what do the fuel gauges say?'

I held a cupped hand to the right-hand side of my helmet and said, 'I can't hear a word, sir.'

An exasperated voice came back: 'Just look at the fuel gauges on the wing, Bloggs, and tell me what numbers the needles are pointing to!'

On another occasion the instruction to 'Roll on the ailerons' came from Him Who Must Be Obeyed. I reached up with my left hand and started to open the cockpit canopy.

'WHAT ARE YOU DOING, BLOGGS?!'

'Well, I was going to get out and go and roll about on the aileron,[29] sir.'

A bit far-fetched I agree, but it got the point across that the student needs to be told what to do with things that are inside the cockpit, not what they operate.

One day I was told to inch the throttle open, so I moved it one inch, paused, then moved it another inch and, at the third movement, a frustrated sigh emanated from the back seat. 'I don't believe a student would do that!'

'Well, one did it to me one day. He was a theoretical mathematics student of some standing. Mind you he had very little common sense,' I replied.

All this theatrical role-playing had one aim: to get these would-be instructors to 'use the right words' and, unlike that great comedian Eric Morecambe used to say, 'in the right order'.[30] It was the sacred 'patter' originated by the great Smith-Barry all those years ago and refined over the intervening years by a host of CFS staff.

When handling the aircraft one tended not to be too silly. However, there were times when one had to explore the student instructor's ability to correct faults, even if he had actually used the right words and demonstrated correctly. Just because the patter and handling from the back seat is good it does not mean that Bloggs will get it right first time.

One of my favourite mistakes to make was one that I had seen often from UAS students. I would just put a small amount of rudder on and correct the subsequent turn by using a tiny bit of bank. This was especially effective if the horizon was not well defined. If 'sir' in the back didn't notice then I would add a bit more of each control until he did. It was a useful teaching point to show that, especially during the very early exercises, it was essential that there was a good, flat horizon outside the front window.

Great fun could also be had during the teaching of aerobatics and I used to try to give each of my student instructors an unexpected departure from controlled flight, often a spin, to see what they would do. This would often show up the difference between someone who had come from a fighter environment to one who was from a transport background. Actually most of the guys came from the latter. Surprisingly, airsickness was a rare event. Although every now and then I would simulate that rather disturbing occurrence because I reckoned, based on my own experience, that their future students would put them through it more than once. They soon learnt that the first thing to get the student to do was to switch his microphone off; the magnified sound of breakfast or lunch being off-loaded could turn the strongest of stomachs! They also learned to avoid the use of the question: 'Are you feeling sick, Bloggs?' This was invariably a trigger to the more sensitive souls!

The initiation of the major emergency of an engine failure was one where I thought that it was important that, once the recovery and forced landing techniques had been taught and practised, the whole thing should have an element of surprise. I was indebted to a staff instructor called Pete Woodham, with whom I had flown as a CFS student. On that occasion we were doing some aerobatics and, after I had recovered from a stall turn with the throttle on the backstop, I pulled the nose up to recover from the dive and tried to increase power. The throttle lever would not move! I tried a little harder, it was still locked on backstop. I told Pete, who was sitting in the front seat. He said he would have a go. I was by now descending steadily at the gliding speed of 70kts. I could see Pete's shoulders moving as he struggled to move the throttle lever.

'No, old chap, it's stuck,' he said. I thought that he would take control at this point. 'Right, you keep control and carry out the forced landing. I'll put out the emergency call. If you make a mess of it I'll be very upset.'

I heard him making a Mayday call, but I was so busy I really didn't listen very hard so I didn't hear the response from Air Traffic Control. As I got down to a couple of hundred feet, with it looking as if we would land in a reasonably flat field with enough room to stop, Pete said, 'OK, well done. I have control.' With that he opened the throttle and climbed away. He laughed at my stunned silence that turned quickly into respectful annoyance at having been so convincingly taken in. I used that trick on many occasions myself, but I could only use it once per student.

The timing of the point at which one must take over control of the aircraft from a student is critical and very hard to judge. Too late and disaster could ensue. Too early and the student won't really learn what he was doing wrong. This boundary is very fine; it is like a cliff edge. So even giving student instructors practice at this has built-in risk. The most dangerous time is near the ground on take-off or landing. I had had my own near disaster on take-off, which I related earlier, so I used to duplicate that, without letting things go so far that we actually left the runway or the grass strip.

On landing the most common fault with real students stemmed from them looking in the wrong place as they tried to hold the aircraft level a few inches off the ground. Instead of looking well ahead, while using their peripheral vision to 'feel' the height and monitoring attitude of the nose against the horizon, they would look at the ground, often just in front of the wing. This usually led to a touchdown too early with just the main wheels. Usually the student's next action was a swift backward movement of the control column, which led to a climb during which the speed would rapidly reduce: a kangaroo hop. This was potentially dangerous because the aircraft could now stall from several feet above the runway and a very bad landing would follow. So one thing I liked to induce was just that situation so that the student instructors could practice taking over and flying off the top of the bounce with a rapid application of full power and very careful control of the aircraft.

After a few weeks at CFS I was feeling much happier than I had when I'd received the news that I was to go there. The job was very rewarding and, on the whole, the pilots selected for the course usually took it in their stride and produced good results, graduating with a satisfactory standard to start their instructional tours.

There were exceptions. A minority just could not achieve the ability to talk and simultaneously fly the aircraft to a high enough standard of accuracy. This was no disgrace and these folk usually went back to their original role or moved into a ground job. But there was one occasion when I felt strongly that the student did not have the right personality to carry off the job as a UAS QFI. I tried my best with him, but he was far too dour and overbearing in his attitude to me as the 'student'. After a while I brought this problem up with Bob Hutcheson and asked him to fly with my problem student.

After the flight Bob looked me out and said, 'Aye, you're right, Mike. It's not something you can put your finger on with any certainty, but I came back feeling more miserable than before I went. He just doesn't have that *je ne sais quoi*. All the words were right and his flying wasn't too bad, but he just wasn't inspiring me to do better. It was like he was just playing the record with all the words on it, but there was no empathy or feeling. In Scotland we would say that he is *guiy surrrly and dourrr!*'

But we had trouble persuading the powers-that-be to move this student on, mainly because personality was not one of the usual judgemental criteria for a pass or fail. If I remember rightly he continued with another instructor until the end of the course. However, I heard later that the UAS he joined was not that happy with him.

One other thing I did with my student instructors was to get them used to standing on their feet in front of other people and talking. Many of them had done that in their previous environments, but more practice in an assessed situation was going to be good for them. While they were still in the conversion phase I would ask each of them to produce a fifteen-minute briefing on any flying topic from their past. After a couple of days to allow for preparation, my other students and I would sit in a briefing cubicle and listen. I would then get the others to critique the talk. It worked quite well and I learned all sorts of things; including how to make a successful landing on an aircraft carrier in a Phantom; how to lay a sonar buoy pattern; how to calibrate an Instrument Landing System; and how to drop paratroopers from a Hercules.

Although I did regret that I did not go back to the front line, I found this job even more rewarding than that of teaching on the UAS.

16 WEATHER OR NOT

Flying from the RAF's highest airfield in small aeroplanes with no navigation aids and only one radio was always going to be an occupation that would inevitably bring with it some weather-related problems. I experienced some of these with fog, overcast cloud and strong winds. Most were safely resolved and often had their funny side.

First a small lesson in meteorology, about fog. Fog is simply cloud that sits on the ground. Cloud is air that is both moist enough and cold enough to condense out the ever-present water vapour into tiny visible water droplets. There are two types of fog that afflict our sceptred isle: radiation and advection.

Radiation fog is formed during calm, cold and clear nights when the heat in the land radiates away into the night sky and the temperature of the ground gets low enough to condense the air touching it; in the first instance this will form dew. But, if a tiny breeze stirs the air ever so gently, then the mixing of the coldest layers near the ground will cause condensation in the layers above. During the longer nights of winter, spring and autumn this effect can go on long enough to form a layer of fog several hundred feet thick. Walking about in it gives no clue as to how deep it is, until it starts to clear, when there will be occasional glimpses of washed out sunlight, gradually getting brighter until the white stuff magically disappears. This is termed 'burning off' and, regardless of the actual conditions, the Met Office will invariably tell you that 'The fog will burn off by 10 o'clock.'

Advection fog is caused by warm, moist air being blown over cold ground, which condenses the moisture in the layers of the air closest to the ground. With this fog there is always a wind, which is part of the process of forming the fog. It is perhaps obvious, but nevertheless true, that this sort of fog happens most frequently near the coast or over hills and mountains. When it occurs over the east coast of Scotland they call it 'the Haar'. Advection fog is not usually burned off but clears if there is a change in the wind direction or the humidity of the air. During the day it may lift as the temperature goes up, but usually only a few hundred feet into a layer of low stratus cloud. When I was in Scotland this sort of weather was described as 'dreek'. The Scots have lots of words for bad weather, probably because they get so much of it. Indeed, that large, hairy, Scottish comedian Billy Connolly once observed that there were two seasons in Scotland: June and Winter!

Lesson over. The first problem I had was with radiation fog. I awoke one morning and drew back the curtains to find that I could barely see the house opposite. 'No point in rushing into work,' I thought. I drove carefully up the hill out of Bourton-on-the-Water, headlights on, in a stream of other folk not rushing to work either. But as we reached the top of the gradient the sun burst out and he certainly had his hat on. In the daily briefing we were told that a lot of our local airfields, like Brize Norton, Fairford and Abingdon were what was known in the NATO Colour Code as RED. That meant that they were essentially unusable, today, due to fog. However, RAF Lyneham was BLUE, that is wide open and Lyneham was going to be our diversion airfield if, for any reason, we could not land back at base.[31]

I went down to the squadron and found that my student instructor and I had the first slot. My man was going to try to teach me some instrument flying, specifically how to fly a radar guided approach known as a PAR.[32] As he was quite well into his course I sent him out to get things going while

I signed for the aeroplane. We taxied out just behind a Jet Provost from the adjacent hangar. I could tell by the dulcet tones and accent on the radio that Captain Jack Snow of the USAF was flying it; he was their exchange instructor at CFS at the time.

Jack had just taken off and crossed the airfield boundary as we lined up. As we climbed ahead it became clear that the only ground visible below us was inside a circular hole of about 5 miles' radius; the rest of the world below was white, but there was no cloud above us. As we were staying in the local area, we levelled off at 2,000ft and called the radar controller. I settled into Bloggs mode and listened to my 'sir' droning on about the way that he was doing this and that and giving me control. I did a typical student thing and let the height gradually reduce. After a couple of hundred feet the impeccable patter paused sufficiently for him to tell me to regain the height; I did so but lost 20kts in airspeed. I was trying to wind him up a bit and distract him from his task of talking to me. So it went on and he took over, correctly, to show me what attitudes, power setting and rate of descent to use for a successful approach. We went round for another approach from 200ft, just before reaching what is known as 'Decision Height' (the decision being to land or not). I told him to relax for a while and that I would fly the aircraft until we reached the point where we turned inbound, then I would revert to my imbecilic Bloggs persona.

As we climbed back up to 2,000ft I noticed that the top of the fog was starting to spill over the nearby village of Little Rissington and was heading towards the western airfield boundary. I told ATC. Nothing was said, so we set off away from the airfield and called the radar controller. Eventually (these things took time at 90kts!) we were handed off to the final controller and started the PAR. At about 3 miles to go he suddenly said, 'Message from the Duty Instructor. You are diverted to Lyneham.'

'Why?' I asked.

'Fog on the airfield,' was the reply.

By now we were at 2 miles and 600ft. I looked out ahead and said to ATC, 'I can see the first 300 yards of the runway so I'm going to land on that. Changing frequency to the tower.' I told the man in the back to relax and I carried out a short landing on the bit of tarmac and concrete that wasn't yet covered in fog. As we cleared the runway onto the grass we went into the fog bank. A voice from the tower said: 'Please call the Duty Instructor when you get in.' That wasn't a total surprise. I would have asked for an explanation if I had been up there. I called him and assured him that we had done nothing naughty and that there had been sufficient runway and visual cues left for me to have made a successful landing, witness my unbent aeroplane. He was satisfied. I was just glad not to be droning south-westwards to Lyneham.

The next odd happening was on a day when the cloud cover was total and not entirely all of it was above something known as 'safety altitude'.[33] This meant that descending into cloud, without knowing how low its base was, might end up as a disaster by flying into something solid before seeing it. There were lots of TV masts, power station chimneys and hills around the Cotswolds, so in these conditions it was only really safe to descend if you had a reliable navigation aid (not fitted in the Chipmunk) to pinpoint your position or a radio on which you could call a radar controller for guidance to a safe lower altitude.

My student and I had climbed to above the unbroken layer of stratocumulus and we were flying in the clear blue at about 6,000ft doing our thing. As soon as we had no need to talk to ATC we used a special 'quiet' frequency, so that we were not constantly interrupted by chat on the radio. Because of the cloud layer we could not do all of the exercise, so I asked the man in the back to take us home via a radar controlled descent into the visual circuit. He made the appropriate radio call on the correct frequency. No reply. He tried again. Silence. I tried but to no avail. We changed frequency. Still no joy. Either our transmitter was not working or our receiver had packed in. There is an emergency procedure for this situation and that is to fly a pattern of timed equilateral triangles. So I asked my student to time me and I made a sharp 120° turn to the left; I flew straight for two minutes and then turned again, another two minutes and then another turn. That should have made a triangular track over the ground. However, there was a 40kts wind at 6,000ft that day so the shape would be distorted. We had lots of fuel left so I could carry on for ages yet.

After a while my man spotted another Chipmunk closing on our starboard side. I straightened up and he came into a close echelon port position. I tapped the side of my helmet to show that I had no radio and he pointed at me to indicate that I should formate on him and follow him home. I did so and we descended into cloud. After three or four minutes hanging on to his wing in the murky greyness we popped out of cloud at about 1,200ft. We were headed towards base and I stayed in formation for a pairs landing. Subsequent investigation found that the radio receiver had indeed failed. Following my occurrence report Chipmunks were eventually equipped with a separate emergency radio operated from a battery. It was a bonus to discover that this rarely used procedure actually worked.

Some years later, at a party, I met an Air Traffic Control officer who had served at Brize Norton in 1970, so I related the story to him. I was astonished to learn that it was he who had spotted my manoeuvres and had alerted Little Rissington to send someone to fetch me home. He confirmed that as he plotted my track on his radar display the triangles were distorted by the wind and he had to get a second opinion as to whether this very rare emergency procedure was actually happening.

Now we come to wind. In winter the weather was not great so our flying rate was often restricted. I was sent off to do instrument flying exercises with a student instructor. It was cloudy, raining and extremely windy. A cold front was passing through. I thought that it was a bit of a waste of time because the air was very turbulent and that was not ideal for the task. However, the course was behind the line and the Boss was pushing us hard to catch up.

We were part-way through the second part of the exercise when the wind veered to the north-west and increased even further. It was now beyond our crosswind limit and was not forecast to change much. Then the radar failed. The cloud base was too low for any other sort of approach so I was told to divert to Brize Norton, the home of RAF Transport Command's fleet of VC10s. This time I acquiesced and set off towards Brize. Their radar was working so we were sent out towards Oxford for a PAR. On the way in, not making much headway at 90kts, I asked for the surface wind. Even on Brize Norton's westerly main runway the crosswind component of the wind was too strong to allow us to land. We broke cloud at 600ft so I broke off the radar approach and called the local controller.

'Do you have any other runway or a grass strip that I can land on?' I asked.

'Sorry, it's runway 27 or nothing,' came the cheery reply.

'OK. I'd like to do a low-level circuit at 500 feet and land on the intersection of the main runway and the disused runway.'

'You're clear to do that.'

So I turned in early and lined up on a north-westerly heading, aiming at the large diamond shape of the concrete and tarmac where the two runways intersected. I had to judge the angle of approach visually, but having operated from grass for quite a while now that was not too hard. I dropped full flap and flew at 55kts with plenty of power on. We were making all of 30kts over the ground. I touched down, into wind, just inside the start of the black stuff and had stopped by the time that we reached the white line in the centre of the runway. But that wasn't the hardest bit. I now had to taxi my diminutive steed on what seemed like miles of taxiways to reach the main parking area. The wind was playing havoc with my attempts at steering and the brakes were starting to fade. The man with the red bats, not being used to little aeroplanes, wanted us to park tail into wind. I stopped and beckoned him over. After shouting loudly in his ear he got the message and pointed us in the safer direction of the wind on our nose. We returned to base after an excellent Transport Command lunch when the weather had cleared up and the wind had abated.

Another tale involving the wind was much more fun. The weather had been poor for a few weeks and the Station Commander, who was a bit of a megalomaniac, had instructed all the flying units to work on Saturday mornings until the various courses were back on track for their graduation dates. Although it was only about seven years since the RAF had stopped working on Saturday mornings there was a lot of discontent with that edict. The Boss hatched a plot to make a protest at this rather overbearing imposition on our weekend. After all, we were working flat out for five days.

'Four of us will come in at 7 a.m. and get airborne before the morning briefing at 0800 hours,' he suggested. 'We will fly in close formation round and round over the Briefing Room and then land and pick up our students. That should make a point! OK?'

I thought that our Jumping Jack Sprackling was playing with fire, but it was a great bit of leadership. I was one of the select four and flew as No 2 on Jack's right wing. The other two guys flew on the left wing and in the box, line astern on the Boss. We got airborne and formed up. The wind was very strong; the Met man had said that it was over 60kts at 2,000ft above mean sea level (amsl). We would fly at 600ft above the airfield so we would be at 1,800ft amsl, so the wind would have been at least 55kts. The air was quite stable so it wasn't too bumpy and we could hold formation reasonably well. The Boss lined us up, into wind and slowed down to 55kts with half flap down. We clung on. We were barely moving over the ground. It was 0759 hours as our dearly beloved station master arrived at the briefing. I was too busy to look down, but apparently he looked up. By the time that the briefing had ended, about ten minutes later, we had hardly moved. We were told afterwards that all the boys loved it. The briefing could hardly be heard for the unco-ordinated throb of four Gipsy Majors and the Station Commander got more agitated throughout the proceedings. The rest of the staff were astonished that we were still there, overhead, when they emerged, blinking in the bright morning sunshine.

I never did find out whether Jack was hauled up in front of the Lord and Master, but he didn't suddenly disappear to pastures new. It was a great jape.

17 SKYLARKING ABOUT

In the early 1970s virtually all of the half dozen or so RAF flying training establishments had their own formation aerobatic team. At RAF Linton-on-Ouse in Yorkshire, No 1 Flying Training School (FTS) ran a four-ship Jet Provost (JP) team called 'The Blades'. Across in North Lincolnshire, at RAF Manby and the College of Air Warfare, there was another four-ship team of JPs known as the 'Macaws'; the name being a play on the mnemonic of the

Manby College of Air Warfare! And, at No 3 FTS based at RAF Leeming in the North Riding of Yorkshire, yet more QFIs were giving up their summer weekends to thrill the crowds. But this time it was just two of them. The pair of JP5s was called 'Gemini', an obvious sobriquet for a duo.

At the RAF College at Cranwell in Lincolnshire resided yet another four-some of JPs. They operated under the rustic title of 'the Poachers', a reference to the famous folk song about a countryman of that county who indulged in the illegal snaffling of the squire's game birds. Perhaps they had considered and discarded the other Lincolnshire based nickname 'the Yellow Bellies'!

Meanwhile back at CFS there was not one team but three! The Red Arrows based at RAF Kemble operated nine Gnats, the Jet Provost squadrons of CFS supported another four-ship of JPs; the team had once been a six-ship but economy got in the way! In deference to the CFS crest (more of which later) they were known as the 'Red Pelicans'. And last, but by no means least, the Chipmunk squadron of CFS had a four-ship team of Chipmunks called 'the Skylarks'. It's a shame that the remaining flying unit at CFS, who oper-ated the twin-engined Vickers Varsity didn't join in; they could have called themselves 'the Heavy Mob'! Altogether Flying Training Command was operating seven formation teams. By then the RAF had decided that the erst-while practice of front-line squadrons providing formation teams for public displays was not cost-effective. So the official, full time job of representing the service at airshows was the job of the gallant lads of the Red Arrows.

So, not long into my first summer at CFS, I was asked if I might be inter-ested in joining the team for the following season in 1972. Don Merriman, who was leading the team in 1971, knew that he was leaving the squadron later in the year, so a space was going to become available. I was delighted to be asked and said that I would look forward to it enormously. So, as an intro-duction to travelling airshow life, I was invited to fly the spare aircraft to a few of the summer's venues. Even better!

So one Friday afternoon, five little Chipmunks were specially cleaned up for us to take away for an airshow. This one wasn't far away: just 'up the road' at RAF Upper Heyford. In reality RAF Upper Heyford was USAF Upper Heyford. The operational squadrons were USAF F-111s of the 20th Tactical Fighter Wing. We arrived in style, a total contrast to all the screaming jets and titanic transports that were turning up for the static and flying displays on the following day.

As is usual, there was a party on the evening before an airshow. Later in life I sometimes wondered at the wisdom of this, but I always enjoyed them! That night it was held in the Officers' Club and we were allowed, nay expected, to remain in our flying kit. In those days the wearing of flying over-alls was not usually allowed in the public rooms of RAF Officers' Messes, so this was a bit of a treat for us 'limeys'. A good time was had by all. Except that at one point in the evening a lady in the circle I had joined asked me how old I was. With my chubby face and blond curls I looked quite a bit younger than my 27 years. Anyway the lady was insistent, so I told her. She had been at the martinis for some time and asked me how old I thought that she was. In my experience that is always an invitation to disaster, so I shied away with some fairly non-committal remark. However, this southern belle was emboldened by the aforementioned intake of martinis and asked me to look carefully at her face and imagine it without make-up, as if she had just woken up in the morning. I tried hard not to see that as some sort of obscure invitation for later. 'OK,' I thought, 'I'll play along with your game.' Actually, when I looked hard, there were some lines and crow's-feet that I bet that she wished weren't there. She was not, by any means bad looking, but she had done a good cover-up job before she had come along to the party. I also took into account her figure and the probable age of the man she was with, whom I supposed to be her husband. 'Here goes,' I thought.

'Twenty five,' I said boldly; thinking that was safely complimentary. In return I received her present martini over my head! And I thought that I had been both cautious and gallant! You just can't win when it comes to a woman's age.

The airshow went well. The spare aircraft wasn't needed and the Skylarks did a creditable display in the fresh wind that was constantly blowing them towards the crowd line. We departed after the show and flew back to our very quiet airfield later that Saturday evening. When we got back I overheard Paddy Cullen come out with an example of his wonderful Irish blarney. He had had some trouble keeping in formation in the aircraft he had been allo-cated, fleet number six, because he believed that it was twisted and needed some re-trimming.

'Dat number six is an owld bucket,' he declared vehemently. 'Oim not takin' dat one again, so oim not!'

My next trip away with the team was to the Royal Naval Air Station at Yeovilton in Somerset. When we flew in transit we remained in a five arrow formation and then arrived in echelon starboard for the break to land. As 'the spare' I was number five. The usual party and the next day's airshow went as well as expected. I was not assaulted by any women and thoroughly enjoyed watching the various displays; especially a pair of Belgian F-104 Starfighters who just did lots of high-speed passes at a very low altitude.

We were cleared to depart before the show had finished as there was a need for us to land back at Little Rissington before 6 p.m. We took off in formation and I tucked myself under Paddy Cullen's tail (he was the team number four). We turned left and were allowed to climb over the technical site, which is where the people, fairground and all the stalls were. Suddenly a small red balloon appeared in front of me, it had a string and a label attached to it. I think that my propeller burst it. Whoever had paid for it in the hope that it would break some distance record was going to be deeply disappointed. As we flew back I wondered whether they were watching it ascend at the time.

By now the team had been in existence for only four seasons, from 1967, the year I had passed through CFS as a student QFI. By the end of the season I had enjoyed the experience of travelling to airshows and I had also flown some formation aerobatic practice sorties; at that stage on the 'QT'. Despite the fact that by then I had done a lot of formation flying, in jets and pistons, not a lot of the time I'd spent clinging onto someone else's wing had involved going upside down. Using a light, low-powered aircraft for formation aerobatics is a much bigger challenge than flying, say, powerful counterparts like the Pitts Special, Zlin or Extra. Aircraft like those give the pilot so much more flexibility of manoeuvre and make regaining or maintaining position so much easier. So, in my little Chipmunk, staying where I should have been was a challenge, to say the least. It felt like I was bending the throttle lever for much of the time trying to get more power than the motor would give me, just to keep up! Another thing that I learnt was that if you are required to stay in position when upside down then there is a disconcerting change in the way that the lateral control has to be used. Because the aircraft are inverted then the roll control works in the opposite sense. To move away from the leader you have to move the stick top towards him; just the opposite of upright flight. In that case moving the stick towards the leader will make the aircraft go closer!

However, although a very interesting and somewhat scary experience, that was not a manoeuvre that was particularly applicable to the Chipmunk – because in inverted flight the engine stopped! The major consideration for all light aircraft teams will always be the wind. Even for high performance jets a strong on-crowd wind can be a problem that needs a bit of thought and application. But for relatively slow aircraft, like the Chipmunk, any appreciable wind, apart from a light zephyr, needs pre-show planning and meticulous execution.

With a wind along the display line then timing adjustments have to be continuously applied to make sure that the formation doesn't disappear over the downwind horizon and that the crowd goes off to buy ice creams halfway through your show. The effect of the wind is even more important when, as the Skylarks did, the formation splits into two pairs and has to ensure that any crossovers are made at the display datum, which is normally at the centre of the crowd line. So the upwind pair has to extend their timing before their manoeuvre and the downwind pair has to cut down theirs so that the effect of the wind is negated and the show stays well centred.

The big advantage of a light aircraft formation display is that, if correctly flown, it stays right in front of the crowd the whole time. There might not be the screaming high-speed passes and enormous loops, with fiery afterburners on show, that the fast jets do, but it is, or at least should be, an all-action event in a small piece of sky right in front of the public's eyes.

At the end of the summer it was announced from on high that the two CFS teams, the Red Pelicans and the Skylarks would be disbanded. Economies had to be made and these disbandments were among them. So I would not be spending 1972 as part of a formation team. Anyway, other events would soon overtake any possibility of staying at CFS that long.

18 PROBLEMS, PEOPLE AND PELICANS

A problem that occasionally afflicted some of our flying at RAF Little Rissington was down to a certain supersonic aircraft project: Concorde. That wonderfully beautiful construction of the 'white heat of technology', as Prime Minister dear old Harold Wilson had put it, was, of course, a joint Anglo-French project. The French-built prototype, Concorde 001, had flown from Toulouse in March 1969, captained by André Turcat. The UK prototype, Concorde 002, was built at the British Aircraft Corporation factory at Filton, north of Bristol, from where it made its first flight on Wednesday 9 April 1969. This time the captain of the crew was Brian Trubshaw. Many years later I was privileged to meet and briefly work alongside Brian. He was a real gentleman and a knowledgeable and skilful test pilot. However, I always secretly thought he looked more like a gentleman farmer than the usual image of a test pilot. That first flight of Concorde 002 was not very long and the final landing was made at RAF Fairford, from where the remainder of the long British flight test programme was carried out. It was there because RAF Fairford had a very long runway and was not very busy. However, it was only a few minutes flight time away from Little Rissington; by Concorde anyway.

To ensure that this priceless flying machine was kept well away from the swarming hordes of Gnats, Varsities, Jet Provosts and even Chipmunks operating over the Cotswolds, procedures had been put in place to give Concorde sole rights to certain bits of sky whenever it flew. The exact details were published every morning that those four roaring Rolls Royce Olympus engines were going to propel this new Queen of the Skies into the wide blue yonder.

In common with all flight test programmes, things rarely went exactly to plan so the projected restrictions were activated only when the test team were aboard their supersonic tube with a firm intention of slipping the surly bonds of earth. Then a broadcast would be made on all frequencies and aeroplanes could be seen darting all over the place to quit those pieces of airspace that were now out of bounds.

Depending on the actual flight profile, Concorde did not always head in our direction. But when she did it was a sight, and sound, to behold. That white slim-line fuselage, with those wonderfully curved delta wings attached, made it look like some fabulous and mythical bird ascending into the bright blue summer sky. And if one was on the ground the howl from the intakes as she approached and the chest-drumming roar of the efflux as she passed overhead and climbed away were unique sounds, surpassing any similar noises one had heard before. Everyone stopped what they were doing and stood with eyes shaded and mouths agape in wonder. Little did I, or perhaps any of us, realise then how poorly the commercialisation of the project would progress and how relatively short Concorde's unique service life would be. Nor did I know (how could I?) that I would actually be at the Paris Air Show in June 2003 and see the arrival of one of the last Air France Concordes, a final flight on delivery to *Le Musée de l'Air et de l'Espace*. As it taxied past where I was standing, with an international gathering of test pilots, I don't think that there were many dry eyes. Of course, none of those steely-eyed, lantern-jawed aces was going to admit it!

Although not, like Concorde, a highly advanced piece of flying machinery, things did occasionally go wrong with our De Havilland of Canada's excellent little trainer. Thankfully the engine was very reliable, as long as you looked after it properly. But one day, while teaching forced landing technique one Gipsy Major engine did nearly let me down, almost literally. My student instructor was demonstrating a forced landing without power. He had done it quite well and had correctly opened the throttle at regular intervals on the way down from 5,000ft to make sure that the plugs were not oiling up.

He had chosen what looked like a good field from a mile up, but as we got closer I could see that it was very wet and had a half-grown crop of winter wheat in it. I was just going to point this out when he opened the throttle to climb away and the engine just coughed and started to die. I took control. I'd signed for the aircraft and if it was going to get bent then I was determined that I would have a hand in it. As I started to slow down, to ensure that our touchdown would be at the lowest possible speed, I thought that I would just try opening the throttle once more. I opened it as slowly as I dared, as we were now only a few feet from the soggy ground. Blow me down, the engine responded normally! We almost had been committed to a landing somewhere in deepest Gloucestershire and now I was able to climb away, raise the flap, and head back to base. The engine continued to run normally, but I climbed to 3,000ft and joined the circuit overhead base for a practise forced landing, which I got the student to fly and talk about as he did it; there was no point in wasting the opportunity! The engineers found that there was a bit of oil kicking around in a couple of the cylinders and the engine was removed for reconditioning.

One of the things that could not be checked by the pilot before flight was the final fastening of the access panel on the right-hand side of the engine. It hinged upwards and had to be opened by the ground crew just before starting the engine. Doing this gave them access to place the cartridges in the engine starter breech. This meant that we had to rely on the ground crew to fasten the panel back into place. But on 6 November 1970, only a few minutes after take-off, this panel swung upwards and started to flap about in the wind. I was worried that it might tear itself loose so I took control and made a rapid return to the runway. The panel did stay in place, but it was pretty bent by the time we got back on the ground. One technician was reprimanded.

Another rather strange failure happened just a week later, on 12 November 1970, when I was flying with one of our older students who was on a refresher course, regaining his QFI category before going to instruct at RAF Church Fenton. He was Flt Lt Charles Spooner, who had been the Station Flight Safety Officer at RAF Khormaksar in Aden in 1966 when I had experienced an engine failure on take-off there in a Canberra.[34] We were climbing to the west to do our flying exercise when a loud, rapid thumping noise started up. Instinctively we both looked at the engine gauges – nothing amiss. Then Charles said, 'The rubber walkway on the left wing is flapping about!' I was sitting in the front and I looked down and could see that the rubber strip that protected the wing where we got in and out was still attached at the front end, but had become unstuck behind that and was writhing about in the slipstream, noisily bashing the side of the fuselage. The only thing to do was to turn round and go home, avoiding the over-flight of inhabited areas in case it came off and dinged someone on the head. I was beginning to wonder just how many things could come loose!

As it happened the rest of my eighteen months at CFS passed by with no other notable aircraft-related problems; the Chipmunk was a simple little aeroplane and the TLC from our engineers kept it going safely and consistently. They were great people and every now and then we would give them short flights; it was called 'Air Experience'. Not all of them volunteered but those that did usually enjoyed it. Some asked for aerobatics, some specifically asked not to do aerobatics and some were ambivalent. On one occasion I was flying one of our two lady ground crew. She asked if we could do a loop, so once we were well away from the airfield with sufficient height I dived to get the speed up to 130kts and pulled up round the loop. When we were back in level flight I asked how she liked it; she said she would like to do another one. So I repeated the exercise. As I pulled the 3G to start the manoeuvre there was a little 'Ooh!' from the back seat. I asked if she was all right and she said, rather hesitantly and demurely, 'Yes thank you, sir.' When we had recovered from that I asked if she wanted to try a barrel roll.

'No thanks, sir. I think that we'd better go back now,' she replied.

'Are you feeling all right?' I asked.

'Oh, yes, sir. It's just that when we looped the second time my left bra strap snapped.'

Well, she was a woman-shaped woman, so her assets suddenly weighing three times normal must have been a bit too much for her chest restraint equipment.

Another piece of equipment that was a letdown one day was my RAF issue watch (Aircrew, for the use of). I flew a sortie in the morning and realised during the flight that the watch had given up the ghost, in fact the minute hand had fallen off. As I was flying twice again that afternoon I rushed down to the Main Stores building before they shut for lunch. Having got there I found one of the brown-coated civilians behind the counter. I told him my problem.

'Oh ahrr, sir,' he responded. 'You'll 'ave to get it officially classified as U/S.'[35]

'Why? Look at it,' I said.

I showed him the timepiece. The minute hand was rolling about in the bottom of the glass. 'That's definitely U/S, isn't it?'

'Ahrr, that may be so, sir, but it's not my place to say so. You'll 'ave to take it to technical stores and get them to put a label on it describin' the fault.'

My lunch-hour was rapidly receding over the horizon. 'Where is tech stores?' I asked as politely as I could. He gave me directions and I went down various corridors and through a couple of doors only to be confronted by a sign on the door: CLOSED FOR LUNCH, REOPEN AT 1330.

'I give in,' I muttered through clenched teeth. Then I noticed an adjacent door slightly ajar and a voice coming from within. I knocked and the same voice invited me to enter. There was one of the Supply Branch officers looking up at me from his desk and holding the phone. He signed off his call and said, 'What can I do for you, old boy?'

I told him my tale and he said, 'No problem, old bean. Give me the offending article and I'll do the necessary.' Within a couple of minutes I was on my way back to the brown-coated retainer in Main Stores. 'I bet he's gone to lunch,' I thought. But he hadn't. I presented him with my little trophy, duly labelled and classified as well and truly broken.

'I'll 'ave to check the stock.'

He disappeared into the maze of shelving and rustling noises emanated. When he reappeared I noticed straight away that he was not carrying a watch.

'We've only got one in stock,' he said – with a perfectly straight face.

'But I only want one,' I replied, no doubt with a slightly mystified expression.

'Ahrr, that may be so, sir, but we 'ave to keep one in stock for an emergency.'

'This is your lucky day!' I said, with a big smile. 'Here I am – your very own emergency. I have to get airborne in less than an hour's time and I must have a watch,' I told him. Thinking that it might help a 'jobsworth' like him I added, 'It's in Queen's Regulations: pilots must not fly any of Her Majesty's aeroplanes without a suitable chronographic timepiece.'

That failed to impress him. I asked to use the phone. I rang the Officers' Mess and asked to speak to the OC of the Supply Squadron; he eventually came to the phone. I apologised for interrupting his lunch and related my problem. He asked to speak to Mr Browncoat. When the latter put down the phone he disappeared back into the warren without a word. This time he returned with a small box, made copious notes on various forms, which he then got me to sign and handed over the box. I opened it and inside was a brand new, glistening 'aircrew' watch. Success! But I only just got airborne on time, with very little nourishment inside me; lunch is definitely a time of day and not a meal for aircrew.

Occasionally an aircraft needs what is known as a 'Full Air Test'. This is something required at least on an annual basis and sometimes after major maintenance activity. With the Chipmunk being such a basic little flying machine, even the Full Air Test only took just about half an hour's flying time. The best bit was in completing two specific requirements: to fly the aircraft at its maximum permitted airspeed of 173kts and to check for full and free movement of all the flight controls while airborne. It was possible and expeditious to blend these two into one manoeuvre.

The first part required quite a steep dive; even at full power it was difficult to get the Chippy above 120kts in level flight. The engine was fitted with a fixed-pitch propeller so, due to complex aerodynamics, as the speed increased so did the rpm. Above about 130kts with the throttle fully open the rpm began to exceed the design limit for the engine. So, during the Stuka-like dive to 173kts, the throttle had to be pulled back to hold the engine rpm at or below its limit. At 173kts the noise of the air rushing by the rather leaky canopy was quite loud; there was a distinctive whistling, like a gale going through a haunted house. Once the maximum speed had been achieved and nothing untoward had occurred a 3G pull up to the vertical was the best next move. This vertical climb would be held until the speed, which was now disappearing rapidly, fell to near zero, at which point all three flying controls could be exercised over their full range before the little aeroplane gave in to

Mr Newton's excellent force of gravity. There usually followed an unceremonious back-flip into a near vertical dive again. After recovering from that it was, 'Home James and don't spare the horses!'

Over my time at CFS I flew with about fifty students. Only some remain memorable forty years later, mostly for good reasons. Dick Woollacott was one of my first student instructors and he allowed me to cut my CFS teeth on him with great good grace. Malcolm Swinhoe and Geoff Rolfe were both very likeable chaps who soon picked up the patter and flew the exercises well. Geoff lived in a cottage halfway up the hill from Bourton, so I occasionally gave him lifts to and from work.

Around Easter 1971 two new students appeared for me to torment; sorry, I mean mentor. They were like chalk and cheese. Lt Neil Thomas RN was a tall, rather sophisticated and debonair, blond-haired ex-F4 Phantom pilot and Flt Lt Ian Gillespie was a short, rather swarthy, straight talking pilot who had come from flying the mighty Avro Shackleton. An aircraft that was a direct descendant of the Avro Lancaster and often described as forty thousand rivets flying in loose formation. They say that you can tell a Shackleton pilot, but you can't tell him much – mainly because he's deaf from sitting for hours on end between two pairs of throbbing Rolls Royce Griffin engines. Ian was a bundle of fun in the air, especially when I tried to upset his patter with outrageous 'Bloggs' behaviour. I later met Ian at RAF St Mawgan in Cornwall, in those days the home of half the RAF's Nimrod force. He was again a squadron pilot, this time on the 'Mighty Hunter', back in the bosom of Coastal Command. We were in the mess for the evening meal. We were both in flying kit as I was staging through St Mawgan on a trial sortie from RAE Farnborough flying a BAC-111. After we had completed the usual interchanges of queries on how things were I asked, 'Are you just off to the simulator then?'

'Oh no,' he replied, 'We're off on patrol – *practising* for the simulator.'

One day I went into work and was told that I was going to have charge of Sqn Ldr Ian Dick during his refresher course. At that time I didn't know him personally, but he had been a well-known member of the Red Arrows when I had passed through CFS four years previously. Ian, or 'Sir' as I called him at the time, seemed to be a happy character, with a great set of teeth that were often seen in his ready smile. As I should have expected from his past flying record he had a great set of pilot's hands; although it took him a little time to get used to using his feet whilst airborne. However, we only flew together three times as he was pulled off the course, from whence he had been scheduled to command Cambridge UAS, and instead was given command of the Red Arrows. Ian's smile suddenly got even bigger. Apparently there had been some problem within the team about the person who had been appointed as leader; this was known as a 'Team Misery'. Ian Dick went on to head the team for three years and, thirteen years later, he would be a tutor of mine at the RAF Staff College.

Another memorable student was Flt Lt George Smith. He was old enough to be my dad and was refreshing his skills before being posted to RAF Church Fenton and the Elementary Flying School there. When George had filled in his paperwork I noticed that he had first become a QFI two years before I was born! I met him again some time later and he related an interesting story. A new course of students had arrived and there was the usual 'Meet and Greet' in the Officers' Mess bar. One of the new students came up to George and asked, 'Are you Flt Lt George Smith, sir?'

'Yes,' George replied. 'Why?'

'Can I be one of your students, please, sir?'

'Well, we don't actually organise it like this. But why do you ask?'

'Because you taught my dad to fly, sir,' came the response from the baby-faced lad.

George told me that at that moment he suddenly felt older than he ever had before.

The official coat of arms of CFS bears a shield on which there are heraldic representations for all three armed services: an anchor, a sword and a pair of wings. Above the shield are a helm and crest and the latter takes the form of a red pelican. This bird species was chosen because of the legend that the pelican pierces its own breast with its beak to feed its young with its blood. This is supposed to represent the nurturing the school gives to its students. I certainly sweated blood at times!

The presence of the pelican on the crest gave rise to the school being presented with a real, live pelican. This happened on 2 February 1962 at the graduation dinner of No 210 Course. The bird, named Patrick, after the commandant of the day, Air Commodore Pat Connelly, had been purchased by several CFS Staff members and given into the care and custody of Mr Len Hill, the founder of Birdland[36] in Bourton-on-the-Water. Until his demise in 1969 Patrick attended most official functions in the Officers' Mess and on the parade ground. For the former he always wore his CFS bow tie.

After almost two years of CFS being pelican-less the graduating officers of No 254 Course had a surprise parting gift: another pelican. They had named him Frederick, after the resident commandant, Air Commodore Freddy Hazelwood. I remember the occasion well, as the young, virile and amazingly strong bird pulled poor old Len Hill into the dining room, resplendent in his CFS bow tie – the pelican that is, not Mr Hill.

Frederick's first official function was an appearance in the 1971 annual Freedom of Cheltenham parade; I was there too, but on a float, dressed as a First World War pilot alongside a student from the Gnat course, John Blackwell, who, ten years later would go on to lead the Red Arrows. Later Frederick was commissioned as a pilot officer and attended many more dinners, reunions and official events. On one occasion he took a sizeable chunk out of the nose of Flt Lt Terry Francis, a member of the Red Pelicans Jet Provost formation team, when Terry leaned too far forward to make some disparaging remark to the bird. Served him right!

Frederick moved in royal circles too. We had a visit from our Commandant-in-Chief, the ever charming and gracious Queen Elizabeth the Queen Mother. As was to be his lifelong duty, Frederick was there. Then on the afternoon of 12 July 1971, when I was in the control tower, doing my stint as the duty instructor, a Jet Provost landed and taxied in. It was flown by HRH the Prince of Wales, who was undergoing his basic flying training at the RAF College at Cranwell. He had arrived to attend the annual reunion dinner of the CFS Association, where he would be introduced to Pilot Officer Frederick. HRH's instructor at the time was Dick Johns, who had been on my CFS Course four years previously; Dick went on to become Air Chief Marshal Sir Richard Johns and Chief of the Air Staff. Perhaps it is whom you know, after all? In similar vein, after meeting Prince Charles, Frederick went on to get promoted to Flight Lieutenant and he remained the official school mascot until dying of natural causes in December 1986. I think that the natural causes may have been exacerbated by all that time he spent smoking and drinking at dinner nights. How he got commissioned as a flying officer I just don't know: I never saw him fly!

19 EXTRA CURRICULAR ACTIVITIES

I made mention earlier of my participation in one of the Freedom of Cheltenham Parades; CFS had been awarded that peculiar and particular honour some years beforehand. It meant that the unit had the right to march through the lovely spa town with bayonets fixed and standards flying. The year I participated I got an easy number by being allocated to stand on a float, even if I did look a bit of a Charlie in that old long flying coat and leather helmet. But it wasn't long before I was given another couple of parade tasks. Hence I had to spruce up the rarely worn No 1 uniform and spit and polish the even more rarely used Oxford pattern shoes (Officers, for the use of).

The first occasion was when I had to command a representative party of men to be marched down to the local church and War Memorial on Remembrance Sunday. As usual for mid-November the weather was cruelly cold. We all had to wear our inappropriately named British Warm Greatcoats. And all that time I had spent on the uniform underneath was wasted – nobody saw it! We had a couple of practices with the chaps, overseen by the Station Warrant Officer, always known as 'the SWO'. He did a lot of shouting at the men, but I got away with a few heavy hints. The day went as well as could be expected in the freezing northerly wind; at least it didn't snow. I always think that those who decided to stop the First World War in November just did not have the well-being of future generations of military personnel at heart. Much more effort should have been made to bring the whole ghastly thing to a stop during the summer of 1918.

The next time I had to strut about and shout a lot was for the Commander-in-Chief's annual inspection. I was a lowly flight commander on a parade with two squadrons of three flights each. During rehearsals our rather per-nickety and often grumpy OC Administration Wing, a tall Wing Commander pen-pusher with a bristly moustache, took the part of the C-in-C. It was a good choice because the C-in-C was a much nicer chap, so the rehearsals were much more of a trial. On the second run-through, when he got to my flight he inspected every man intently and had just reached a rather short airman in the centre of the middle rank. The good Wing Commander was not at all pleased with the state of the lad's headgear; I've no idea why, it looked perfectly respectable to me. Anyhow, he made his dissatisfaction very clear and then glared at me and said, 'Ask the SWO to take that man's name.' I turned to the SWO who simply nodded; he had heard the instruction per-fectly well without me having to relay it across the three-foot space that lay between the three of us.

As we advanced slowly down the rank I overheard the following inter-change behind me.

'All right, me lad, give us yer name,' growled the SWO.

'I can't, sir,' came the reply.

'WHAT? GIVE ME YOUR NAME!'

'I can't, sir.'

'WHY? What do you mean you little twerp!'

'Well I can't sir, because you took it yesterday.'

There was an outpouring of rage from the SWO and poorly stifled laughter from those within earshot.

Later in the year, the Commandant-in-Chief of CFS, Her Majesty Queen Elizabeth the Queen Mother, was due to make one of her periodic visits. This time I was 'volunteered' to go to the Officers' Mess on the day before the visit to participate in the dress rehearsal. This was a really good deal because we were to be served the full meal. The only drawback was that when I got there I was given a nametag on which was inscribed 'Mrs Sparrow'. I was to take the part of the wife of the then boss of the CFS Gnat squadron, Sqn Ldr Mike Sparrow. We hung about in the anteroom for a while, and then a party of folk arrived with one of our WRAF officers playing the part of the Queen Mum. After the whole thing had been timed we went in for lunch and took our places. The top table folk trooped in and we sat, prayed and attacked. The food was really nice and there was wine, so no flying that afternoon.

Apparently everything went well on the day; it always does if you practise enough! However, there was one exception. When the Queen Mum shook the antique silver pepper pot over her main course the top came off. Panic ensued while the plate was taken away and replaced and the offending antique article removed; the pepper pot not the Queen Mother! Throughout, as was her wont from decades of practice, the lady smiled sweetly and chatted graciously to her neighbours at the table. Apparently she said to one of them, 'How funny, that happened to me last time.' I supposed that certain heads rolled later.

On the flying front there were other diversions in which we could participate. One was that all CFS staff pilots could be checked out on other aircraft of the school; I bet that doesn't happen these days. I had already, through dint of knowing a few people, been cleared to fly the Jet Provost Mark 5, which I had not flown before. This version, the latest and last of the RAF's first jet-powered, basic trainer had a pressurised cockpit. The Mark 5's new canopy profile made the aircraft a little bit more attractive, although the JP was never going to look streamlined. The pressurisation meant that there were now no limits on the time that could be spent above 25,000ft, as there were with the earlier marks. The aircraft handled much like the Jet Provost Mk 4, which I had flown during the second half of my basic flying training. I only flew just over fifteen hours in the JP at CFS, but it was great to be able to keep in touch with the higher, faster regime of jet aviation after four years away from it.

Then came another opportunity for further widening of my experience. The Boss had received a call that there was an offer for someone to go to RAF Kemble for a week and do sufficient flying to go solo in the Gnat. I had narrowly missed the very first Gnat course so this was right down my street. In May 1963 I was selected to go to RAF Valley to train on the Gnat; however, the aircraft and training system was not quite up to speed when I passed out of basic flying training. Instead I had been sent to one of the last courses on the venerable DH Vampire. So, when the Boss asked for a volunteer to go to Kemble, I jumped at it. Mind you, I had no competition from anyone else on the squadron; they all thought that I was mad to get in such a small and fearfully

fast flying machine as the Gnat. I had flown in the back of the Gnat a couple
of times before that. Once with my neighbour from across the road in Roman
Way in Bourton-on-the-Water, Red Arrows pilot Chris Roberts. Then I had
flown as a passenger on a couple of sorties with guys from the Gnat squadron.
But getting into the front seat and being taught by an instructor, with the prospect of going off in the tiny jet on my own, was absolutely fantastic.

So I had a week off from the Chipmunk Flight and travelled daily down
to Kemble to fill a gap in my aviation portfolio. Before I started my training
at Kemble I had managed to get hold of a copy of the Pilot's Notes for the
Folland Gnat TMk1 and had spent quite some time studying it. After the first
morning going through a series of rapid-fire briefings on the aircraft's various systems it was into the simulator for me. This was a very simple machine,
especially when compared with today's high fidelity, state-of-the-art devices.
However, it served its purpose quite adequately in helping one to learn the
checklist and to deal with various in-flight emergencies. The most important
of these were to do with the hydraulically powered flying control system.
There were a couple of mnemonics that helped one get through the drills in
the right sequence, so avoiding any form of cock-up that might lead to the
situation getting worse rather than better. The mnemonics were STUPRECC
and CUBSTUN; but I can no longer remember all the words that they stood
for. I expect that ex-Gnat pilots whose memories are better than mine will
now be shouting some strange words at the book and anyone nearby will be
wondering if they have gone slightly dotty!

By the middle of the week I had flown three conversion sorties. At first
I had a little difficulty with the circuits and landings in that I was not accus-
tomed to using more than 30° of bank angle in the landing pattern and I was
no longer used to rushing towards the runway at 130kts. There was a saying
that you didn't get into the Gnat – you put it on. It really felt like that. Once
seated in the front cockpit it was actually quite difficult to see any other part
of the aircraft, except for the long tube that sensed the airspeed sticking out
in front. Once near the ground it felt like you were sitting on a supersonic
skateboard; one's posterior was less than three feet from the ground. Because
the wheels stuck out of the fuselage at a slightly odd angle it was possible to
get into a rapid lateral rocking motion under braking during the landing run.
The only way to stop this disturbing effect was to stop braking – easily said,
but when you can see the end of the runway rushing at you at a good rate
of knots – very hard to do. After a couple of times you get used to it and the
waddling motion gets less with practice.

After three sorties the management were happy for me to go solo. However,
the autumn weather had other ideas. On Thursday morning the journey to
Kemble had taken twice as long as normal; there was thick fog all the way.

The Met Office did not that day issue their usual, 'It'll clear by 10 o'clock' forecast. I sat in the crew room waiting for it to improve and it did, but not sufficiently to send me off on my own. There was worse to come. The forecast for Friday was no better. So I was advised not to even turn up – it would be a waste of time. So, once more I failed to go solo in the Gnat! But watch this space!

A month later I had seen the one and only CFS-operated Gloster Meteor T7 flying. It was one of the pair of historic trainers flown by the school, the other being a De Havilland Vampire T11. The man flying the Meteor was Sqn Ldr Bill Waite, whose day job was Chief Ground Instructor. I chatted him up in the bar one Friday evening and asked him if there was ever any chance of getting in the back seat when he was flying. He affably agreed that there was and that he would call me. These sorts of conversations happen all the time at Happy Hours and rarely does anything actually come of them. But Bill Waite was a good stick and a few days later he called me up and asked if I could be available for a flight in the Meteor on the afternoon of 10 November. I checked with my flight commander and he said that he was happy for me to go, so I called Bill back and told him that I would be there.

After a short briefing on bailing out (there were no ejection seats in the T7) we climbed aboard, closed the greenhouse-like cockpit canopy and Bill started the engines, the noise from which was very subdued. After a few more checks we taxied out. It was like being in a Rolls Royce, it was so smooth and quiet. Although the cockpit oozed the sort of vintage layout that I had got to know and love when I was training on Vampires, the design of the cockpit canopy made it feel somewhat claustrophobic. That, and sitting in the back seat, made it extremely difficult to see out forwards. How Meteor instructors taught students to fly approaches and landings I'll never know!

However, Bill was going to do most of the flying – I was just along for the ride. We took off and climbed to the west and up at 10,000ft Bill stalled and turned and aerobatted. Then he let me have a few minutes in control. I was still taken by the Meteor's classic smoothness. The flying controls seemed well balanced and harmonised, if a bit on the heavy side, the throttles moved smoothly fore and aft on two rails and the thrust was easily sensed and controlled. It was great to be flying a twin-jet again and making flowing curves in a blue autumn sky. All too soon Bill took control again and we set off back for him to practise approaches and landings, including one with an engine at idle to simulate its failure. The touchdowns were all as smooth as everything else and when we finally stopped and dismounted I expressed my gratefulness.

'That's OK, old boy,' he replied. 'You can buy the first beer next Friday.'

Another small job that came my way was to fly a BBC cameraman for some film being made about the Red Arrows. At first I thought, 'this has to be a joke, how do I keep up with them in a Chipmunk?' When I asked for further information I was told that I had to fly alongside and over the team's minibus on its way down the Fosse Way from Little Rissington to Kemble. I was to be authorised to come down to 100ft and told not to annoy anyone on the ground or frighten any horses or motorists. My passenger was one Reg Pope, whose name I have seen in TV credits many times since.

Reg was a very nice chap but he had an enormous camera for the confines of the rear cockpit so we put him in the front and flew with canopy half open. We received the rendezvous time and orbited over the Fosse way just south of Bourton-on-the-Water. After a short time we spotted the minibus and started to chase it. Despite flying at the lowest safe speed we overtook it so I then flew a series of passing shots. Because of the open canopy and the size of his camera Reg couldn't say much, so I just tried my best to put us in positions where he might be able to get something useful for the film. I never did see the final version so I don't know whether any of it was used. But I didn't care – it was twenty-five minutes of fun.

Another extra-curricular event came in the unwelcome guise of a two-month, supposedly career enhancing, course at the Junior Command and Staff School (JCSS). This took place at RAF Ternhill in Shropshire and was usually referred to as the 'Jackass' course. I went there for the first two months of 1971. Although there was a large 1939 pattern Officers' Mess, just like the impressive brick buildings found on most RAF stations, the JCSS student accommodation was in wooden framed buildings with bedrooms and an occasional bathroom. These had undoubtedly been erected as temporary accommodation during the Second World War, but were still in use thirty years later. They were barely warm enough in the bitter winter weather of that year and I vividly remember that, on the first night, after turning off my bedside light, I could see a vertical strip of orange light from the street lamps coming through the wall in the corner of the room! The next morning I pushed the wardrobe firmly into the corner. It probably wouldn't stop the draft through the hole, but at least I wouldn't be able to see the light.

The course was all about the things that junior commanders should know. Such as Queen's Regulations, Air Force Law, how to write letters and reports in the format known as 'Service Writing', public speaking, a wider understanding of the various branches of the service and lots of practice at sword drill with aluminium sticks, much like kids would use to play pirates. The sword drill was to try to make us fit to lead flights of airmen and airwomen on formal and official parades. I quite enjoyed it, but after half an hour my tiny right hand was frozen. I suppose that much of the syllabus was learnt by osmosis but my main memory is of fellow syndicate and course members, many of whom I would bump into later, as is often the way of service life. One of the JCSS directing staff was Sqn Ldr George Etches, my first CFI at

Glasgow UAS. It was good to see him again and I spent a delightful evening at his home.

Much less delightful was the day when I slipped on the icy steps coming out of the mess. My ankle rapidly inflated to twice its normal size and I was put in a service ambulance and taken to a hospital in Wolverhampton for X-rays. There was a suspicion of a fracture but nothing was truly broken, so the extremity was strapped up and I was given a basket load of painkillers. Be thankful for small mercies, I told myself. At least I wouldn't have to stand on that freezing parade ground any more waving my aluminium stick about. It was good to get the course behind me; one more step on the ladder that I still wasn't convinced I needed to be climbing.

It was whilst I was at Ternhill that I heard some dreadful news. On 20 January, while working up two new pilots as the Synchro Pair, two Red Arrows Gnats had collided. All four pilots died. They were Johnny Haddock, John Lewis, Colin Armstrong and Euan Perreaux. Only a month or so earlier I had seen all four of them celebrating the start of the Christmas break at the Inn for All Seasons on the A40, south of Little Rissington. They were all very merry thanks to the excellent ale served there. Euan Perreaux had been a member of my CFS course and was a popular man. I later found out that someone who had seen the accident, from the roadside public viewing area at Kemble, had rung the local radio station and they put the news out almost immediately. One of the Red Arrows' wives heard the radio report and soon there was a full-scale welfare emergency at base. I believe that this disgracefully irresponsible media behaviour was the start of the strict regime where the media cannot release news of fatalities to service personnel until the next-of-kin have been informed. It was a sad day made all the worse by thoughtless behaviour.

The final diversion from normal duties that came my way did so right at the end of my tour. One of the newer staff instructors, Ian Ray, and I were detailed to do some 'Aid to the Civil Powers' flying, similar to that which I had done in Scotland. We would be flying policemen again, but this time to help with road traffic control for the annual Cheltenham Gold Cup Race Meeting. On 14 March 1972 and the following day Ian and I flew half a dozen sorties watching and reporting on the traffic on all the roads around Cheltenham and Gloucester. It was interesting and undemanding flying, the main problem seemed to be the communications between the various airborne and ground-borne Mr Plods. 'Twas ever thus. And, what's more, we were never given any decent racing tips.

No 239 Squadron RFC, St Omer 1917. Actually most of my CFS course members dressed up for the spoof photo for the RAF Little Rissington Officers' Mess Summer Ball, 1967. (Author's collection)

Formal Squadron photograph at summer camp, RAF Bicester 1968. Front row, L–R: Plt Off Ian McCoubrey, Fg Off John Barrow, Flt Lt Bob Hutcheson, Sqn Ldr Arthur Pullen, Wg Cdr John Greenhill, Flt Lt Andrew Bell, Flt Lt Colin Adams, Flt Lt Ian Montgomerie, myself. (Author's collection)

Instructors and policemen of Exercise Maigret at Scone in September 1968. The UAS's wooden huts can be seen in the background. (Author's collection)

Informal group photo at the summer camp of 1969 at RAF Abingdon. (Author's collection)

Last one airborne's a sissy! Summer camp at RAF Abingdon, June 1969. (Author's collection)

Acting Pilot Officer Gavin Mackay about to board a UGSAS Chipmunk at Glasgow Airport. (Gavin Mackay)

When we said close formation, we mean *close* formation! (Gavin Mackay)

The author (left) and fellow instructor Flt Lt Hector Skinner about to commit aviation. (Gavin Mackay)

The author (front) flying 'his' Chipmunk, WP 967, over the Erskine Bridge, which was still under construction in 1969. It was opened by Princess Anne on 2 July 1971. (Gavin Mackay)

The 'view' from the back seat of a Chipmunk. (Gavin Mackay)

A formation of three UGSAS Chipmunks over Glasgow Airport in 1969. (Gavin Mackay)

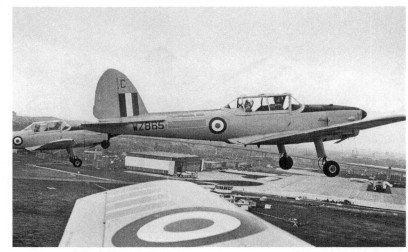

Our 'Red Sparrows' arrival at Old Warden on 2 July 1969, photographed by one of the students. (Author's collection)

The CFS Commandant-in-Chief, HM Queen Elizabeth the Queen Mother, receiving the Sword of the Freedom of the Borough of Cheltenham. (With permission of the CFS Association)

Ian Ray and I relax during our three days of airborne highway patrol duty during the spring 1972 Cheltenham Gold Cup Meeting. (Author's collection)

A B2 of 231 OCU starts up. (Author's collection)

The ergonomic slum that was the Canberra T4 pilots' cockpit. (Author's collection)

T4 WT 488 en route to RAF Kinloss, 23 January 1973. (Author's collection)

Navigator Dave Terry and myself pose beside a B2. (Author's collection)

My old mate Ian Ray together again as he re-qualifies me as a Chipmunk instructor so that I could check out pilots for the ATC summer camps at RAF Cottesmore. (Author's collection)

Canberra T4 WE 192 in the red-and-white training livery. (Author's collection)

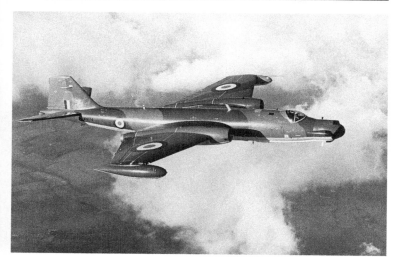

Canberra T17 WH 874 of No 360 Squadron, RAF Cottesmore. (Author's collection)

A copy of the AID Certificate of Safety for the first flight of the Canberra prototype VN 799 on 13 May 1949. (Author's collection)

CERTIFICATE OF SAFETY FOR FLIGHT.

M.A.P. Form 1090.

From :—
Inspector in Charge, A.I.D.,
The English Electric Co. Ltd.,
East Works, Preston, Lancs.

To :—
The English Electric Co. Ltd.,
Warton Aerodrome,
Nr. Preston, Lancs.

I HEREBY CERTIFY that the aircraft defined hereunder :—

Type.	Engine(s).	Serial No. or Registration Mark.
B3/45 Prototype	RR.Avon R.A.2. A13/A617963 A14/A617964	VN.799.

has this day been inspected including the engine(s), the engine installation(s) and instruments and is in every way safe for the undermentioned flight(s) :—

Purpose of flight(s) Initial Taxying & Flight Trials in accordance with schedule of Flight Tests & Design Certificate dated 5/5/49.

Authority* Contract 5841/CB6(b). To take place

from WARTON Aerodrome with Mr. R.P. Beamont. as Pilot.

NOTE.—Any alterations, repairs or adjustments made to this aircraft subsequent to the issue of this certificate renders it invalid, and no further flight may be made until the certificate is renewed.

	Signed.	Date.
1 INITIAL TAXYING (LESS ENG. ENGINES)		7th May 1949
3 INITIAL TAXYING (WEA SHORT ENGINES)		8th May 1949
2 TAXYING & HIGH SPEED RUNS		9th May 1949
4 Flight		11th May 1949
5 Flight & Taxying		12th May 1949
6. 1st Flight		13th May 1949

(*13706—7252: Wt. 42659—3381 3m Pads 1/44 I.S. 700 *Contract, A. N. D., etc.

Canberra PR9 XH135 lifts off. (Ray Deacon)

A Canberra PR9 in its later life on Operation Herrick in Afghanistan. (Ray Deacon)

20 WHAT NEXT?

When I had arrived at CFS my 'Desk Officer' had promised me that I would be there for a maximum of two years. The Desk Officer is the man up at the RAF's Personnel HQ who has the unenviable task of matching people, with all their qualifications and their foibles, to specific appointments. But at CFS there was an in-house staff officer who liaised with the personnel folks; therefore we had an on-base buddy to help organise what we wanted to do next. It also so happened that this staff officer man was none other than Flt Lt Don Merriman, who had been on the Chipmunk Squadron staff with me for about a year. It was in autumn 1971 that Don contacted me and said that he thought that I could possibly be moved on in the spring. He wanted to confirm that the choices that I had expressed in my Annual Confidential Reports (ACR) were still valid. I confirmed that my first choice was for a posting to a Buccaneer squadron in Germany, second choice to Phantoms in Germany and third choice to a Canberra PR9 reconnaissance squadron in Malta or Cyprus.

In the spring of 1971, following the advice I had received from Jock Wingate at RAF Kinloss in the summer of the previous year, I sought out the appropriate form and applied for selection to the Empire Test Pilots' School. Once completed, I gave it to Jack Sprackling, who read it and then asked about my educational qualifications. I told him that I had eight O-levels and pointed out that academics would be examined during the selection process. He said he would send it up the line. A few days later he gave it back to me.

'I'm sorry, Mike, but the CFI and Station Commander won't support your application. They feel that you don't have the right academic or flying background,' he explained. I was miffed that they would not endorse my application. I had more than the minimum number of hours required, I had an 'Above Average' assessment of my flying ability and nowhere did the application ask for a degree, or even A-level academic ability. Oh well, on with the motley!

In the meantime my Red Arrows neighbour, Chris Roberts, had told me that the team was looking for a new team manager for the coming season and that there was a move afoot to make the manager's post a full three-year appointment. This had not been the case previously; the practice had been for the manager to do one year in that post and then move onto the team. This had led to a lack of continuity in a very important job. The Red Arrows' team manager was responsible for all the planning and support arrangements for the pilots during the hectic display season: food, accommodation, baggage and press relations amongst many others. The manager, known as Red 10, would fly the spare aircraft ahead to displays and ensure that everything was set up in accordance with the team's pre-show requirements. He was also the team's commentator for every display. The best thing about the job was that it was counted by the personnel folk as a ground tour, despite the fact that the manager got to fly the Gnat throughout his time with the team.

I told Chris that I would be delighted to apply, so he put my name into the pot. The nine pilots of the Reds have a big say in who is in the team; in fact they have a veto. However, I did have to undergo an interview with the commandant, Air Commodore Freddy Hazelwood. I turned up in my best uniform and shiny shoes, was let in by the ADC and threw the commandant the smartest salute I could muster. He asked me to sit down and relax, so I took off my hat and did so, but not too much. He astutely explored my motives for wanting the job, so I told him honestly about why. One vital question was, 'Would you be hankering all the time to get into the team or will you be content to stay as the manager for three years?' I knew that this was the vital point of the exercise and answered, 'No, sir. I'll be perfectly content to stay as the team manager throughout my tour.' And that was the truth. Then he started to look into details about how it would work for me if I stayed in my hiring in Bourton. I told him that I now had three neighbours who were in the team: Chris Roberts, Alan East and Ted Girdler. We chatted some more about the other things I would wish to do if I did not get the manager's job. I told him of my wish to go back to Germany flying the Buccaneer or the Phantom. He nodded wisely, as air commodores do, and then brought the interview to an end. I stood, replaced my hat, saluted and departed. I felt that it had gone well; all I could do now was to wait.

I didn't have to wait long. A couple of weeks later Chris told me that the other contender, Flt Lt Bruce Donnelly, had been selected. As expected he got more votes from the team than I did, as more of the team knew him and his background was more favourable in that he hadn't spent the last four-and-a-half years flying a small, slow aeroplane. I was very disappointed but not really surprised. The hardest thing to bear came much later when I learnt that Bruce joined the team at the end of his first year. So much for that idea!

So back to Plan A. After some time I bumped into Don Merriman in the Mess. 'Ah, Mike, I wanted to have a word,' he said, acting very much the staff officer. 'We've just found out that the Rolls Royce Spey engines in the RAF's Phantoms have a serious problem and that they have cancelled the next few conversion courses for at least six months.'

'What about the Buccaneers?' I asked. 'They have the same engine, but without the reheat.'

'The Buccaneer force has put all conversion training on hold as well, but probably not for as long as the Phantom OCU.'

'OK, what next?' I responded.

'I'll look into the other options and get back to you,' he said and went on his way.

So now it was Plan B or was it Plan C? Meanwhile I was doing my day job of training Chipmunk instructors; oddly enough, many of my student QFIs ended up going to Glasgow. It was during the summer of 1971 that I had taken the chance to visit my old UAS at their Summer Camp at RAF Marham. It was good to see some of the QFIs that I had trained now at work and some of the students with whom I had flown with at the beginning of their training now about to finish. The CO, Sqn Ldr Barry Dale, gave me the impression that he was happy with the standard of the CFS graduates that he had received, so I was pleased with that. But one sadness happened while I was there. The area from which the UAS was operating was near the Station Fire Section's practice ground and sitting there in the middle of it, thankfully not yet burned, was a No 16 Squadron Canberra B(I)8; it had belonged to my old squadron during my first tour in Germany. I walked over to take a look and it was actually my old jet, XM 272. It had someone else's name on it now, but it was like coming across the grave of a friend you did not know had died. I took a look inside. The smell was still the same; all Canberras had that unique odour. Someone had removed the stick – otherwise I would have taken it. It was a poignant moment in a happy, summer's day.

Events unfolded about my onward move. First, I was offered a chance to stay at CFS, move to Examining Wing and, with Ian Ray, help bring the Scottish Aviation Bulldog into service to replace the Chipmunk. I was asked to think about it, but that didn't take long. I felt that if I did take up the offer I would be stuck in the instructional light aircraft world for good and never get back to flying jets at low level, which was what I really wanted to do. Then there was mention of a new Hunter Wing of two squadrons that had been set up at RAF Wittering to keep trainees flying while the Spey engines were modified. However, Don thought that might not be applicable to me. He offered me my third choice, PR9 Canberras in Cyprus or Malta, where I would become one of the squadron's QFIs. I accepted. It might not be low-level and it was recce and not strike/attack. But I knew the Canberra and the PR9 version of the aircraft was the ultimate one. Moreover, the prospect of living on an island in the Mediterranean for three years was very attractive.

By February 1972 I had a posting notice to No 36 Refresher Course at No 231 Operational Conversion Unit in my hand. Since I had passed through the Canberra OCU in 1964 it had moved from RAF Bassingbourn to RAF Cottesmore in Rutland. I had to report there on 29 March.

An OCU does just what it says on the tin. Pilots and, where appropriate, all the operating aircrew of a particular aircraft type, go to the OCU for their final phase of training before reporting to a squadron. At the OCU they will be taught everything related to the aircraft and its operational role. They will fly training sorties until they reach the required standard for a safe transition to a squadron, where some further training may be needed for specialist roles. Essentially the OCU completes the full flying training cycle. For people like me at the time, there are shorter courses to give what is known as refresher training for those who have already qualified on type. So it was time to pack the bags, get the removers in and take the three of us north to England's smallest county.

PART FOUR

THE CANBERRA OCU (AGAIN!)

Teachers open the door. You enter by yourself.

Chinese Proverb

21 BACK TO THE FUTURE

At Cottesmore I was allocated an OMQ: No 4 Heythrop Road. The address was a reminder that we were in the heart of hunting country; all the roads on the officers' married patch were named after hunts. Our house was very near the technical site and behind the Officers' Mess and our kitchen and living room windows overlooked the airfield itself. Within days of arrival I had discovered that there was a bicycle store from where I could sign for a black upright, gearless bike to use until I was posted out. As I lived so close to the part of the station where I would work it seemed foolish not to take up this facility.

The HQ of the OCU was in what had once been an airmen's accommodation block and was just a few hundred yards from home. All the essential facilities and offices were in the building with the exception of our flying clothing. That was in the Operations Block at the top of Heythrop Road. Cottesmore had first opened during the RAF expansion of 1938 and was originally used for training. The first operational aircraft based there were the Vickers Wellesleys, Fairey Battles and Handley Page Hampdens of various bomber squadrons. In 1954 Cottesmore became a Canberra base with Numbers 15, 44, 57 and 149 squadrons arriving. These Canberra squadrons practiced high-level bombing missions, but their stay was short lived; by 1955 they had all moved elsewhere.

Then, for almost twenty years, Cottesmore was a V-bomber base, with Handley Page Victors and, later, Avro Vulcans. These aircraft were on quick reaction alert (QRA) duties and carried Britain's nuclear deterrent. The Canberra OCU moved to Cottesmore in 1970, after the V-bombers moved out. The other squadrons that moved in to occupy this very large airfield with its 9,000ft-long runway were two Canberra squadrons, Nos 98 and 360, and No 115 Squadron, which flew the Armstrong Whitworth Argosy turbo-prop transport aircraft. No 360 squadron was equipped with the Canberra T Mk17, a highly modified version of the B2, instantly recognisable by the many protuberances on its nose. This squadron was a large unit, jointly operated by the RAF and the Royal Navy and used in the electronic-warfare training role for NATO armed forces.

Nos 98 and 115 squadrons were radar and approach calibration squadrons, previously operated under the aegis of the by-now defunct Signals Command. All these assets had been absorbed into Bomber Command under the direction of No 1 Group, with its HQ 20 miles up the A1 at RAF Bawtry, near Doncaster. Cottesmore was a busy base and I was glad that I wouldn't be there for too long. I was looking forward to warmer climes.

The refresher course started with the usual week of ground-school lectures and a visit to nearby RAF North Luffenham for the Aeromedical Training Course and a session of dinghy drill training in the swimming pool. On 10 April 1972 I climbed aboard a dual controlled Canberra T4 for the first time in five years. But it was like coming home. The smell, the effort of strapping in, the difficulty of seeing out ahead and the rather haphazard instrument panel were all unchanged.

It was strange to be wearing a lifejacket, leg restraint garters and an oxygen mask again and to be removing safety pins from the seat before going flying. In fact on one occasion I had reverted to Chipmunk days and forgot to take a lifejacket with me. As the aeroplanes were a minibus ride from the Station Operations Centre, where the flying clothing and safety equipment was housed, this did not impress my instructor. On another occasion, still getting used to strapping into ejection seats again, I attached the quick release connection from my lifejacket to my very near neighbour's survival pack. He looked down when he was looking for the connection to attach to his own lifejacket and said, 'We'll have to come to some arrangement.' I eventually cottoned on to what he meant. In some respects, and with hindsight approaching nostalgia, strapping into the Chipmunk and getting airborne was such a simple and easy job.

Nevertheless I flew my nine aircraft conversion sorties within a couple of weeks and was ready to pass on to the QFI Conversion course. This was flown with the CFS agents, Ken Allan and Pete Perry. Now I had to sit in the right-hand seat and operate the throttles with my right hand and the control yoke with my left. To give better access to the cockpit and the navigator's cabin at the rear, the right-hand seat was mounted on a beam across the fuselage. This meant that it could be pushed back for the occupant of the left-hand seat to get in, forward for the directional consultant to clamber into his cubby-hole behind the pilots and locked into the middle position when ready for flight. That meant that the right-hand man had to learn to strap in hanging forward at an angle of 30°. It just went to prove that you can get used to anything if you do it often enough. After another month I had mastered all that the people who wrote the reports wanted of me.

When I arrived on the OCU the Boss was Sqn Ldr Bob Taylor, an urbane man with a friendly approach. However, he was on his way out of the RAF; he was to become the manager of Birmingham International Airport. His replacement was none other than the newly promoted Sqn Ldr Don Merriman; the very same ex-CFS personnel staff officer and fellow Chipmunk QFI with whom I had worked at Little Rissington. I was chatting to someone in the crew room about going on to become a squadron QFI on the PR9 when another officer said, 'Oh, that's a coincidence, so am I.' He was Flt Lt Norman Gill, who was shortly to be posted to Malta. I thought that I would therefore be going to the other squadron, based at RAF Akrotiri in Cyprus; a secret smile crept shyly across my face – I thought that Cyprus was the better option. It would not be long before I found out the truth.

22 NOT MOVING ON

The new Boss, Don Merriman, invited me in for a chat during the course of which it became clear to me that I was going nowhere else. I was replacing the Malta-bound Norman Gill on the staff. I was both hugely disappointed and a bit angry. It seemed to me that I had been misled, or that negotiations had taken place so that Don could keep me on the staff of his new unit. If it was the latter, then it was sort of flattering, but I'd much rather have gone overseas and flown the PR9. Now my next three years would be spent sitting in the most uncomfortable cockpit ever devised by man for man. I was not a happy bunny. It seemed to me that the RAF did whatever they wanted with you regardless of what you told them you would like to do. But that's the nature of service life. Protecting democracy from within an organisation that, by its very nature, does not practise it.

On 1 June 1972 I started work as a Canberra QFI with my first student pilot, Dave McIntyre; by the following evening we had flown three sorties together. He made a good start to his new career as a Canberra pilot. As in my day on the Canberra OCU, the crews went through the course together and the navigators usually flew the T4 sorties with their allocated pilot. Another of my student pilots at that time was Keith Breadmore; his navigator was Chris Knight. On one of their early sorties, in fact the first that trained them in all aspects of operations using only one engine, known as asymmetric flight, one of the engines actually failed. So I had to carry out a single-engined recovery to base and landing. Thankfully it went well and was a useful, if unwelcome, demonstration that once in a while the old Rolls Royce Avon did actually give up the ghost in flight and a good lesson in how to deal with the problem.

On another occasion, just four days later, we were climbing out of Cottesmore on a north-easterly heading, passing 20,000ft on our way up to 41,000ft. Keith said that he could smell something odd. The man in the back agreed. I told Keith to keep flying the jet and I took off my oxygen mask and sniffed. There certainly was a strong smell of something hot, possibly oil. There was also a grey mist forming in the cockpit. I was about to ask Keith to make a rapid descent when he said that he was not feeling so good. I took control, put out an emergency call and asked for directions towards the nearest active airfield. I closed the throttles, extended the airbrakes and opened the bomb doors while pushing the nose down to make a rapid dive to below 10,000ft. I also turned off the pressurisation and opened the little porthole, known as the Direct Vision or DV panel, on the right-hand side of the cockpit canopy. By now Eastern Radar, with whom we had been operating, had directed us towards RAF Cranwell. They handed us over to Cranwell air traffic control and I made a prompt approach and landing. Keith was recovering from his bout of nausea well and both the nav and I had suffered no ill effects at all; well apart from a lot of ear popping as we were hurtling earthwards. After turning off the runway and cancelling our state of emergency, we taxied in to our indicated parking spot where there was an ambulance waiting for us. As I stopped the engines I looked across and saw a medical officer in attendance. It was an ex-Glasgow University student whom I had known well – Ian McCoubrey – now a Flt Lt and a real medical officer in the real air force (well at Cranwell!).

We greeted each other like the old mates that we were, much to the amusement of everybody else. We were then taken to the Station Medical Centre, more usually referred to as Sick Quarters. There Ian examined us for ill effects and blood samples were taken. One thing that was obvious was that Keith was suffering from mild carbon monoxide poisoning. Ian said that it was because Keith had already smoked three cigarettes that morning so had predisposed his body to the ill effects from the fumes. When all the medical bits had been completed I telephoned our engineers back at base. They agreed that we could fly the jet back to Cottesmore, below 10,000ft and unpressurised. The trip home took all of fifteen minutes. A slight overfilling of the engine gearbox oil tank had caused our problem, with the spillage burning and the fumes getting pulled into the air conditioning system.

I was now into the swing of things but still learning. There were various challenges that reared their head occasionally. With four flying units at Cottesmore the airfield was a very busy place. No 115 Squadron's twin-boomed, turbo-prop Argosy transports tended to fly very big circuits of the airfield and seemed to take ages to get anywhere. This made it sometimes very difficult to co-ordinate the correctly sized circuits we had to show our students. The guys on No 98 Squadron, who flew Canberra B15s, were a well-behaved lot who didn't bother us much. But some of the pilots on 360 Squadron were much more gung-ho; I put it down to the bad influence of all those Fleet Air Arm pilots and observers. Their operations meant that they often flew in formations, usually in pairs but sometimes in fours, and their arrivals back into the circuit could be a bit over-enthusiastic. I didn't really blame them; compared to my tour on Canberra B(I)8s in Germany their job didn't give them much room for free expression. However, they often cut inside our students who were being taught to fly a normal sized circuit and, occasionally, even made disparaging remarks on the air. Very poor form! However, I did once respond to such a radio call later by reminding its sender that he too had once had to learn to fly the Canberra properly.

Something that all pilots are very aware of is the effect of reduced pressure on various parts of the body. Because the Canberra, and most military fast jets, are not pressurised to the same degree as airliners then any climb to altitudes above 30,000ft will inevitably lead to cabin altitudes of more than 20,000ft. Rapid ascents and long exposure to reduced atmospheric pressure can cause the nitrogen, which is always present in the blood and gets there via the lungs, to bubble out, especially in the joints, such as knees and elbows. This brings on decompression sickness, also known as 'the Bends'. It's exactly the same affliction that can affect underwater divers if they come up from depth too quickly. I never experienced this problem, but those that have speak of sharp pain in some or all of their joints and even headaches and vertigo; not a good thing when you are flying an aeroplane.

To offset the possible onset of 'the Bends' the proportion of oxygen to nitrogen being breathed is increased automatically by the oxygen regulator. For folk undertaking long, high-altitude flights then 100 per cent oxygen is breathed both before and during the flight to help purge the nitrogen from the blood. The most common symptom of the effect of flying at a high cabin altitude isn't normally felt until, like that of a few pints, the morning after. This symptom is usually first noticed not by the sufferer but by their nearest and dearest, who will arrive downstairs and complain, loudly of course, about the volume setting on the TV or the radio. That's because our gallant aviator is, until it is lovingly pointed out, suffering from a temporary deafness. The nitrogen that bubbled out of the tiny blood vessels in the inner ear, behind the wall of the eardrum, has been reabsorbed during the night, but not replaced. So the air pressure outside the ear is now larger than inside and the effect is to push the eardrum inwards so that it is now too taut to work properly. A quick pinch of the nose and a blow will pop the eardrum back into its proper shape and the noise of the world will return to normal. The secondary effect of this is to cause the subject to immediately readjust the volume on the broadcasting media.

As the aircraft climbs or descends everyone with normal ears will suffer from this pressure differential in flight and swallowing can quickly sort it out; that's why they dish out sweeties on some commercial flights, especially to the kids. Some aircrew have sinus trouble and that is more serious, as the pain can be really intense. So we never flew with a head cold. For some folk the problem is caused by the passages to and from the sinus cavities being too narrow. If that is the case then surgery has to be carried out; this is known colloquially as a 'rebore' and is a very unpleasant procedure. I have known three pilots who have had to undergo this rather medieval torture. I visited one in hospital once; his face was twice its normal size and he looked like he had gone ten rounds with a professional boxer.

The final and equally painful outcome of the change in air pressure during a climb afflicted me on 26 July 1972. If there is an abscess under a tooth a very small gas bubble can develop inside the gum, near the tooth's root. As the cabin pressure reduces then the bubble expands and puts pressure on the nerve of the tooth. It is very painful and gets worse with increasing altitude. On this occasion, as we climbed I felt the toothache start. After thirty minutes it was excruciating so I asked the student to fly me home. Once on the ground I went direct to the Dental Section where I was examined. Sure enough there was an abscess under one of my molars. For once I was really glad to get that jab of novocaine and let the Fangmeister do his stuff. The next day I flew with Ken Allan to carry out, as it says in my logbook, a 'Tooth Air Test'. It passed.

By now I was flying between twenty-five and thirty hours every month. A pace of life that was busy but not frantic. So much so that I discovered in the early days of my tour of duty that two Chipmunks were detached to Cottesmore for the summer to give air experience flights to the Air Training Corps cadets who came for summer camps during their school holidays. A call had gone out for any Chipmunk experienced aircrew to volunteer for such duty. I thought that with around 1,200 hours on type, I should qualify – so I volunteered. After a quick check flight with the man in charge I started flying cadets. Suddenly it didn't seem that long since I had been one of those small figures waddling out with a parachute strapped to their posteriors and being lifted bodily into the back seat. In fact it was twelve years. Flying the cadets was great fun and a good diversion from the daily grind.

23 INTERESTING TIMES

By the early 1970s there was increasing pressure on the defence budget. While the government of the day and its predecessors had reduced the nation's worldwide commitments by withdrawing from bases to the east of Suez, a large re-equipment programme was under way to modernise the armed forces for warfare in the latter part of the twentieth century. In the RAF the Hawker Hunter had been replaced by the Harrier and the Jaguar; the Shackleton by the Nimrod; the Canberra bomber versions by the Buccaneer and Phantom; the Wessex helicopter by the Puma; the Hastings and Beverley transporters by the Lockheed Hercules and the Lightning also by the Phantom. The spiralling upwards costs of new technology was driving more and more projects towards a multi-national solution. The Jaguar and Puma were Anglo-French co-operative ventures and the Multi-role Combat Aircraft (MRCA),[37] which was nearing its first flight, was a tri-national collaboration between the UK, Germany and Italy. The V-Force was being phased out and the responsibility for the UK Independent Nuclear Deterrent handed over to the Royal Navy, with their new, very expensive, nuclear powered submarines, armed with lots of Polaris Intercontinental Ballistic Missiles (ICBMs), each fitted with multiple nuclear warheads.

Of all those now replaced aircraft some of the Canberras survived, but in much reduced numbers and in unarmed support functions. The most important of which was in the photo-reconnaissance role undertaken by one UK-based and two Mediterranean-based squadrons. There were also Canberras being operated by the Royal Navy's Fleet Requirements and Development Unit (FRADU) from RNAS Yeovilton, where they provided training targets for RN Air Direction operators, both ashore and at sea. Nos 85 and 100 Squadrons at RAF West Raynham, in Norfolk, and No 7 Target Facilities squadrons at RAF St Mawgan in Cornwall provided airborne targets for UK air defence forces. Then there were the two Cottesmore-based units, Nos 98 and 360 squadrons. In the slightly shadier world of electronic intelligence (ELINT) there were a couple of Canberras with No 51 Squadron and, in the world of Research and Development, perhaps another twenty with the Radar Research Squadron at Pershore in Worcestershire, the RAE at Farnborough and the A&AEE at Boscombe Down. Finally No 56 Squadron, based in Cyprus with their Lightnings, had a couple of Canberras to provide their own target facilities. That meant that, including the OCU's holdings of the aircraft, there were still well over 120 Canberras in RAF and MOD service.

This led to the required throughput of trainees for the OCU being moderately high, although nothing like it had been when I had attended the

Canberra Bomber Course in 1964. All those bomber squadrons in Cyprus, Singapore and Germany had now gone. Nevertheless, the courses came at monthly intervals so our turnover was high. With the advent of new, shiny and sharp-pointed machines, like the Harrier, Jaguar, Buccaneer and Phantom, the best graduating students from the flying training system were selected for those types. That meant that we tended to receive the guys from the lower end of the ability range. Another frequent arrival at the OCU was the V-Force co-pilot who had failed to achieve captaincy. Often he came to us via a ground tour.

Although the quality of some of the students had changed, not for the better, the Canberra had not. It was still an aircraft that sorted out the men from the boys. Mishandled it was a killer, especially after an engine failure. It was a totally manually operated flying machine. No autostabilisers and, with the exception of the PR9, no powered flying controls and no autopilot. It was big and relatively heavy; a fully loaded PR7 weighed in excess of 25 tonnes. The power-to-weight ratio was moderate and the aircraft's response to turbulence was not comfortable.

So we had our work cut out. Some of the students arrived knowing that they had not been selected to go to the sharp end of the RAF and were not well motivated. Some had very low levels of innate skill and soon found themselves well behind the aircraft and the rate of progress we had to ask of them. We often had student pilots under review, the first step of which was to give them a change of instructor. This had a twofold benefit: it allowed a second opinion and it lifted the possibility of a personality clash.

I received a student this way in August 1972; to save embarrassment I won't give his name. He was one of the ex-V Force co-pilots I mentioned earlier. He had flown three years as a co-pilot on the Vulcan, not made the grade for the switch to the captain's seat and then spent two years on the ground as a bombing range officer. He came to us after a refresher course on the Jet Provost, with a less than complimentary report, and flew nine or ten sorties with one of the other instructors. His name came up regularly in our regular staff meetings as someone who might need additional effort. Then it was decided that a change of instructor would be the next thing to try. I won that particular 'prize draw'! So I went flying with him. He was a real 'curate's egg': good in parts, but not enough parts and the bad ones were the dangerous ones. He had difficulty keeping on top of things generally and especially when flying using only one engine.

After several sorties he was making slow progress, but not as much as I would have liked to see. Then we went into the night flying phase. On the first sortie he was so bad that after forty minutes I called the whole thing off and we landed. His biggest problem was in not adapting to the correct technique for aviating in the dark. Whatever the owls and bats do makes no difference – for us ordinary human beings, to whom flying is not natural anyway, night flying is an awkward business. There is usually not much in the way of a horizon, from which we mere mortals draw our orientation *vis-à-vis* the ground/sky interface; that is – which way is up? In the dark we need, just like when flying in cloud, to use the artificial aids given to us by way of the flight instruments. This helps us to monitor what the aircraft is doing compared with what we've asked it to do. But at night we are not always inside clouds and neither are all the other folk out there committing *aviation noir* with us, so we still have to watch out for them. We also need to see useful things like towns, major roads and other illuminated landmarks to check on where we are. Finally when we need to land and get back into the light, we need to be able to see the airfield and its runways. So we have to fly using a mixture of instrument and visual flying techniques. Doing one in exclusion to the other will bring disaster.

This guy was doing too much visual and not enough instrument flying, especially in the circuit pattern. The correct technique for making any manoeuvre, like starting a turn, is to look out in the direction you wish to turn and make sure you are not going to bump into anybody. Then transfer all your attention to the instruments to roll into and set up the turn at the desired angle of bank, speed and, if landing, the correct attitude and rate of descent. Once all that is achieved, hold everything as it was and look out into the turn again. When you are sure that the sky isn't previously occupied, back to the instruments … and so on. This pilot's poor technique, despite my constant reminders, was leading to poorly executed approaches, which inevitably lead to bad or inaccurate touchdowns.

After two more sorties I went back to the Boss and told him that I thought that my student still had not achieved a safe standard to go off on his own at night and opined that he might be better employed elsewhere. However, the Boss, who was under pressure from above to graduate as many crews as possible, asked me to give him one more trip. I reluctantly agreed and the next night I gave the lad another intensive briefing. Before he went 'solo' in the B2 he had to demonstrate the capability to deal with an engine failure on take-off and a subsequent safe circuit and landing using one engine.

We went off to Waddington, near Lincoln, to practice a radar approach and visual circuits and landings. After about twenty minutes he had actually flown the aircraft better than on the previous three evenings, so on the second take-off, from a touch-and-go landing, I chopped a throttle back at 140kts. He recovered satisfactorily and, flying totally on the instruments, which was acceptable for the moment, he climbed ahead, carried out the checklist actions and levelled off at the circuit altitude of 1,500ft. It was then that things

started to go wrong. When he set the power on the operating single engine
he used the figure he should have used when flying on two engines. Then he
looked out to turn back towards the airfield. By the time we had reached a
position known as 'downwind' opposite the runway the speed was dropping
too low. The staff navigator in the back prompted him when it got to 10kts
above the minimum speed of 140kts. He then cottoned on and increased the
power and adjusted the rudder position to keep going straight. Then he did
the pre-landing checks, which included lowering the landing gear. But he did
not put on some extra power to offset the increase in drag. Now he was getting flustered. I told him to calm down and fly as I had told him to. He called
air traffic control, 'Bravo 06, finals, three greens, to roll.'[38]

He rolled into the turn as he was looking over his shoulder for the runway.
WRONG! FLY THE INSTRUMENTS! He over-banked slightly and the
nose went down too far. I firmly reminded him to look at his flight instruments and sort it out. He saw the speed increasing too much because the
nose was too low, so he reduced power. About one third of the way into the
turn he was too low and was still looking out to see where the runway was.
Why? It had not moved – it was still where we had left it! Things were now
going from bad to worse. He raised the nose, the speed started to drop and the
navigator called 'Speed 140 knots!' At this he pushed the throttle wide open. It
was the engine on the inside of the turn and as the thrust came on the aircraft
rolled to the right and the nose pitched down.

'I HAVE CONTROL! RAISE THE UNDERCARRIAGE!' I com-
manded, in as controlled a manner as I could muster, while simultaneously
pulling one throttle back and opening the other, lowering the nose to get a
safe speed while the engine spooled up, at the same time trying to roll the
wings level. At this stage I was locked onto the flight instruments. We were
descending into the blackness, well short of the runway with not a great deal
of speed. I pulled the stick back as much as I dared and, as the thrust of both
engines started to kick in, the nose started to rise. I looked at the altimeter
and it was coming down to 200ft. I kept pulling and noticed the runway lights
appearing in the top of the canopy. I just watched them and kept pulling. The
nose came above the lights and the navigator called '100 feet'. Phew! That was
a close thing! I called Air Traffic Control to tell them that we were returning
to Cottesmore and I flew the aircraft all the way home myself. After I had
got my breath back I told the occupant of the left-hand seat that I would be
recommending that he be 'chopped', that is, leave the course.

When we got back the navigator told me that he was within a millisec-
ond of ejecting. I reflected on the incident and came to the conclusion that
I would never again let myself be talked into pushing on with anyone who
had already demonstrated to me that they did not possess the aptitude or

ability for the successful completion of their training. It was my fault for pushing the guy beyond his level of ability. He was asked to seek further employment, well away from aeroplanes.

In contrast and thankfully, I had many more and much better students. They were usually the ones straight from advanced flying training on the Gnat. Some came a little disappointed that they did not get onto a sharp-end squadron, flying Harriers or Jaguars. However, they soon came to respect the Canberra and its demands on their talents. These students were a joy to teach. They learned quickly and, even when they faltered, they soon picked themselves up, dusted themselves off and started all over again. Two particular guys in this category were Dickie Sutcliffe and Steve Solomon. The former really enjoyed the course and went off to fly PR9s. I was very flattered when he left because he gave me a copy of Richard Bach's book *Jonathon Livingston Seagull* with the inscription 'You will enjoy reading this because you enjoy your flying as much as Jonathon.' I still have the book today and have read it more than once. It was a very nice, and true, thing to say. A few years later I was very sad to learn that Dickie had lost control of the Hunter he was flying off South Wales, had crashed into the sea and never been found. I just hoped that he went through that magic door in the sky like Jonathon Livingston Seagull.

Steve Solomon was an enthusiastic young fellow, reasonably talented, fun to fly with but had to have his keenness tempered occasionally. He passed the course well and went off to No 85 Squadron at RAF West Raynham. One incident I remember with Steve was on a Friday when he wanted to go to RAF Valley on the Isle of Anglesey, for some sort of reunion with his mates I believe. I arranged to take him there in a T4 as part of his training. We arrived at a very windy Valley, landed and taxied to our parking position. However, the ground crew parked us with our tail into the gale, a really bad idea for an aeroplane with manually operated flying controls, as they will be blown violently about and might even be damaged. I tried to signal them to let us park the other way round but they either couldn't or wouldn't understand my hand signals. I shut the engines down and lowered my seat back and unstrapped. Steve hung onto the flying controls, which were trying their best to thrash about alarmingly. I dismounted and went over to the recalcitrant men. It was very hard to make myself heard in the wind, which was blowing at about 25 or 30kts, but I attempted to explain that the aircraft's control system could be damaged. One of them said that we could not turn round here under our own power, but that he would ask for a tractor.

'Make it urgent, please,' I said.

'Well it is lunchtime, sir,' was the rejoinder.

I knew that Steve had to get away so I stood in the spot vacated by my now swung-back seat and hung onto the controls while he unstrapped. Then he had to squeeze past me to exit and go off for his dirty weekend. I'm glad that no one saw the intimate manoeuvres that we had to do to get him out! I then climbed into the left-hand seat to hold the controls while I waited to be turned about. It was hard work and then a huge gust hit the aircraft and the control yoke went to full deflection crushing the end of my ring finger against the control column. It hurt like hell. But I had to keep hanging on. The throbbing pain just grew and grew, but I didn't dare take my glove off.

After what seemed a couple of lifetimes, but was probably ten minutes, the tractor arrived, hitched up and turned us, at last, into the wind. By now the pain was sick-making so I disembarked and told Steve's navigator, Dave Terry, to get out as well if he wished. There was no way I was going to fly back until I had seen a medic. I got the ground crew to take me down to the Medical Centre and the Duty Medical Orderly took a look at my swollen and battered digit. I explained that I needed to fly home; not only was it Friday but there was a Ladies Dining In Night back at base, to which I had promised the memsahib we would go. The orderly went off to find a doctor.

I re-explained the problem and he took a look at my finger. He was very understanding and came back with four big pills and a tube of cream. He applied the cream liberally, put a finger sock on my hand and said that I should take the pills as soon as I had arrived at Cottesmore. Then he gave me a big wink. I looked puzzled for a moment then I caught on. The pills were painkillers, but he did not want to know that I had taken them and then gone flying.[39] Then he suggested we went to the Aircrew Buffet, aka 'The Greasy Spoon', had something to eat and drink before setting off home; at lunch there I took two of the pills with my cup of tea. I flew back as fast as the old lady would take us, landed and took the other two pills that I had been given with my post-flight coffee. My Cinderella did go to the ball and I anaesthetised myself with red wine and port. Fortunately Saturday was a slow day.

Life progressed on its inexorable path. I had established a bit of a reputation for being a sympathetic person with those that were struggling, although I still demanded the best out of everyone with whom I flew. I tried my best not to 'nit pick' as some did. In any debrief after a sortie I would try to highlight the most important thing that needed attention as well as give praise when improvement had been shown. I also became the instructor to whom future senior executive officers were allocated. I had under my wing both the new Station Commander and the replacement OC Operations Wing. When teaching these 'Sirs' one had to be honest but diplomatic. For instance, on one occasion, I was asked to fly with a group captain on his Instrument Rating Test (IRT); I was by then an Instrument Rating Examiner (IRE). We flew the sortie but he had not achieved the required accuracy in several parts of the test. When we had landed he said to me, 'Well, how was that?'

'What do you think, sir?' I asked.

'Perhaps not my best,' he said.

'No. Perhaps we'll call this sortie an additional practice, eh, sir?' I suggested.

'What a good idea,' he rejoined.

We flew a couple more 'practices' and he finally got his Instrument Rating on the Canberra.

I felt that I had to be fairly demanding on these senior guys. In their posts as station, wing and squadron commanders they would not fly as often as their subordinates. While they usually possessed more depth of experience they had also usually come from ground tours, often more than one, and had got out of practice in some crucial areas. One of these was in radio communications. I had one Wing Commander who had not flown for well over ten years. The last aircraft he had operated was the Gloster Meteor fighter. One of the major obstacles for him was gaining an understanding of the huge changes that had taken place in the layout of UK airspace, as well as the changes in radio phraseology. In addition, there was the relatively new way that military, non-transport aircraft were now regularly using the airways and other controlled airspace used by commercial operators. The RAF now had a 'Procedural' element to the IRT and that required knowledge of how to join, fly along and leave airways. After five years flying outside such bits of the sky it had all been new to me too.

That same Wing Commander had a nasty shock one day. I had briefed him that there would be a practice engine failure on take-off. He had not had much problem with the flying of these. His single-seat Meteor experience made him very aware and adept at asymmetric flight. But that same single-seat background meant that he was not used to using his navigator to monitor his actions from the checklist. On this particular day I pulled back the starboard throttle as soon as the undercarriage was retracting. He immediately and correctly applied full left rudder to keep the aircraft going straight and started to call out his subsequent actions; none of these were actually done – it's called a touch drill.

'Engine failure,' he called, 'Port HP Cock⁴⁰ closed. Port ...'

At which point he stopped talking and looked across the cockpit at me. His eyes above his oxygen mask were open very wide. I said nothing.

'OK, simulated double engine failure. Simulate EJECT, EJECT, EJECT.'

'I have control,' I said as I opened the throttles and started to climb away from a very low altitude. 'Well done, sir. But what do you think that the subsequent Board of Inquiry would have found?'

'I don't know, some sort of fuel contamination I suppose.'

'Well, you're on the right lines, sir. There was no fuel going to either engine. But why?'

'I don't know.'

'Navigator, what did the good Wing Commander say as soon as he had gained control of the aircraft?' I asked of the man in the back.

'Port HP Cock closed,' he dutifully replied.

'Which engine had failed?' I asked 'Sir'.

'Oh … yes, of course … how stupid of me,' replied the now somewhat abashed occupant of the left-hand seat.

'Never rush the drills, sir. Remember that the leg that you are not pushing with is on the same side as the engine that had failed. Dead leg, dead engine.'

The rest of the sortie went well. The Wing Commander passed the course and took up residence in his office in the Station Operations Centre. There I would work part time for him as the Station Flight Safety Officer.

One day the OCU Boss called me to come to his office. With him was a pilot whom I had not met before. After introductions it transpired that he had flown Canberras previously and had been overseas. The Boss said that he had agreed to give this passing stranger, whom I shall call Ted, a trip in the T4. I was to be the captain and occupy my usual cramped right-hand seat. After all the preliminaries we got airborne and I found that Ted had retained all his skills on the Canberra and I was just along for the ride. We flew for about an hour and then we did a practice diversion to the huge airfield at Thurleigh, the home of the flying units and wind tunnels of the Royal Aerospace Establishment Bedford.

Ted had observed that the way that we now flew asymmetric approaches (using one engine) had changed since his day. Therefore I told him that I would demonstrate one for him and then he could have a go. We asked Bedford for a radar controlled approach to the westerly runway and were positioned by the controller accordingly. As we reached 5 miles from the runway we were advised that the RAE's Avro 748 was making a steep approach to the other end of the runway; something no doubt demanded by the Ministry of Silly Trials. At 2 miles we were asked to break off the approach and climb out to the east again for another attempt. The controller was very apologetic and promised that we would get priority on the next approach.

Once we were outbound at 2,000ft I handed the aircraft over to Ted. 'I'll talk you through it, because we won't have enough fuel to do a third one of these,' I told him.

He flew the aircraft very well and we set ourselves up for the approach with one of the engines throttled back. We turned inbound towards the runway and the controller started to talk us down. As we flew down the 3° glide slope the speed started to increase. Ted did the sensible thing and reduced the power on the one engine in use. I, meanwhile, was concentrating more on the conversations between the air traffic controller and the 748 out to the west of the airfield, just to make sure that we would be able to make our approach and touch-and-go landing. Ted had proved that he hadn't forgotten much and was spot on the centreline and glidepath. The only thing I noticed was that the speed was still quite high. When we passed 600ft we had to make a decision whether to land or not. Ted said that he would continue. I was beginning to be puzzled about how he had managed to get so much speed on. He was about to lower the flaps at 100ft when I noticed a flare being shot from the little caravan that was at the edge of the runway. 'A funny time to scare the birds,' I thought.

We were still going too fast so I took control and started to equalise the throttles and then, as I reached for the button on my side of the cockpit which raised the undercarriage, a huge surge of adrenalin hit the pit of my stomach. The wheels were still tucked away in their little cupboards under the wing! Ted had forgotten to put them down. That's why the alert runway controller in his red and white caravan had fired off a red flare; the standard visual signal that the approaching aircraft did not have its wheels down. I was too relaxed because Ted had thus far shown that he was still a good pilot and I allowed myself to be distracted by listening to the radio. The navigator later admitted that he had missed the call of 'Gear Down'. That had become so close to being my first and only wheels up landing: something every pilot dreads. There's rarely any other excuse than 'I forgot!' I once watched in horror as a Swedish SAAB test pilot landed his trainer on its belly in front of thousands at a Farnborough Air Show. I understand that he joined the Swedish unemployed the following day.

On another day I was flying with a student who was nearing the time for his Instrument Rating Test. He was practicing steep turns with the instrument flying blind on his helmet visor so that he couldn't see out. I was looking out to make sure that we didn't hit anybody. Then I spotted an aircraft, turning equally hard, looking like he was trying to set up for a dogfight. As we got closer to each other I could see that it was a camouflaged McDonnell F4 Phantom in USAF markings. I thought that it was probably from the 'Wild Weasel' wing at RAF Lakenheath. He was burning a lot of gas and pulling hard. One thing that I had learnt in Germany was that pilots of high performance aircraft had to work very hard to out-turn a Canberra. The big wing gave us lots of lift and with full power we could turn in a very small circle with the speed down at around 190kts; that made us an extremely difficult target, despite our size. I told my student to relax and I took control. He lifted his visor and started to help me keep track of our 'opponent'. As the Phantom started to gain an advantage, I used a trick I had learnt on my first tour. I rolled out of the turn and simultaneously extended the airbrakes, opened the bomb doors and pushed the nose down into a 60° dive. The drag from the airbrakes and bomb doors stopped the speed building up too quickly and as we descended I saw the Phantom zoom past us. We had virtually stopped our forward speed right in front of him.

He now pulled up and turned back towards us again. I levelled off to see what he would do next. He descended towards us and pulled into a close formation position on our left wingtip. I could clearly see the pilot. Then it suddenly struck me. Perhaps all he had been trying to do was to get close to us so that he could indicate that he had lost his radio and wanted us to shepherd him down through the cloud cover back to an airfield. By way of a visual query, I held up an arm with an upturned thumb at its end. He dropped his mask, returned the thumbs up, made an exaggerated wiping of his brow gesture and then lit both his afterburners and swung up and away right over our heads. We could clearly hear the roar of his jet exhaust. Obviously his radios were fine and he just wanted to have a bit of fun. I put 'Bloggs' back under the hood and we continued as briefed. It had been a rare and welcome diversion from the daily grind!

24 TRIPS AWAY

One of the things I had missed during my time instructing on Chipmunks were the overseas flights that were such a prominent part of my previous life on the Canberra squadron in Germany. Although the OCU had no formal war role and there was no essential need for us to deploy overseas, our lords and masters at HQ No 1 Group allocated the unit a certain number of annual overseas trips. The aim was to keep the staff pilots and navigators current with the procedures required for such sorties. We didn't argue with this impeccable logic. So, about once per year each pilot and navigator received a blessing to proceed to places far off and, to one extent or another, exotic. Well, virtually everywhere else was exotic compared to Rutland.

My first such 'jolly'[41] was to RAF Akrotiri in Cyprus via a lunch stopover at RAF Luqa in Malta in October 1972. I had visited both Malta and Cyprus regularly in the mid-1960s, during my time on No 16 Squadron. I had been temporarily based on both islands for extended detachments to carry out conventional weapons practice with the Canberra B(I)8 on a number of occasions. Nevertheless it was very agreeable to renew my acquaintance with the Mediterranean and these holiday destinations. On 6 October we flew a total of four hours and forty-five minutes to arrive at Akrotiri by late afternoon. It was as pleasant as ever to be there again and I bumped into many old mates. The RAF, even in those days when it was much larger, was a very small world. Then there seemed to be much less than six degrees of separation between strangers!

On the way back we night-stopped in Malta. We were allocated rooms in the transit Mess, which was usual for those just passing through. I had experienced the place before. The food was not great and the rooms were spartan. However, there was a nice little bar where Joe (it often seemed that all Maltese men are called Joseph) served a very good John Collins. I needed one of those after I had taken a bath in the communal ablutions area. As I had laid back in the nice hot water in my upper peripheral vision I noticed something move. It was a gecko. He was high up the wall, showing off his ability to climb slick vertical surfaces. He must have noticed me watching him, because he then tried to negotiate the curving joint between tiled wall and painted ceiling. He should have arranged for a safety net. Just as he was getting a grip on the ceiling he must have encountered a wet patch. He slipped and fell into the hot water by my feet. He didn't like that much and neither did I. He started swimming, but it looked like he hadn't had much practice. I hopped quickly out of the bath and immediately slipped on the tiled floor. From that level I peered over the edge of the bath to find my little friend in some distress. So, putting any squeamishness aside, I reached in and pulled him out. I grabbed my towel and wrapped him in it. However, most ungratefully he squirmed out of my grip, fell for the second time within a few minutes, and scurried off under the door. I suppose that he recovered more quickly than I did.

Being in Malta reminded me of many pleasant times spent there both at work and play. At the airfield, when I went to the Visiting Aircraft Flight (VAF), I remembered a wonderfully funny story about a USAF F-100 Super Sabre pilot who stopped off at Luqa on his way to the USAF Base at Wheelus on the Libyan coast, east of Tripoli. That was in the pre-Gaddafi days when the UK and USA were friendly with King Idris, the monarch of the United Kingdom of Libya. As was often the case in the late 1960s the VAF aircraft parking area (the pan) was crowded. As the F-100 taxied in he was directed to park and shut down under the port wing of an RAF Transport Command Blackburn Beverley. The Beverley was very large, with a tall, slab-sided fuselage and high mounted wings. There was plenty of room for the Super Sabre. The pilot dismounted looking up in awe at the monster above him. When he walked into the VAF office he asked, 'Say, is that the largest airplane you have in the British Royal Air Force?'

As quick as a flash the flight sergeant behind the desk responded, 'Oh, goodness me no, sir. You should have seen the plane we flew it out in.' What repartee!

Another Super Sabre event I remembered happened while I was on holiday in Malta in 1968. My wife and I had hired a motor scooter for a few days to explore the island and we were headed up the hill, out of Sliema, that went right past the gates of RAF Luqa, just after which we reached the back of a stationary line of traffic. That was most unusual in Malta, as everyone drove around at just less than the speed of light, despite the atrociously surfaced roads. I could see that there was some activity in a field not far away to our left. I parked the scooter and we walked to the front of the line of traffic to see whether it was worth waiting or choosing another route. There were two Maltese policemen looking, as was normal for members of the island's constabulary, very relaxed. I asked them what was the hold-up and one of them pointed to something about 100yd away. It was a USAF Super Sabre with its nose firmly buried in a stone wall, with which Malta is furnished in their tens of thousands. I looked back towards the airfield and saw that there was a Super Sabre-shaped hole in the 10ft-high chain-link boundary fence; it was a bit like something from a *Tom and Jerry* cartoon.

That evening, on our way back from sightseeing we called into the Officers' Mess for a drink. In the bar was an American gent with his leg in plaster, regaling all who would listen with his latest 'war story'. Apparently he was on his way from the UK to Wheelus when the engine quit. As the F-100 has only one this was not good news. He made several attempts to get it going again, but to no avail. When he was considering ejecting he saw the island of Malta and the friendly ATC controllers, with whom he was now in contact, offered to help him make a 'dead stick' landing on Runway 06 at Luqa. As an eye-witness ATC officer told me later: 'He must have been doing well over 200kts when he arrived over the runway. He selected his braking parachute out, but the speed was too high and that simply tore away. Then he raised the landing gear, but by the time he passed the control tower he was still going like a bat out of hell. There was a spectacular amount of sparks and we thought that he was bound to catch fire. Then we realised that he was still going too fast for the arrestor barrier to do any good, so we put it down. The fence didn't stop him, neither did the first two stone walls. But the third did!' He was very lucky to get away with only a broken ankle.

RAF Gibraltar was the setting for 1973's 'jolly', from 24 May to 29 May; Flt Lts Gordon Campbell and Roy Smith were down the back. Roy was the navigator and Gordon was another instructor just filling the third seat to enjoy a weekend away in 'Gib'. Our mode of transport was Canberra B2 WJ 674. On the first day we flew to RAF St Mawgan in Cornwall, where we refuelled and stopped for the night. The plan now was to head south-west until we reached the longitude line of 10° West. Then we would follow that line on the chart, due south, until we were abeam Gibraltar. It was then a relatively short easterly leg, along the coast of the Portuguese Algarve, descending into Gibraltar and avoiding Spanish Airspace like the plague.

During the leg south, along the 10° West meridian, Roy kept giving me changes of heading to try to hold us on the line in the changing winds up at 41,000ft. A regular pattern of a correction to the left followed, about twenty minutes later, by a correction to the right. When we turned left to head for the Rock I asked Roy if he had actually been on his track line for the past two hours.

'Oh yes, my boy. I was on track at least ten times,' he replied.

By international agreement the Spanish allowed UK military aircraft to use only the airspace to the west and south of Gibraltar. That wasn't a very big area, especially as the centre of it was a 1,300ft high lump of *terra firma* that was often obscured by its streamer of cloud. The runway was 6,000ft long and lay across the narrow neck of land that joined Gib to the Spanish mainland; at its western end the runway protruded, like a large aircraft carrier deck, over 800yd into the busy harbour.

At the runway's eastern end there was a sea wall that was about 30ft high; that was there to prevent high seas from flooding the runway. The only road off the Rock into Spain ran north, across the runway, and road traffic was controlled via lights operated from the control tower. However, the *bête noire* for the local ATC controllers were cyclists and pedestrians. Although cars could easily be stopped well clear of the runway, the cyclist or walker who went through just before a red light often took several minutes to reach safety on the other side.

The runway at Gibraltar also had unique markings. The sloping surface down from the sea wall, on which we were not to land, was painted with black-and-yellow chequerboard markings. There were also two prominent yellow lines at about one-third distance gone in each runway direction; these were the 'last touchdown' lines. If the aircraft wasn't firmly on the ground before it crossed these lines then a go-around had to be initiated. The Rock itself caused another unique problem. It was not unusual, especially with southerly winds, for there to be a tailwind at both ends of the runway as the wind bent round the Rock. This meant that very accurate speed control would be needed on the final approach, which would always be over feature-less water onto what looked like an inadequately short runway.

Gibraltar is an enthralling place to visit and has a fascinating history. 'The Rock' had been populated since prehistoric times by a whole series of peoples, representing all of the major historic Mediterranean nationalities. However, Gibraltar seems to have spent most of its history under siege. It was in 1704, during the War of the Spanish Succession and after the eleventh siege, that a joint British and Dutch military force conquered the Rock. So 1704 is the year from which modern Gibraltarians take the colony's British genesis. But it wasn't until April 1713 that the Rock was formally recognised as British

Sovereign Territory by the Treaties of Utrecht, when the perpetuity of British rule was first written down. In the year of my first visit there, in 1964, the Spanish had raised the whole question of the rightful sovereignty of Gibraltar at the UN, who had come down on the Spanish side. That was one reason that we had been told to be very careful not to fly into Spanish airspace. I knew several pilots who had found themselves being escorted round the circuit by Spanish Air Force fighters, just to make sure that they stayed within Gibraltar's air traffic control zone!

I had visited Gib on at least two occasions before, when I was stationed in RAF Germany. Nevertheless any landing on that apparently short runway was a slightly tenser affair than landing anywhere else. However, the arrival was fine; I was very happy about that as I had a fellow instructor sitting in the back, no doubt silently taking note of my performance.

Since my last visit, in 1967, relationships between the UK and Spanish governments had deteriorated to the point where the land border had been closed. This meant no naughty night out in La Linea, the small Spanish town immediately across the border from Gib. We would spend the weekend sight-seeing, shopping and visiting the odd restaurant and bar. On the Saturday morning Roy and I went down to the harbour and bought return tickets for the ferry to Tangiers.

The journey across the Strait was very pleasant in the early summer sun. While watching from the deck I kept seeing what I thought were birds flying low over the water and then plunging into the foam. Then I saw them flying out of the water and gliding a considerable distance before disappearing from whence they came. It was then that I realised that I was watching not birds but fish. It was my first ever sighting of flying fish. They were fascinating quicksilver creatures. Dolphins also appeared to 'fly' in formation with the bow of the ship gleefully breaking the surface in graceful arcs.

Disembarking in Tangiers reminded me strongly of Tripoli in Libya, which I had visited occasionally during my first operational tour. There were the same sights and sounds (and smells!), the same small brown boys pestering to sell you something banal, like overpriced bangles or fly whisks. And there was that North African paradox of the threatening welcome from many of the bearded market stallholders. We wended our way, through all these dis-tractions, up the hill to the old part of town and its Suhq, where there were narrow winding alleys, thronged with people engaged in all manner of com-mercial activities. At one point a young blond 'Arab' proffered us hashish; I declined his offer and headed for the nearest restaurant where we sat on low cushions and ate couscous from a large brass dish on a low table. It was an authentic taste of the Maghreb; the toilets were also authentically fragrant and equipped in Arab style!

After a few hours ashore the ferry was due to sail back to Gibraltar, but this time via Algeciras on the other side of the bay from Gibraltar. Because the Spanish land frontier was closed to anyone coming from Gibraltar, the only way that folk could visit the Spanish mainland at Algeciras was to catch the ferry to Tangiers, but stay on board and alight at Algeciras on the return trip. Then it was OK; what a way to run a country! Actually this prohibition was harder on the local Spanish people who, in great numbers, worked on The Rock. The Gibraltarians didn't like their physical isolation much either, but the UK was ensuring that all necessities kept coming in by sea and by air.

Gibraltar had its own little airline. Not surprisingly it was called Gib Air and they operated two or three venerable DC 3s. They flew into North Africa and Portugal, but, at that time, not into Spain. On every visit I made to Gib and saw their aircraft parked out on the vast areas of tarmac at the airfield I harboured a secret desire. That was to get a set of ladders and a pot of paint and put a Y and an O in front of the airline's name on each side of their old flying machines: YOGIB AIR![42] We returned to Cottesmore, via Istres in the south of France and RAF Waddington, to clear HM Customs, on 29 May, having had a very enjoyable weekend in the sun.

Other trips away were definitely not 'jollies'. Three times I journeyed north, back to Scotland, to carry out some training flights, basing myself once at RAF Kinloss and on two occasions at RAF Machrihanish. The Kinloss and one of the Machrihanish detachments were, ironically, to get away from poor weather in England's East Midlands. That was so that we could at least try to keep up with the relentless requirement to graduate our students on time. In fact, the three days at Kinloss, on the Moray Firth, was a detachment of two aircraft. The other instructor was a wee Scotsman called Ian 'Dobs' Dobbie, another Cold War Warrior who had come through the rigours of spending three years on No 16 Squadron. We had shared a couple of years at RAF Laarbruch together and I was really pleased to see him arrive at the OCU and join the staff. I was flying with Steve Solomon and, apart from upsetting OC Ops Wing once for some misdemeanour so trivial I forget what it was, the trip went well. We flew four successful instructional sorties each, while the rest of the OCU back in Rutland languished in fog, snow and ice.

The first detachment to Machrihanish was in October 1972, with a student called Terry Cairns. Terry went on to fly the Canberra for the whole of his long RAF career. He retired beyond the normal retirement age of 55 because his extensive experience on the Canberra was needed right up to its last service flight in July 2006; that means that Terry flew this one type, in a variety of guises, ending with the biggest and best, the PR9, for thirty-three years: a remarkable achievement.

My second detachment to Machrihanish was with Gp Capt. Alan Jenkins, the man about to assume the Station Commander's hot seat at Cottesmore. RAF Machrihanish was a bit of an anachronism. It was built during the Second World War on a flat neck of land on the Mull of Kintyre, not far from the fishing port of Campbeltown. The runway is 10,000ft long and the airfield was one of several built for the emergency use of USAF bombers during the Second World War. By the early 1970s Machrihanish was used as a reception and staging post for some transatlantic military traffic, but had no resident aircraft. There was also a US Military detachment there, whose esoteric business was highly classified. The conjunction of these factors: a very long runway, its isolation and the US presence may have inspired conspiracy theorists to assign a mysterious role to the place. Many of their theories about its use by 'spy-planes' over the years may well have some truth, but it is now no longer in MOD hands.

RAF Machrihanish was a good place for us to go. We generally had the place to ourselves, so the students could concentrate on flying in the visual circuit and the radar pattern without much interruption. The long runway gave an added safety factor and there was plenty of free airspace nearby. However, the isolation was easily sensed. Glasgow, as the crow flies, is just 50 miles away, but the shortest road journey to Glasgow is 138 miles and would take well over three hours. The small Officers' Mess was very dated, but comfortable enough. But I had a big surprise when I ran a bath. The water was the colour of whisky! I asked about this and was told that it was normal. The drinking water was similar, but it was perfectly safe to drink. However, I took that as a sign that we should not imbibe the water, rather its look-alike beverage, especially the single-malt, Highland or Island varieties.

These short trips away always added a bit of variety to what could easily become a training process that had within it a great deal of repetition. Sometimes it was difficult to keep one's enthusiasm up. But it was the student pilots and navigators who did that. They were not just the subjects of our endeavours but also the inspiration for us to keep on doing our best.

25 PROFITS, COFFEES AND THE THURSDAY WAR

When I discovered that No 360 Squadron was often over-tasked another perk came my way. Although the squadron had a relatively large establishment of aircraft and aircrew, it had to do its nefarious electronic work all over NATO, in such locations as Portugal, Italy and Germany. So, on occasions, they found themselves tasked to support the training of the RAF's interceptor fighter force or the Royal Navy's anti-aircraft frigates with an aeroplane available but no pilot. So I volunteered to be a locum on call. At first I was given a morning's introduction to the aircraft and its systems, followed by a simple training flight after lunch. Looking at the T17 from the outside, from the pilot's cockpit rearwards it looked much like any other Canberra. However, the nose was what Prince Charles might have called 'an ugly carbuncle'! The lumps and bumps mounted around the nosecone contained the transmitters and receivers for the electronic wizardry that made the aircraft what it was: a flying bundle of potential confusion to radars and radios and their users.

From the inside, sitting in the pilot's seat, there were two advantages. The first was that one could not see the unattractive front end of the aircraft and the second was that the T17's cockpit was very much like that of the B2. The performance of the T17 was marginally lower than the B2 because it was slightly heavier and there was a small amount of extra drag from the aforementioned protuberances. One major on-board difference was that there were no bomb-bay doors; the bomb bay was now packed with electronics and access to that area was by removable panels. The second major difference was that the large amounts of electricity needed to run all this kit was produced by turbo-generators driven by air bled from the engines.

Nevertheless, all the required actions and checks to achieve flight were very familiar and once we were up and away everything felt just the same. In the back was a navigator, or observer if it was one of the Royal Navy guys, and an Air Electronics Officer (AEO). The latter was the responsible adult who kept an eye on the other two and operated all the magic kit. The AEOs were very much the lead men for the mission because it was they who selected the type of radar jamming required, messed around with the defenders' radio communications and called for 'chaff' to be released. The pilot's job was, obviously, to fly the aircraft and ensure that normal ATC procedures were complied with and do the bidding of the 'customers' and the other crewmembers. The navigator's job was to ensure that the aircraft ended up in the right place at the right time, heading in the right direction for each training exercise.

The 'Chaff' was bundles of strips of aluminium foil, cut to varying lengths to match wavelengths of the radars to be affected; that length has to be half the radar's wavelength to be effective in jamming the operator's screen. This metallic rain had been invented and first used during the Second World War. Although, as early as 1937, the inventor of radar, Dr R.V. Jones, had suggested that clouds of metallic strips could interfere with the return signals, it was not until 1942 that a lady called Joan Curren of the Telecommunications Research

Centre first proposed the use of foil-backed paper strips for radar counter-measures. It was her head of section, A.P. Rowe, who first gave chaff the code name 'Window'. The paper made the strips lighter so it descended more slowly than plain foil, and prolonged the interference effect. The Air Ministry and War Department suppressed the knowledge of Window until the characteristics of German air defence radars were better understood. Window was first used in anger on 24 July 1943 during Operation Gomorrah, the so-called Battle of Hamburg, during which the city was bombed for over a week. Aircraft of No 76 Squadron were equipped with chaff dispenser chutes and twenty-four crews had been specially trained. These Window aircraft went in ahead of the bomber streams on Hamburg. The result was a dramatic drop in the number of aircraft lost approaching and over the target area.

The Germans had developed their own version of Window, which they called 'Düppel', and they used it on many of their bombing raids. It was especially effective for them during the so-called Mini or Baby Blitz of Operation Steinbock from 21 February to 29 May 1944. As the use of radar developed after 1945 the 'technology' of chaff radar countermeasures developed. However, the concept remains simple and, as long as the lengths of the chaff match the half-wavelengths of the radars, it is still an extremely effective way of making radar targets apparently disappear, and thus become immune to attack by radar equipped guided missiles or aircraft.

Hence the need for the continued training of any radar-directed air defence forces. Although the effects of chaff can be and are simulated in operational flight simulators, the added reality to exercise scenarios that No 360 Squadron's operations brought was invaluable. That is why they were so often over-tasked. They were the only NATO unit able to give this sort of experience to fighter controllers and fighter pilots alike.

After a couple of familiarisation exercises I flew my first air defence exercise on 23 March 1973; it was an 'Exercise Coffee'. Then I flew an 'Exercise Profit' sortie a few days later. As far as I remember there wasn't a lot of difference between 'Coffees' and 'Profits' except the names and they didn't mean anything either – they were just random. We flew over the North Sea off East Anglia at the height the radar folk wanted us to and the Lightning fighters were directed onto us as the target. Then the AEO in the back did his best with whatever was at his disposal to put everyone off their stroke. As far as I was concerned all I had to do was what I was told by the radar controller or the navigator. At the end of the exercise, when we had stopped confusing them, the Lightnings usually flew past us very close with their afterburners fully alight. Unless the weather was bad at base, that was the most exciting part of the trip. But it was great to be doing something different and vaguely operational again.

Every Thursday the Royal Navy Fleet Training School held an exercise in the English Channel south of Chesil Beach and Portland Bill, in an area of the sea they called 'the Deltas'. The exercise did have a formal name, but it was universally known as 'The Thursday War'. No 360 Squadron were normally tasked with supplying up to four aircraft for this 'Grey Funnel Lines' extravaganza. The flight profile was to fly from Cottesmore in formation at high level and then descend into the exercise area to be directed by the land-based radar units into positions from where we could be set up for the air defenders on their ships to see what we could do to confuse and disrupt their efforts.

My final trip in a T17 was interesting. It was a night sortie, in formation with another T17, operating over the southern North Sea with Lightnings from RAF Wattisham. I hadn't flown in formation at night for several years, but it is like riding a bike, you don't forget what to do and how to do it. When we had finished and the 'fighter boys' had made their usual close and noisy passes over us, we climbed to about 25,000ft to return to Cottesmore together. As we were getting close to base, descending and passing about 7,000ft, I heard a thump from somewhere on the nose, just ahead of me and to the right. I had, by now, had enough birdstrikes to be pretty certain that was what it was. I checked all the relevant engine dials but nothing appeared amiss and there was no other sound, such as that of rushing air. So I decided to keep following my leader and go home for my night flying supper.[43]

After we had landed I went round the front of the aircraft with my torch (Aircrew, for the use of), illuminating the nose. There was a slightly bloody dent and, in the joint of two alloy plates, a few brown feathers. I was the Station Flight Safety Officer at the time so I knew that the Ministry of Agriculture, Fisheries and Food had a man who would identify the type of bird from just a few feathers, so I prised them from the aircraft skin. The next day I wrote my report and sent the aforementioned plumage off to the man at the MAFF. A few days later I received a phone call from the MAFF man himself.

'It was a song thrush, old boy,' he said.

'What on earth was a song thrush doing at night and up at 7,000ft?' I asked, intending the question to be rhetorical.

'Well, until you bashed it out of the sky, it was flying,' came the unnecessary reply.

He then went on to tell me that birds are often caught up in the rising currents inside thunderstorms or large cumulus clouds and there have been birdstrikes as high as 30,000ft. I wondered how they managed to keep going without little oxygen bottles strapped to their backs and tiny masks over their beaks. I thanked him for his enlightening information and bid him a good day. You live and learn; shame about the song thrush though.

All the sorties with No 360 were interesting. Listening to the AEOs reciting all sorts of literature into the ether, singing silly songs and obviously having success with the electronic wizardry as controllers and fighter pilots alike couldn't find us on their screens. It was an education in an area of air operations to which, hitherto, I had not given much thought.

26 THINKING ABOUT THE FUTURE

In RAF life one is reminded annually that in three years time one is going to be moved on. The Annual Confidential Report (ACR) has many boxes to be filled, usually by one's superiors, but there is a very important section which is for one's choices for the next appointment. Although holding a permanent commission (PC) and therefore, potentially, a 'career officer', I had yet to find anything, other than flying, that I could imagine doing. I was still hoping to be posted to a front-line squadron where I could fly something more modern than a Canberra or a Chipmunk. I thought that it shouldn't be too difficult; after all, there were not many aircraft types now in service much older than those two. I was still entering Buccaneer, Phantom and Jaguar in the three boxes; hoping beyond hope to go back to the low-level, attack role in Germany.

I had learnt that one could arrange a visit to see a personnel staff officer, who at that time resided in London. So I arranged a meeting with him. I had also discovered that Barry Nelson, an old friend from No 16 Squadron days, was at the MOD and that he lived on a boat moored on the Regent's Canal. So, after making the appropriate phone calls, off I set and met up with Barry. We went to the boat for lunch and then, on a bike with which he had provided me, we set off in close formation for the office. I arrived there a little later than the appointed hour and not a little dishevelled and sweaty. The occupant of the office to which I was directed was a Wing Commander who was obviously a bit peeved that a flight lieutenant had kept him waiting. 'This is not starting well,' I thought. I didn't know the half of it!

'Well, young man, how are things going at Little Rissington?' he urbanely enquired.

There was a bit of a pause before I said, 'I'm not at Little Rissington, sir,' wondering if he had someone else's file in front of him. 'I left there eighteen months ago.'

The fluttering of paper as he rifled the file in front of him was followed by: 'Oh yes. Cottesmore isn't it? Are you happy there?'

I gave him the brief version of the change to my expectations on arrival at the OCU and my strong desire to get back to the front line.

'Ah yes. But you hold a PC so we have to start looking at a meaningful junior staff job for you. It will be good for your career.'

I didn't wish to disabuse him of the idea that I wasn't sure that I wanted 'a career' other than flying, but he was insistent.

'You have been getting good assessments and you now have a recommendation for promotion. But you have been flying for over ten years now. We are looking at an ADC[44] tour for you. If you do a good job for your principal you should then get promoted. Then we can give you a good quality staff job. Then it's onwards and upwards, my lad.'

The only upwards I wanted was in a cockpit, preferably going onwards at a good rate of knots. By the time he had finished planning out my life I didn't know whether to throw myself in the Regent's Canal or go to the pub. In the event I did neither and caught the train back north in a blue funk. *How do I convince people that all I want to do is fly?* I wondered.

Some time later I was thinking about the next move when a thought came back to me. Why not try applying for the Empire Test Pilots' School (ETPS) again? Because of the less than supportive response I had received the last time I applied, at CFS, I was not hopeful. But I did think that *if* I got into ETPS that would virtually guarantee me another four years' flying. And, hopefully, not all in museum pieces.

One night, shortly after that minor inspiration, I was in the control tower acting as the OCU Duty Instructor; we had to do this whenever solo student pilots were flying at night. Also up there was an officer from No 360 Squadron, one Flt Lt Dicky Duke; he was doing the same thing for his squadron. We got to chatting and he was asking what I might do next. I told him that I wanted to apply for ETPS but that I was a bit unsure about my academic ability.

'It's funny that you should say that,' he said. 'I thought about applying once, but never got round to it. But now I'm too old to apply and I'll never know whether I would have got in or not.'

The impression that Dicky's word made on me ran around inside my head for most of the night. The next morning I found the appropriate paperwork, filled it in and put it in the Boss's IN tray. I was determined not to end up wondering for the rest of my life, like Dicky had. I needed to know.

A few days later, after I had just landed, I got a message to go and see the Station Commander ASAP. As I was the Station Flight Safety Officer I assumed it was something to do with that. I rang his PA and asked if I could show up in my flying suit. After a small pause I was told that it would be fine. I grabbed my hat, hopped on my bike and cycled down to Station HQ.

'Come in and sit down, Mike,' the group captain said. 'I don't know what to do about you, so I thought that I'd see what your opinion was.' This sounded a bit ominous to me. It was also unusually democratic, but I still wasn't sure what his quandary was.

He could see my rather blank look, so he continued: 'I have here in my hand two pieces of paper,' he said, in quite a good imitation of Neville Chamberlain. 'One is a Special Recommendation for promotion to squadron leader and the other is a recommendation for you to go forward for selection to ETPS.'

'Oh, yes, sir.' It was all I could think of to say. At the time one had to be a flight lieutenant to go for selection to ETPS, so one course would exclude the other.

'Now if I waved a magic wand over your head,' (I found this image was difficult to hold on to) 'and said, "You are now a squadron leader", what would be your reaction?'

This was getting more like a surreal interrogation session than a chat.

'I would ask "What's the job that went with the promotion?" If it was a ground tour I would say, "No thanks, sir".'

'So let me get this right. You would rather go to ETPS as a flight lieutenant than be put on a ground tour as a squadron leader?' he asked, fixing me with a beady eye; well both beady eyes actually.

'That's about the long and short of it, sir,' I replied. I tried not to show the delight and the concomitant small frisson of panic at this likely fixation at zero of my future promotion prospects.

That afternoon the OCU Boss, Don Merriman, called me to his office. 'I've just had a conversation with the Station Commander,' he said. 'Is it true that you would rather be a test pilot than a squadron leader?'

I replied in the affirmative.

'Good. Now I know where we all stand. I will make sure that your application for ETPS is fully supported all the way up.'

So that was it. I wasn't sure what would happen if I failed the Selection Board, but I didn't want to think about that now. I had to somehow get my academics up to speed.

Some time later I went, with Don, to the CFS Association's Annual Reunion and there I met a chap called Tom Gilmour, who had passed through ETPS some years earlier and was now working at Brough in East Yorkshire for the erstwhile Blackburn Aircraft Company. He told me that I needed to obtain a book by some American author, with a bizarre name like Cyrus P. Thomson, about calculus. I can no longer remember its title or the author's real name but it put me on the right track. I went out and bought *Teach Yourself Calculus* and started working my way through that. Our new junior engineering officer on the OCU was a young fellow who rejoiced in the name of Ellis Artus. I knew Ellis because he had been one of our RAF Scholarship students at Glasgow UAS. So I asked him if he would help me occasionally with the maths, if I got stuck. He agreed.

So I started to sit down at home in the evenings and do mathematics. I had spent one year in the sixth form at grammar school, before leaving to join the RAF, so I had done the introduction to differentiation and integration. But I needed to go further and there were only a few months before the selection process the following June. Now all I needed was confirmation that I would go forward to the interviews.

That happened a few weeks later. I received a copy of the message and it gave all the names of the candidates for selection. Although I didn't recognise any of the names, I noticed that one of them, Flt Lt John Thorpe, was from nearby RAF Wittering where he was no doubt flying the Harrier. A few days later I was in the Flight Safety Office and the phone rang; it did that often. But this time a voice announced: 'Hi, this is John Thorpe here. I saw your name on the ETPS Selection Board list and I wondered whether we could travel to Boscombe Down together?'

'Yes, by all means, that would be great,' I told him. 'It will be good to have someone to talk to on the way. Why don't I pick you up at Wittering, as it's en route?'

He gave me his address and a week or two later I was at his front door. John came out with his bag, said goodbye to his wife and folded himself into the passenger seat of my car. He was very tall. On the journey we shared our RAF life stories. He was flying the Harrier and had been doing so since it entered service. He was part of the first squadron to fly it; appropriately No 1 Squadron. The odd thing was that, because he was too tall to fly the Gnat, he had done his advanced training on the Varsity, which was usually the trainer of choice for those destined for 'heavies'.

After a couple of hours on the road we arrived at Boscombe Down and went to the Officers' Mess. We booked in and found our rooms in what appeared to be a collection of rather well-worn, single-storey buildings at the rear. It looked like they had been erected a long time ago to increase the accommodation in the rather small 1920s building that served as the Officers' Mess. We dined and met others who had arrived to endure the two days of tests, interviews and cross-examinations that we were to undergo.

The next morning it started. We were taken to an old barrack block on the northern edge of the vast complex that is the Aeroplane and Armaments Experimental Establishment (A&AEE) Boscombe Down. This was, a notice board outside announced, the ETPS ground school. Written tests in maths and aerodynamics kicked off the day. Then we were interviewed by panels of ground instructors and flying instructors, known at ETPS as 'Tutors'; perhaps a bit more upmarket and academic? That was Day One. We repaired to the Mess Bar and compared notes over drinks. We received a certain amount of friendly joshing from the course in residence, most of it hinting that we ought to leave now and that we had no idea what we were letting ourselves in for.

That night I did not sleep too well. I had found the whole day a bit of a trial and felt that I had probably fallen short in the academics department. The following day was the one for the final Board Interviews. An array of senior officers sat behind a table, with a civilian at one end. I entered, and saluted.

'Flight Lieutenant Brooke?' the gentleman in the centre seat enquired.

('Starting with the hard ones?' I thought.)

However, discretion being the better part of almost everything, I simply replied, 'Yes, sir.'

'Please sit down.'

So I took the only seat on offer, right in the firing line of this impressive panel.

After the usual introductions the interview focussed primarily on my motivation for wanting to be a test pilot. I was also quizzed about the aircraft that I had flown, they asked me what I thought needed improving and why. The interview was long and intensive, but finally the man in charge, an air commodore, brought it to a close.

I returned to the Mess, changed out of my best uniform back into travelling kit, and waited for John. It was a longish wait as being a 'B' I had been interviewed early and he was a 'T'. When we finally got on the road and drove up the hill away from Boscombe Down, John looked across at me and said, 'Well, I don't know about you, but I don't think I'll be seeing this place again.'

I readily agreed.

We did not know just how wrong we were. Between us we would spend over a quarter of a century there! After I dropped John off at Wittering I drove home and collapsed exhausted into an armchair in front of the telly with a large gin and tonic close by. What a trial it had been!

When I went back into work, everybody was asking how I had got on.

'Don't worry, I won't be leaving here any time soon,' I told them. Now it was a case of waiting a few weeks for the result. When the letter arrived it went to the Boss.

That morning I had taken Flt Lt Dave Peet off to do a practice IRT. During the trip we made an instrument approach at RAF Finningley near Doncaster. After this I took control and asked for clearance to return to Cottesmore following a visual circuit. While I was doing that the controller asked me for my altitude and heading outbound back to Cottesmore. I passed him that information.

'Can you make an altitude of 8,000ft within 5 miles of the airfield?' he asked.

'I sure can, sir,' I said, doing my very poor John Wayne *Flying Tigers* impression.

So I flew a flapless approach and from the touch and go landing applied full power and raised the nose to hold 160kts. With only 3,000lb of fuel on board we climbed like a homesick angel. I turned onto a southerly heading and called, 'Passing 8,000ft at 3 miles. Not bad for an old girl, eh?'

When we arrived back and were rolling down the runway after landing, the local controller called me, saying, 'Bravo 06, please call your squadron commander as soon as you get to a phone.'

'Roger,' I replied, wondering if some old, boring, senior person at Finningley had complained about the manner of our departure.

Once inside the technical site offices I found a phone and rang the Boss, waiting for some sort of ticking off.

'I bet you're wondering what you've done wrong, aren't you?' enquired the Boss.

'What me, sir, no sir, it was someone else,' I replied.

'Now I know you have. But that's not important. I thought that you'd like to know that I've just received notification that you *have been accepted* for ETPS and you will start in January next year. Congratulations Mike.'

Trying not to jump up and down too much I simply said, 'Thanks, Boss, that is good news.'

It took a while to sink in.

27 DISASTER STRIKES

All my life I had been prone to put on weight. I was a 'bouncing' baby. At school I was a 'chubby' boy. As a teenager I was tending to become 'fat boy'. However, I was no couch potato. I enjoyed playing sports: football, basketball, tennis and those athletic events that had anything to do with throwing things. This exercise and occasional dieting took me into adulthood without me becoming too rounded a figure. But I had to keep watching my consumption of food and alcohol. The RAF had introduced me to squash (the game not the drink!) and, although never really good at it, I enjoyed it and at Cottesmore I was playing two or three matches a week. The squash court was immediately behind our garden, but a short cycle ride away.

The Officers' Mess was just beyond the squash court so, while I could take regular exercise not far from home, I could also eat and drink in almost the same location. Between the end of Heythrop Road and the road entering the Mess was a large area of grass bisected by a hedge. In that hedge was a gap, just wide enough for an officer on his bicycle, so that became my regular shortcut to both the squash court and the Mess. That was until one wintry Friday night when I had been at Happy Hour. After a couple of hours in the bar I set off home for my dinner. As usual I cut across the grass heading for the gap in the hedge, which I could just make out in the light of the distant street lamps. I entered the gap at speed and the next thing I knew there was a loud noise and I was flung over the handlebars to land in a messy heap on the muddy ground. Despite the anaesthetic properties of several pints of ale, it hurt. My RAF raincoat (Officers, for the use of) had been torn quite badly and my hands, face and arms were scraped and muddied.

I then began to wonder where my bicycle was. I looked around and saw it standing bolt upright part way through the fence, staring at me with the one eye of its lamp. I went over to find out why it was there and I was here. It was soon evident that at some time since I had last used the shortcut the Ministry of Works and Bricks had put a picket fence along this side of the hedge! In the dark I could not possibly have seen it, so my high-speed arrival in the gap had been firmly arrested and I had continued, in a no-doubt graceful arc, over the fence and hedge to land ungracefully a few feet beyond. I had to walk all the way round to recover my bike and then cycle slowly home. My eventual arrival was not greeted with much sympathy or offers of first aid. After all I had been at the Mess with 'the boys' for what was now over a couple of hours and I looked and smelled a little like a gentleman of the road.

Although unpleasant, especially as the various aches and pains from the multiple impact points kicked in, this was not the disaster referred to in the title of this chapter. Nor was the embarrassing explanation I had to give to the aged retainer in the Clothing Stores to obtain a replacement raincoat. No, what happened over the next few months was to have a bigger impact on my life.

The throughput at the OCU was inexorable, with long and short courses coming through. This timetable meant that at least once every month, and sometimes more often, there was a 'Meet and Greet' or a Farewell party in the Mess for each new or departing course. On top of which was the relentless round of normal Mess and Unit social functions. All this convivial activity led to irregular meals, too much booze and lots of late nights. Meanwhile, work went on and so did the weight. After some disparaging comments, I decided to do something about it. I determined that the first thing that I would reduce was everyday food so that I could still participate, as expected of me, in the many social functions. After all, they say that there's a pork pie in every glass! Lunch would also be replaced with something lighter; Pot Noodles were then new and all the rage, so I squirreled away a load of those in my desk drawer. I, like most aircrew, drank coffee during the day. So I would take it black; the Carnation milk we used was fattening, so I would go without it and use sweeteners instead of sugar.

With fortitude and resolution and more exercise the weight started to drop off. I was very pleased and redoubled my efforts; I probably became a bit of a diet bore. A few weeks into this regime I started to get stomach pains, usually a few hours after eating. When they became so bad as to wake me during the night I decided to visit to the doctor.

The Station Medical Officer (aka 'Doc' or 'the Quack') at Cottesmore was a squadron leader about whom people said you felt better by just going to see him. He smoked like a chimney, the air in his office was always a fog of blue smoke, and every lunchtime he could be found in the Mess Bar quaffing ale. He had some sort of skin complaint that made his forehead look like the surface of Mars: all red and pockmarked. He was definitely not a good advert for his profession.

When I went to see him he prescribed some antacids but didn't enquire as to my eating habits. These pills helped a bit but not enough. As a 'born again' hypochondriac I had a copy of a Reader's Digest *Medical Health* book at home so I scoured that. I deduced that I might have diverticulitis. A few weeks later I went back to the doc to tell him that things were not much better and that the pains were getting worse. I bounced the d-word idea off him. He muttered something disparaging and gave me more pills. This went on for some months.

Then, one time after I had been night flying, I got home and went to bed. By three in the morning I was in agony. My wife called the emergency medical doctor and a locum arrived to find me writhing about on the bed. He immediately diagnosed a gastric ulcer, which he thought may have perforated, and called out the ambulance. A couple of hours later I was in the RAF Hospital at Nocton Hall, near Lincoln. During the one-hour journey I had been given pain-killing injections and was feeling a little better. I was put in the care of a gastro specialist, Wg Cdr Bill Larkworthy, who came to see me the next morning. He told me that I would be undergoing an endoscopic inspection. That would entail a mild anaesthetic and then a flexible tube being pushed down my throat. The tube was a fibre optic that would enable the doctor to examine the inside of my duodenum and stomach. The mild anaesthetic was really quite pleasant, giving me a feeling of floating gently just above my bed; but, from what little I remember, the rest of the procedure was pretty unpleasant and I ended up with a very sore throat.

After the good doctor had looked down my insides he announced that there were indeed a couple of duodenal ulcers and that immediate treatment was required. However, he said that he wanted to test an experimental regime on me.[45] He told me that it was difficult to get aircrew quickly back to flying status using traditional treatments. The one he was going to use on me was based on experiences in India. It involved chewing gum that had been mixed with liquorice extract and healing drugs to cure the ulcers, saliva also being a good antacid. The bad news was that I had to chew three pieces of this gum, each for four hours per day, only stopping to eat or sleep! After being given a huge box of the cubes of gum I was discharged. However, my medical category had been downgraded from A1G1Z1 to A4G3Z4.[46] This meant that I could no longer fly, I had to be employed on light ground duties and banned from going overseas. When I asked how long this would continue I was told: 'At least six months, old chap; but I'll be having another look down there in four months' time. So off you go and keep chewing.'

It was now late October. Six months' 'grounding' would go well beyond the start of next year's ETPS course. I was devastated. The first thing that I did was to write to the CO of ETPS, Group Captain Alan Merriman. I told him what had happened and asked if I could have a place on the 1975 course. When his reply came I was shocked to discover that I would have to go through the whole selection procedure again. I showed the letter to Don Merriman, hoping that the good group captain might be some kindly uncle and that he could pull a few strings. Sadly that wasn't the case, but Don took the letter to the Station Commander, Gp Capt. Jenkins, with whom I had flown during his conversion course. Despite his best efforts he was told that his hands were tied by the way that the selection procedure was done. OC ETPS had explained that each annual selection board is done against test flying posts that would become available during the following year and each place was allocated on a competitive and not an absolute basis. When it was explained to me I could see the sense of it, but I was still crushed. I made my mind up to do exactly what the medics wanted me to do and to get fit and flying again before the summer of 1974 and go forward again for selection to ETPS.

28 GROUNDED

By the beginning of November 1973 I was back at work. Some time earlier Flt Lt Mike Phillips, an ex-PR Canberra man, had been posted in to take over from Colin Westwood as the Chief Ground Instructor (CGI). Because I could no longer fly, it was decided that I would take over as CGI and so release Mike Phillips to become my replacement as a Staff QFI; he was, understandably, a very happy bunny. I was also still the Station Flight Safety Officer so I could keep busy with that as well.

I kept on chewing the magic gum, but it soon became a bit of a chore – had I bitten off more than I could chew?! One of the male nurses at the hospital had given me some advice. He was of Asian stock and he told me, 'There are only three things that cause gastric ulcers: hurry, worry and curry.' So I tried to avoid all three. The other thing I had to avoid was alcoholic drink. Because of their inherent acidity fruit juices were off limits as well. I'd just have to get used to drinking milk at parties. When I got back to base I had a word with the bar staff and they kept a bottle of semi-skimmed in the fridge for me. It did raise eyebrows at first but everyone soon got used to Brookie the Milky Bar Kid!

I worked my way through my first course's period in the Ground school, teaching emergency systems and pilot-related topics such as the aerodynamics of flight on one engine, that is asymmetric flight. The first thing I had to teach on that topic was how to spell it. I soon got used to my first ever non-flying appointment. However, there were unexpected advantages. For example, a weather forecast was only required to ascertain if one should equip oneself with a raincoat or not. Regular hours and a proper home-cooked lunch were also things that I didn't really know I had been missing. I'd always subscribed to the aircrew credo that lunch was a time of day not a meal. Of course, this slower pace of life and regular meals were all just what the doctor ordered. On which subject I learnt not long after I returned to duty that our SMO, the 'Pocked Doc', had received some sort of rocket for not diagnosing my condition earlier.

So life went on. Our second child, Peter, had been born in the April of 1973, also in the RAF Hospital at Nocton Hall, so I was much more available for giving a helping hand with him and the now 3-year-old Sonia. Peter had a hiatus hernia so he was soon an expert projectile vomiter. One day I came in from the office and found him playing happily on the floor, so I picked him up and held him high above my head. He was laughing and gurgling with delight. Just then my wife came in, looked at the baby and me and said, 'I wouldn't do that if I were you, he's just been ...' She didn't finish the sentence as little Peter's last meal cascaded down all over me. I handed the child back to his mum and retired to clean up.

Peter was quite ill for a while and became very dehydrated. But with treatment he improved and by the age of 10 months or so the hernia must have repaired itself because the problem went away.

Sonia was by now a 3-year-old, bouncing, bubbly little toddler and had a wonderful laugh that was very easily induced. She was a bundle of fun and mischief. But one evening I got home, feeling very tired, and was asked to go up and read her a bedtime story. Obediently I went upstairs, tucked her in and then knelt alongside her bed and started reading the Ladybird book that was currently in favour. After some time my wife, who had been preparing dinner, came up to find out where I had got to. She came into Sonia's room to find me fast asleep with our daughter sitting up 'reading' the book to herself. Oh the shame of it!

During 1973 we were given notice that all the married quarters were going to be fitted with central heating and double-glazing. Wonders of wonders; the RAF was catching up with the twentieth century! Of course, as is their wont, they did the job in the depth of winter, taking the windows out BEFORE they put the heating in. For a couple of weeks it was perishing cold. Our house faced east across the open airfield. There was no high ground between us and the Ural Mountains and the east wind off the Fens could cut like a knife. Eventually the job was done, just in time for the first warmth of spring. The tank for the heating oil was in the garden, behind the detached garage. One day, when Sonia's cousin was visiting, she came running into the house shouting, 'My river's running into my sea.' For a few seconds we were all baffled, wondering what strange imaginary game was she up to now? Then I thought that I'd better go out and check. As I rounded the wall of the garage I could smell it. Then I could hear it. Then I could see it. Sonia had opened the drain cock on the oil tank and central heating oil was cascading out onto the ground. I turned it off. About half the contents of the tank had been lost. Worms were leaving the ground as fast as they could. I was in shock.

The first thing I did was to find a screwdriver and remove the circular tap from its spindle. The next working day I called the local manager of the MOD Works Department and said that I thought that leaving the drainage control in place was a bit foolish, citing this experience as evidence of my opinion. That started a blame game, which I eventually won with the help of the RAF Station Works Services officer. I was reimbursed for 100 gallons of oil. What's more, Sonia learned a valuable lesson about fiddling with things she didn't understand.

Christmas came and went; a very abstemious one for me. By now, after three months of chewing for twelve hours a day, the muscles in my face and the saliva glands beneath had all become over-developed. I looked even more like an overfed hamster and face ache was a new fact of life for me. In January, Wing Commander Larkworthy called for me to return to Nocton Hall for another endoscopy, to see how things were going. The result was, he admitted, astonishing. One ulcer had disappeared completely and the other was much diminished. He told me to keep chewing, gave me some other drugs to accelerate the healing and asked me to come back in early February.

At this second inspection of my innards he declared that there were now no ulcerations in my duodenum and that he would write a report and recommend that I be returned to an unlimited medical category and flying. Result! As soon as I could I contacted ETPS to see whether I could join the course, which had started only a few days previously. However, on the receipt of the news of my grounding they had chosen the best of the previous summer's non-selected candidates to replace me, so I still had to go through that gruelling two-day selection process again and hope that I made the cut for the 1975 Class.

29 FLIGHT SAFETY

During my first tour on Canberras I had been 'volunteered' to take over as the Squadron Flight Safety Officer (SqnFSO) and had been sent back to Blighty to attend the appropriate course in London. In the armed forces it is virtually impossible to take up any extraneous, or as the RAF puts it 'secondary', duty without undertaking a course. The job of a SqnFSO is to make sure that everyone is kept up to date with the latest flight safety issues, by constantly keeping the topic well publicised; to attend Station Flight Safety meetings; and to initiate and follow up reports from squadron aircrew of safety related incidents.

When I had settled in at Cottesmore I was told that there was going to be a vacancy as the Station Flight Safety Officer (SFSO). My friend and colleague Gordon Campbell was the SFSO when I arrived, but he was in the throes of leaving the RAF for employment as an airline pilot. So I understudied Gordon for a while and then assumed his duties when he departed. I had my own office in the Station Operations Centre just round the corner from the office of the OC Operations Wing. On flight safety matters he was my 'Boss' and I was responsible through him, to the Station Commander, for all matters pertaining to the safety of flight operations at Cottesmore. However, and unusually, I did have the right of direct access to the Station Commander should I feel that was necessary.

As a 'secondary duty' it was much better than many others on offer, such as Mess Secretary or Unit Inventory Holder. It was directly connected to flying and the post carried a lot of weight, which meant a lot of responsibility. However, for most of the time it was routine. It was also continuous, there was no let-up in the 'traffic' across my desk of reports, minutes of meetings, new publicity and directives from above.

A few things out of the routine and ordinary came my way during my tenure of office. The first was the Long Grass Policy. Birds and airfields do not mix, especially where the operating aircraft use huge vacuum cleaners as their motive power. One bird down a turbojet aero engine can cause catastrophic failure. The trouble with airfields is that there are enormous areas of well-tended grassland and often warm concrete and tarmacadam. These are attractive to a wide variety of birds, both resident and visitor. The worst and most frequent at Cottesmore were lapwings. These are grassland birds of medium build and who love getting airborne at the slightest disturbance and then doing lots of wild aerobatic manoeuvres. To make matters worse the larger rooks and crows from the surrounding farmland often joined the lapwings to consume the insects and invertebrates in the soil. Then there were huge flocks of starlings that descended to feed during the day, before departing at dusk for their roosting areas in vast wheeling, fluid clouds of blackness.

The Long Grass Policy was the result of a study by the folks at the MAFF who had determined that grassland birds did not like walking around if the grass was about 6 to 9in high. I wondered why; perhaps it tickled their nether regions too much. But, whatever the reason, the suggestion was that airfields should not crop their grass areas to look like bowling greens, as had been the practice, but to adjust the cutters to give the required height. I got involved because Cottesmore was chosen as an airfield upon which this proposal would be evaluated. Until then we had used a variety of bird scaring tactics: exploding shells fired from a Verey pistol, recordings of alarm calls played from fire vehicles touring the airfield and our very own falconer, with his Harris hawks, peregrine falcons and other assorted birds of prey. On the whole we had managed the problem but with a lot of effort. If simply growing the grass to the right length would make all the birds go away then I was all for it.

I gave a briefing on the topic at the next Station Flight Safety Meeting and, in conjunction with the Airfield Works Services team, we set about growing the grass. We started with the target of about 9in. Of course it didn't happen immediately and it was many weeks before it arrived at the required length. I had never expected to have a job that involved watching grass grow! Two problems then came to light. Not all the grass was strong enough to stay upright at that length, so some areas were still popular with our avian friends. The other was totally unexpected by us or by the MAFF. The new habitat became a superb breeding ground for slugs and snails. So much so that these slithering, slimy little beasts started to overflow onto the runway in sufficient numbers as to become a flight safety hazard on their own. As they were squashed by the aircraft wheels running over them the resulting slime noticeably reduced the braking coefficient of parts of the runway. Several pilots, especially early in the day, reported skidding unexpectedly as they braked after landing.

The upshot was that we were asked to cut the grass to 6in. When this happened the gastropod problem went away. What's more the birds did not return in their previous numbers. However, the mowing men said that it wasn't easy to keep the length at 6in. Eventually various trials led to a length of 10–15cm being the target. I'm not sure whether the Long Grass Policy is still adhered to these days but, once we had refined it, it made a big difference.

However, it soon became apparent that the bird invasion might return, but from a different source. It was during 1973 that work started on the creation of England's largest[47] reservoir – then known as Empingham Reservoir but later as Rutland Water. This undertaking was due to take three years to complete but would bring in its train an increase in the number of birds in the skies around Cottesmore. The centre of the reservoir was only about 5 miles (as the crow or any other bird flies) from the centre of the airfield. It was going to be a big concern for the future. However, the other side of the coin was that the new attraction for the birds may make Cottesmore's grass passé and so there would be fewer of them actually on the airfield, where they could do their worst.

The biggest and most tragic happening while I was SFSO was a fatal accident to one of the OCU's student pilots during a night sortie. I was off-duty at home when, from our kitchen window, I noticed the flashing blue lights of fire vehicles moving rapidly across the airfield. I immediately hopped on my bike and cycled the short distance to the Ops Centre. There I was told that a B2 from the OCU had crashed only a couple of miles north-east of the airfield. I knew that the fire crews would be there by now so the only useful thing that I could now do was to get everything ready for the inevitable Board of Inquiry. As I was doing that the Station Commander and the OC Ops Wing arrived and started the usual instant inquiry of their own.

I had made sure that the folk up at Group HQ had been informed as they would pass the sad message up the line to HQ Bomber Command and then things would kick off, quite rapidly, with the appointment of the members of the Board and their arrival at Cottesmore, probably by the middle of the following day. I stayed on to do as much as I could without getting in the senior men's way and then pushed off home.

The next day I was required to set up a room for the Board to use. First I tried to find out as many facts about the accident as I could. The pilot was a student on his first night 'solo' in the B2. He had been briefed to carry out a practice single-engine overshoot from a radar-guided approach and it was during that part of his trip that the accident had happened. The navigator, a member of the OCU staff called Max Murray, had ejected when he was sure that the lad up front had lost control. The pilot had also ejected but unfortunately too late for the seat to be able to do its job correctly. He had been found still in the seat, clutching the face blind initiation handle, with his legs at odd angles and very evidently suffering from severe internal injuries. He was pronounced dead by the doctor at the scene.

Other than the navigator there were no eyewitnesses. There were, however, ear-witnesses. The aircraft was abeam the Fox Inn, a public house and hotel on the A1, when things went awry. Someone there heard a strange noise at the time of the accident. The description was compatible with the sound of a jet engine surging. A surge is when the demand for air into the engine cannot be met, the compressor in the engine stops working efficiently and the thrust then reduces dramatically. A surge is common if the throttle is opened too rapidly at low airspeed or under conditions of extreme sideslip.

The members of the Board of Inquiry and a representative from the Aircraft Accident Investigation Branch arrived as expected during the late morning of the following day. I took them out to the crash site, which in accordance with regulations was under guard. The aircraft was remarkably intact, there had been no significant post-crash fire and the two ejection seats lay where they fell. Initial visual examination of the front end of each compressor showed that neither engine had been rotating at high speed on impact; indicating the possibility that they were both at or near flight idle and, therefore, not producing much thrust.

The Board sat for several days and finally came to the conclusion that the student pilot had mishandled the practice single-engine overshoot so badly that he had lost control of the aircraft. At 600ft above the ground that left him with no option but to abandon ship. The odd thing was that he used the face blind to initiate the explosives in his seat.[48] For many years aircrew had been taught to ignore the 'top handle' and use only the lower firing handle between their legs. The reason for this was that trials had proved that it saved at least one second in escaping from the jet. That doesn't sound a lot but it can represent a lot of height if the aircraft is falling out of the sky. It was a sad time for us on the OCU; fatal accidents were rare and the poor lad's instructor found it particularly hard to deal with.

My time in the SFSO's shoes came to an end when I returned to flying in February 1974. There were no more serious events during my tenure of office and I was glad to hand over an empty in-tray to my successor.

30 A SILVER ANNIVERSARY

When, in late 1973 I was looking over some old documentation in my office I was reminded that the Canberra had been in RAF service since 1951 – that would be 23 years in 1974. *But*, I asked myself, *when did it first fly?* I discovered that this was on the afternoon of Friday 13 May 1949. My immediate thought was that Wg Cdr Roland 'Bee' Beamont must not have been a superstitious chap. My second thought was that 1974 would be the 25th Anniversary of that momentous first flight of the first British-built jet bomber. Surely we here at the epicentre of Canberra operations should do something to mark the passing of this considerable landmark? I gathered my thoughts and went to see OC Ops. He liked the idea and then had one of his own.

'OK, Mike,' he said with a large smile. I knew what was coming. 'You draw up some possible things we could do, look at dates and then come back to me. When we've tidied it up we'll go see the Station Commander.'

I had broken the skiver's golden rule: if you don't want to be lumbered with a job don't suggest it to your superiors. Not that I was a skiver – far from it. But give a senior officer an idea and he'll give you the job.

A couple of weeks later it was official. We had presented our ideas to the great man and he had fully supported the proposal to celebrate the Silver Anniversary of the Canberra at Cottesmore in 1974. He told OC Ops to be in overall charge of the planning and execution, but the good Group Captain thought it a good idea if I was the Project Officer. They are all the same!

As I was still medically grounded it gave me something to fill my time, so I threw myself into the task. The first thing was to set the date. When that had been fixed, which took some negotiation, we then had to fit things into our outline programme. Sadly I now have no recollection of the exact date that was chosen, but I do know that it was not 13 May. I then started by making numerous phone calls to Canberra squadrons, because I wanted to have a line-up of as many different marks of the star of the show as possible. I also telephoned the RAF Museum to find out whether they had any useful items they could lend us. The call also went out to any past Canberra aircrew that might be able to come up with any historic mementos or relevant items that we could exhibit.

As the New Year came and went the task seemed more daunting than ever. We were getting a very positive response from most places. More and more material was being offered and I now had an impressive line-up promised for the static display. The marks of Canberra that should be attending were B2, PR3, T4, B6, PR7, PR9, SC9, B15, TT17, T19 and T22. I have made mention of some of these marks elsewhere; indeed I would end my career with all of them in my logbook. The most unusual of them all was the SC9. This was a unique aircraft. It was a PR9, XH 132 that had been built and then modified by the Northern Irish aircraft company Short Brothers Ltd for radar trials. The main modification was to the nose, in which was mounted an Air Interception Mark 23 'Airpass' radar with two other tracking devices in ugly protrusions above and below. The AI 23 was the radar that equipped the Lightning interceptor fighter and, as in the Lightning, the radar display and all its controls were operated by the SC9's pilot. The aircraft was also wired for other radars and electronics to be carried in special wingtip pods. The first time I saw the SC9, as it arrived for the following day's celebrations, I thought that it was an even worse desecration than the carbuncle on the front of the T17. But I supposed that it was doing important and no doubt highly classified work with the Radar Research Establishment down at Pershore in Worcestershire. Little did I know that a few years later I would find out all about that work at first hand; and fly the SC9 into the bargain.

By the time the big day had arrived everything was in place. The Officers' Mess was decorated with lots of photographs from the Canberra's past and the Operations Centre Briefing Room was set up as a cinema to show the historic films we had received; it was my job for the day to compère these. The line-up on the airfield, as close as we could make it to the Mess and Ops Centre, was complete and before we knew it the great and the good started to arrive. The programme for the day was for everyone to be welcomed by the Station Commander, told what there was to see and where. A buffet lunch was laid on in the Mess and we invited our guests to walk around the various locations and enjoy the day. The weather was fine and dry so brollies and wellies were not required. The day was to finish with a formal dinner.

Being stuck in the Ops Centre I did not see much of the rest of the show, but I had seen it all being set up. One very nice surprise for me came early in the day, before I had started my duties as Master of Ceremonies in the 'cinema', and that was the arrival of a Puma helicopter. Once it had shut down and stopped its rotors out clambered one Group Captain 'Trog' Bennett, my old boss from No 16 Squadron at RAF Laarbruch; he was now the Station Commander at RAF Odiham in Hampshire. I was so glad to see him again and pleased that he had received a very well deserved promotion. Sadly we didn't have time for a long reunion because I had to get him to the welcome event fairly smartly.

It all seemed to go well and most people seemed appreciative of the effort we had put in to make the celebration worthy of such a superb record-breaking aeroplane. One highlight for me occurred during one of the afternoon showings of the two films, both of which were in colour. One of them showed a visit in the 1950s to the Hashemite Kingdom of Jordan by an RAF Canberra squadron. In this film there was a sequence of a very youthful King Hussein climbing aboard a Canberra B2 flown by the squadron commander, one Sqn Ldr Ivor Broom. The royal person had to sit on what was known as the Rumble Seat, a very simple fold-down affair next to, but below, the pilot. The back support for the occupant was a broad canvas strap that was clipped onto each side of the passageway from the navigator's cabin to the nose.

After we had watched the film I pointed out that the, now, Air Chief Marshal Sir Ivor Broom was sitting in the audience. He received a well deserved round of applause. He then got to his feet and told us all of an episode that was not recorded on film. After King Hussein had got himself comfortable and he was ready to go, Sir Ivor taxied out and lined up on the runway for take-off. He ran up the engines, released the brakes and had, almost immediately, to reapply them. As the aircraft had started to accelerate the King's upper body had disappeared from view and his feet were now up alongside the pilot's right knee! The strap at the back of the seat had not been secured correctly and under the acceleration the regal body had been thrown backwards with nothing to restrain it. Once the aircraft had stopped the navigator came forward and fixed the problem and the trip went ahead as planned. Fortunately His Royal Highness saw the funny side of the incident and the crew did not end up in Amman Prison.

Sir Ivor was actually retired by the time of this visit but, as a group captain, he had been the Station Commander of Cottesmore in the 1960s. It is a mark of the man that one of the first things he did was to visit the headmistress of the primary school to see how she was and thank her for helping to educate his children over ten years previously.

We had a very large number of visitors throughout the day and about 140 of them stayed for the Black Tie Dinner in the evening. At that splendid affair the senior guest, Marshal of the Royal Air Force and past Chief of the Air Staff Sir Dermot Boyle, regaled us with some amusing stories of the time that he took a detachment of Canberras from his squadron, No 101, to South America. I think that the best of his tales was when one Canberra was left behind at an airbase in one of the host countries, while the others made a flying visit elsewhere. An RAF Senior NCO from the support party was left behind to keep an eye on it. During the morning a group of host nation officers arrived and started to look over the wondrous machine. After a while they took up conversation in broken English with the RAF 'guardian'.

'Tell me, 'ow 'igh can eet fly?' asked one.

'Oh, well above 40,000ft, sir,' was the honest reply.

'Can eet fly 'igher zan ze Meteor fighter?' asked another.

'Oh, easily, sir,' came another honest response.

'Do you sink zat ze Meteor could shoot eet down?'

'Not a hope, sir,' the NCO proudly said.

The visitors thanked their 'host' for all the information, took their leave and departed. Later at a reception Sir Dermot discovered that the country was about to place an order for a good number of Gloster Meteors but had now decided not to. Their neighbours had just ordered Canberras.

By the end of the day we had a lot of very happy people, none more so than the team that made the day the success that it was. I finished my evening, or early morning actually, in a corner of the bar having one of those long and meaningless conversations that too much alcohol brings with OC Ops. He was also a very happy bunny. The departures of our visiting aircraft the next morning were, apart from the PR9, gently done. I bet most of the guys had been breathing 100 per cent oxygen from the moment they strapped in!

31 LICENSED TO TRAP

When I returned to the OCU, with my shiny new medical category proclaiming me once more fit to fly, I wondered what I would be doing. Mike Phillips had filled my instructor's appointment and nobody else had departed. The Boss soon put me out of my misery with some very good news. I was going to move into the office of the CFS Agents for the Canberra and take over from Sqn Ldr Pete Perry who was leaving for pastures new. The CFS Agency scheme operates throughout the RAF with CFS-licensed QFIs. These guys carry out visits to squadrons to check on piloting and airmanship standards. CFS Agents are usually based at the OCU of the relevant aircraft type. The scheme was not mandatory; Station Commanders had the option to invite the CFS Agents to visit the squadrons under their command. In practice there were very few that did not issue an annual invitation. The agents also undertook the categorisation of all QFIs on their particular force, as well as any re-categorisation and refresher flying of previously qualified instructors on type.

However, the first thing I had to do was to prove that I had not forgotten how to fly the Canberra or instruct on it, so I flew a couple of check flights: the first, by day with Don Merriman and the second at night with Sqn Ldr Dickie Lees, one of the two CFS Agents. The first went well enough but on the second, in the dark, during a touch-and-go landing at RAF Leeming in Yorkshire the port main wheel tyre unaccountably burst, so we came to a shuddering halt on the runway. That meant an overnight stop at Leeming, the RAF Training School at which I had done my basic flying training. Although I had left there twelve years before I was pleasantly surprised to find the same two bluff Yorkshire barmen, George and Arthur, still at the beer pumps in the Officers' Mess Bar; they both said that they remembered me because I had looked so young when I was there. Well, I was only 18!

We flew the repaired T-Bird back the next morning and I found that, despite the incident, I would still be joining the CFS Agency office at the OCU. The fact that I had nearly wrecked a jet the previous night was obviously not an issue. I spent the rest of February regaining my Instrument Rating and generally getting back up to full speed. By mid-March I was declared 'operational' as an agent. I was now what was universally known as a 'Trapper'; it seemed so bizarre to me that I was now one of the clan that squadron pilots did not look forward to seeing, less still flying with. I wondered how I would best do the job without becoming too unpopular and pedantic; which was what a few Trappers I had known certainly were.

Apart from visiting squadrons our job was also to prepare instructors for the OCU and the squadrons in the field. I spent the rest of March and most of April teaching, and learning from, a great guy called Pete Diggance who was staying on the OCU as a staff QFI. Pete was an ex-member and leader of 'the Macaws' Jet Provost formation team from RAF Manby, an inveterate pipe smoker and a man of great dry wit. We had some fun together as he got to grips with sitting in the right-hand seat of the T4 and making it do what he wanted while he talked about it.

Then Dickie Lees told me that we would be making our first visit, leaving on 16 April to go to the Mediterranean. This smacked of 'the good old days' on No 16 Squadron and our exercise 'Southern Ranger' overseas training flights to all points south and east. Dickie announced that we were going to visit No 13 and No 39 PR squadrons in Malta and No 56 Squadron Target Facilities Flight in Cyprus.

We flew in a Transport Command Comet 4 from RAF Brize Norton to RAF Luqa in Malta, settled into the Officers' Mess and then made our courtesy call on the Station Commander. He was pleased to see us and instantly showed that he was leading from the front by insisting that he be examined; I was relieved when Dickie said that he would fly that sortie. We then went to call on the commanding officers of Nos 13 and 39 squadrons to make our arrival known and to plan the programme for the nine-day stay. At that time No 13 Squadron was flying the PR7 and No 39 the PR9 versions of the Canberra. Their roles were complementary, that was to undertake PR tasks anywhere within the southern areas of NATO and the CENTO regions to the east of the Med. The PR9s had previously been based at RAF Akrotiri in Cyprus.

The PR7 was essentially a grown up version of the original B2/PR3 model that had first entered RAF service in the early 1950s. It had the second-generation RR Avon engines giving 7,500lb of thrust, extra fuel tanks in the wings and in the rear half of what was originally the bomb bay. So the PR7's range and endurance exceeded that of all its predecessors. The front half of the erstwhile bomb bay was now the flare bay; from where 'n' million candlepower photoflash flares could be released to illuminate targets at night.

The PR9 was the last version of the Canberra to be built. Although its ancestry could clearly be seen in the plan-form of the broad un-swept wings and the placement in them of the engines, in many other ways the PR9 was the ultimate development of this distinctly British aircraft of which over 1,300 were built. However, aficionados of the US licensed-built Martin B-57 might argue with this suggestion, as the last of that line had a wing of almost twice the 69ft span of the PR9 and huge turbofan engines of twice the thrust. And that was no mean feat because the PR9's motive power came from one of the ultimate versions of Rolls Royce's Avon, the Mk 206, giving over 11,500lb of thrust at maximum output. This was the same variant of the Avon that had gone into English Electric's other world beating aircraft, the Lightning; although in that guise it was given reheat, or afterburning, to increase the thrust even further.

As Dickie and I had flown out courtesy of RAF Transport Command we had pre-arranged the use of the two T4s based at Luqa. So as soon as we could, we got our programme going. The aim was to fly with a representative proportion of the pilots and it was the squadron's job to offer up the bodies for torture. We might reject someone who had flown with us during the last annual visit in favour of someone who had not yet been 'trapped' and we would certainly want to fly with the squadron's own instructors and at least one of the executive officers. The whole philosophy was to make sure that no unsafe trends were appearing in the way that the pilots were flying the aircraft. We had no remit to test their operational competency, however, any comment relevant to that would be allowed. My view was that once the Station Commander had arranged a visit, 90 per cent of what we wanted the squadrons to do would have been completed before we arrived. Pilots' Notes and Aircrew Manuals would have been dusted off, updated and studied once more, the squadron QFI would have flown with a good number of the pilots, especially those with any weaknesses and he would have brushed up their performances. The squadron executives, always known as 'the wheels', would have checked that all the regulatory documentation was correct, updated and that everyone had signed as 'having read and understood' them.

All we then had to do was to fly and write short reports about each pilot and crew that we flew with. It was an open reporting system and the pilot and squadron commander had to read and sign each report before we sent it to the Station Commander. We would fly by day and by night and we had *carte blanche* as to the content of the sortie. Inevitably that would include at least one simulated major emergency, plus a practice engine failure after take-off (EFATO) and at least one landing or go-around on one engine. I used to like varying things a bit and, where possible, throwing in a bit of role-related flying. For instance on one sortie I asked the crew to fly at low level to Sicily and show me some of the low flying routes they used. I set up the circumstances of some practice emergencies or simulated weather conditions so that they had to divert to the airfields of Sigonella or Palermo in Sicily. On one flight we did a practice diversion to Palermo at night and I was astonished to see a huge slab of rock quite close to the airfield, illuminated by the lights of the city. It reminded me of Gibraltar.

One of the great things about this new job was coming across old mates and acquaintances. I flew with two of my ex-OCU students, Dave McIntyre and John Armitage; as I remember they acquitted themselves satisfactorily. Well, they had had a first-class instructor at the OCU! One of the squadron QFIs was Sqn Ldr Tony Terret who had been at Cottesmore on No 115 Squadron flying the Argosy. He was still finding his feet a bit as he hadn't been in Malta long. I also flew with Norman Gill, the QFI whom I had replaced at 231 OCU and who, in my mind, had got the posting to Malta that had my name on it. I wasn't too hard on him: I couldn't be – he was too good! It was great to be back on the island again. My last visit had been a couple of years beforehand and prior to that not since 1966. We had time for play as well as work and were invited to several open-air parties; the weather and the food were invariably delicious. Malta in April still has green bits and the temperatures are very equitable. The sea is still a bit chilly but as clear as gin.

Before we had left Cottesmore Dickie had told me that there was another perk to the job. That was that the 'Trappers' were more often than not offered a chance to fly the squadron's operational aircraft and so find out what the guys we were examining were doing for their day job. Consequently, after a couple of days, I broached the subject with one of the flight commanders.

'Excuse me, sir,' I ventured, hoping that Dickie hadn't been winding me up, 'Do you think that there might be room in your programme to let me have a go at the PR9?'

'Yes, I don't see why not,' was the very agreeable reply. 'I'll set it up for tomorrow, OK?'

It certainly was OK. I was given a set of the Pilots' Notes and a briefing that very afternoon. I took the book to bed with me and looked forward to trying the 'big yin' out the next day. In the morning I flew an examining sortie in a T4 with Flt Lt Jim Ball and his navigator. Once I had finished the debrief and write up, I grabbed a quick aircrew lunch, probably a sandwich and a coffee. Then a very brave chap called Paul Jennings, one of the PR9 pilots, was volunteered to sit in the nose of PR9 XH 167 while I found my way around the cockpit, started the engines and slipped the surly bonds of earth.

The PR9 pilot's cockpit is an offset fighter-style, bubble canopy, much like that of the Canberra B(I)8 that I flew during my tour on No 16 Squadron in RAF Germany. The exception being that on the PR9 the canopy opened upwards and one climbed in, as into a proper jet, from the top. I'd always wished that the same arrangement had been made for the B(I)8.

The navigator's station was in the nose. At least, unlike the B(I)8 navs, he had an ejection seat. Access for the nose occupant was direct from the ground because the nose cone was hinged on its right-hand side. The drawback was that there were only two small side windows. It really was a claustrophobic's nightmare; much like what the Fleet Air Arm Observers on Sea Vixens referred to as 'The Coal Hole', where they sat to the right of and below the pilot. The main view of the outside world for the PR9 nav (navigator) was via a moveable periscope that looked downwards and helped with the alignment for high-level photography and some visual navigation.

Once I had completed all the pre-take-off checks and received clearance from ATC to go, I lined up on the runway, double checked that I had closed the canopy properly and applied the power. The throttles were much smaller than in the other models of Canberra that I had flown and, paradoxically, seemed to move much less distance for lots more power. During this take-off I would be using only 90 per cent of full power; the aircraft was relatively light as not all the fuel tanks were full and this power setting gave me a much lower safety speed should an engine fail. We still leapt off the ground like a startled rabbit. Once above safety speed I increased the power to 95 per cent and climbed at 330kts. We were up at 40,000ft in less than half the time it took in the T4! The PR9 was equipped with hydraulic power to both the lateral and directional controls, which are the ailerons and the rudder. I had tried rolling the aircraft through 60° both ways during the climb and was very pleasantly surprised by both the low forces and the nice rate of roll. If only we had had these luxuries on the B(I)8, low-level formation gunnery would not have been so exhausting. Another luxury was an autopilot, so I tried that out. I had only been allowed an hour in the jet, so I thought that we had better get back before I was called in. After a few circuits I landed with a very satisfied feeling. The PR9 was certainly the most mature and exhilarating version of the Canberra. I had enjoyed my flight so much that after I had enthused about it, I was offered a second one a few days later. On that one I played with the autopilot some more, including making a fully automatic ILS approach to 100ft before cutting out 'George' and landing.

We debriefed the station and squadron commanders on 25 April 1974, the final day of our visit. Then Dickie Lees, our nav, Flt Lt Hally Hardie and I strapped into the Malta-based T4, WJ 872, and flew ourselves from Luqa to RAF Akrotiri in Cyprus. There we were greeted by Wing Commander Martin Bee, the CO of No 56 Squadron, the 'Firebirds'. He had two Canberra B2s and three crews who flew as airborne targets for the squadron's F6 Lightnings. One of the pilots was my old mate from No 16 Squadron and the OCU – Dobs Dobbie. We would be there for just a few days flying just three sorties between us.

On the second day of our visit I was delighted to be asked by Wg Cdr Bee whether I would like a trip in the two-seat, dual controlled Lightning T5. My grin was sufficient answer. I was duly kitted out and we walked together towards XS 422,[49] in its shiny metal and red colour scheme. The jet did not have a ventral tank fitted so I was told that we would be lucky to get more than twenty minutes out of it, especially if we went supersonic. I told 'The Boss' that any time in a Lightning would be OK by me. So off we went; and how we did go! The take-off seemed to be over in seconds and the climb to 36,000ft passed in a flash. I had spent that very short time lying on my back looking out sideways at a horizon angled at about 60° from level. At the apogee, the nose was pushed down and we pierced Mach One almost instantaneously. At Mach 1.5, Martin pulled the throttles back and we decelerated to just subsonic and then he handed control to me to try throwing this exciting flying machine around a bit. I had not much to compare it with but I thought that it felt a little heavier than I had expected. But it was fun. Then he pointed at the fuel gauges and said, 'We'd better get home.' The next thing I knew we were touching down at Akrotiri and the brake parachute was streaming out behind us. I know it was all fast and furious but how could twenty minutes speed by like that?

Martin Bee was an interesting chap. In the early 1960s he had been one of a few select RAF pilots who had been chosen to fly the Lockheed U2; then a US operated photo-reconnaissance 'spy plane'. It so happened that, at RAF Akrotiri, there was a resident U2 detachment. I called them the Alarm Clock Outfit. Every morning at 7 a.m. precisely there was a loud and persistent jet exhaust noise. It was the daily U2 flight getting airborne. The all-black, spindly, long-winged machine climbs at 160kts and an angle of about 45°, so it hangs in the air for a long time. Its smoky engine pours out carbon and noise for quite a while before the odd-looking flying machine disappears into the upper atmosphere, staying up there for well over twelve hours and going on 3,000-mile trips to secret destinations.

Martin Bee arranged for us to go to the U2 Detachment's hangar to look over one of their black birds, known as the 'Dragon Lady'. We met some of the U2 pilots and, after a while, I was allowed to sit in the cockpit. It was very reminiscent of the Canberra, all black with old-fashioned dials and switches. The main 'instrument' right in the middle of the panel was the large, circular glass of the downward looking periscope, much like that in the nose of the PR9. A control yoke, not a stick, operated the flying controls and the engine controls and dials were simple. There was one large throttle. But with that big wing and the relative frailty of the U2's construction it takes a special breed of pilot to fly and operate it for twelve or more hours at a time. As if sitting inside the thing for half a day isn't enough, it takes particular skill to land the

U2 safely. It only has wheels under the fuselage and a fast chase car is used to talk the pilot down through the last 10ft of the landing. The Dragon Lady is also very capricious in any sort of a crosswind.

There was a tale going the rounds at Akrotiri about a U2 that had flown in from an airbase in the Pacific on the far side of the International Date Line. When it landed in Cyprus a young, keen RAF Duty Movements Officer had appeared to meet the aircraft to complete the usual formalities, as was his obligation.

As the pilot stiffly dismounted and took off his space helmet the young officer said, 'Welcome to RAF Akrotiri, sir. The local time is 1800 hours.'

'Never mind the local time, sonny,' came the gruff reply. 'What's the local day?'

Soon we were boarding a Transport Command Belfast to return to the UK. That was an interesting experience sitting in the 'minstrels' gallery', a sort of mezzanine floor looking down over the vast cargo bay. The Belfast was not known for its speed and its service sobriquet was the 'Belslow'. One of the Boscombe Down test pilots, Robby Robinson, had led a proving flight out to the Far East. On the leg between the Arabian Gulf and the island of Gan, Robby sent a message that encapsulated the Belfast's stately progress through the sky. The message read: 'Eight hours outbound. Still no signs of scurvy.'

Eventually we arrived at RAF Brize Norton. A few days later the Turks invaded Northern Cyprus and established a partitioned state; it is still there today. No 56 Squadron were no doubt very busy.

After a month of the usual daily round: re-categorisation, refresher and other such CFS Agent flying we got notice of another visit. This time we didn't have to travel far because the invitation had come from Group Captain Alan Jenkins, our own Station Commander. The units to be tested were Nos 360 and 98 squadrons. The 'visit' was so like our usual routine that it seemed that nothing special was happening. However, we did our job of making sure that folk were operating correctly and safely. Dickie Lees had now left for pastures new and he was replaced by a legend of the Canberra world, Sqn Ldr Paddy Thompson. Paddy seemed positively ancient to me; he had flown the DH Mosquito, which put him in my dad's generation. And that turned out to be not a bad analogy. Paddy was a gentle man, unless you upset him, and he was very supportive of me in my attempts at getting fully to grips with this very special job.

Our next trip away wasn't until September when we were invited by the Captain of Royal Naval Air Station (RNAS) Yeovilton to come down to Somerset and fly with the Fleet Requirements Aircraft Direction Unit (FRADU). The unit was commanded by a naval officer, but staffed by civilian ex-military pilots and navigators. FRADU had a mixed fleet of Canberras and Hunters and their job was to provide airborne targets for the training of fighter controllers and air defence crews on RN fighting ships. The version of the Canberra that they used was the T22. The 'T' designated it as a trainer, in this case for the training of ground or sea based personnel, and the '22' was the last of the series of design changes to the basic aeroplane. This time the base airframe was the PR7, but the cameras had all been removed and the glazed nose had been replaced with an anti-shipping radar with the code name of 'Blue Parrot'. This was the same radar as used in the Buccaneer strike aircraft. The single navigator's station, in the rear cabin, had the radar screen as well as other navigation aids. The cockpit was essentially identical to that of the second generation Canberras, such as the B6 and PR7.

This time we took a T4 from Cottesmore and we also used the FRADU T4 so that we could achieve a good representative series of tests within the week allotted. Some of the guys we examined were getting on a bit. One of them, Paddy said, with a glint in his eye, should fly at night with me. I could tell that there was more to this, so I asked why.

'I knew him when we flew Mosquitoes together,' he responded. 'And I bet he's no better now than he was then.' This revelation was followed by a wicked grin. Sure enough this man bounced along on a base level of a great deal of experience, which offset just sufficiently his lack of natural ability and skill. It was quite a trip. On one occasion he seemed to lose track of what we were doing and where we were! When I did the written report I did not mince my words and suggested that perhaps it was time for him to retire gracefully before 'circumstances' took control and retired him permanently. He was a bit miffed, but I got the impression that he had heard it all before. His line management were a bit more responsive, but he was still flying the Canberra some time later. The best thing about this particular trip was that during it I passed a total of 3,000 flying hours!

I also managed to get myself two flights in the right-hand seat of the dual-controlled Hunter T8 and a flight in the front seat of a T22 Canberra. I had not yet flown the PR7, but the main difference for me was the increased number of fuel gauges. Like the PR9, the PR7 had extra fuel tanks in the rear half of what had originally been the bomb-bay. We flew for two-and-a-half hours on what was known as Exercise Broadway against the frigate HMS *Torquay*. Most of the sortie involved flying at 330kts and 100ft towards the Grey Funnel Line warship, pretending to be a missile. My civilian navigator, Mr Davis, in the back was using the radar to steer me in the right direction. Once the ship had declared that we had done enough we flew to Boscombe Down to carry out an approach and a couple of visual circuits before returning to Yeovilton. As I now knew that I had passed the second two-day grilling, which had happened in June, and would be attending the 1975 ETPS course, I thought that I might as well get a look at the place from the air. The runway was enormous: 10,000ft long and 300ft wide. An interesting optical illusion of being too low and too close on the final approach was very evident.

One highlight of our visit was my meeting HRH the Prince of Wales, although the circumstances of the encounter were, to say the least, a little odd and a bit embarrassing. I had just been flying and I made for what the Navy call 'the heads': the toilets. I went in and found a convenient urinal to carry out my fuel dump. Someone in a flying suit, with naval stripes on the shoulder tabs, came in and stood beside me. I glanced at the newcomer and, with a bit of a start, realised that it was Prince Charles, who was at Yeovilton carrying out his flying training on the Wessex helicopter. I was stuck for something to say in response to his 'Hello,' so I just muttered 'Hello' back. I had been briefed that if I encountered the prince I was not obliged to call him 'Sir', because he was the same rank as I was.

As we went to the sink together, having completed our duties, he probably could see that I was feeling a little awkward and in that well-trained royal manner he said, 'We can't go on meeting like this.' I dutifully, but perhaps a little nervously, laughed in response and agreed that we couldn't. I then explained what a 'Crab'[50] was doing at Yeovilton. We then went our separate ways. Some time later I realised that when he had stood beside me I should have said, 'So this is the royal wee?' But I didn't – another chance that will never come my way again.

Paddy and I had only one week back at base before we were on the road again, this time to the Radar Research Squadron at Pershore in Worcestershire. There I flew several standardisation sorties and managed to get a lift back to Cottesmore in the unit's two-seat Gloster Meteor; the second time I had flown in that wonderful old flying machine. It was as smooth as ever. I was really enjoying this job; it was a shame that most of my flying was still in the T4!

Another week at Cottesmore was followed by a visit to RAF West Raynham in Norfolk to fly with crews from the target facilities units of 85 and 100 squadrons. We had a very full programme there, which took up almost two weeks. I flew with several of my old students and other acquaintances from the past. I also managed to talk my way into flying a couple of typical sorties in the Canberra T19, which was used by the squadrons. On one of them I towed a 'flag' and flew around while fighter pilots made holes in it. The take-off was very interesting because the flag, with its long towing cable, is laid out beside the aircraft on the runway. The take-off technique is slightly modified to ensure that the flag is pulled cleanly off the ground. Once airborne I was not really aware that it was there.

The T19 was a B2 that had, at one time, been modified to carry a radar in the nose. In that role it was used for training night fighter navigators for the Javelin force. Since that big triangular fighter was no longer in service the radars had been removed and replaced with a weight made out of concrete. This made for a really good in-house joke amongst the guys on 85 and 100 squadrons. When they went to other bases, especially American ones, and they were asked, 'What's the type of radar you guys have?' the response was, 'Well it's very secret but its code name is Blue Circle.'[51]

'Gee, how good is it?'

'If I told you that I would have to shoot you.'

32 BACK TO SCHOOL

The year was coming to a close, the nights were drawing in and I was bound for pastures new on Salisbury Plain. Despite having gone through it once, the second ETPS Selection Board in the summer had been no easier than the first. But within a few weeks I had received confirmation of my place on No 39 Fixed Wing Test Pilots' Course. It came as no surprise to find that the school wanted me there a month before the start date in early February because the standard of my mathematics had been only marginally acceptable and I needed extra tuition. Although a little daunted, I was very happy to comply. By Christmas of 1974 I had handed over my desk to my replacement and flown down to Boscombe Down in a Canberra B2 to 'March In'[52] to our next home, OMQ No 10 Bawdsey Road. The house was almost brand new, having been built in 1973 and had only been occupied by the German Air Force exchange student on the 1974 ETPS course.

As I had flown down the afternoon prior to the 'March In' my navigator and I stayed in the Officers' Mess overnight. While we were in the bar, having a pre-prandial aperitif, three officers in uniform came in. They said hello, but stayed together chatting. From their youthful postures and faces I thought that they were three flight lieutenants, but when I looked closer two of them had Wing Commander's rank-tapes on their shoulders; the other one was indeed of the lower rank. I wondered whether they were test pilots and whether they had been flying some new shiny machine on some sort of exciting test flight.

I didn't have the bottle to introduce myself so I just carried on wondering while chatting to my nav and the barman. Many months later I found out that the Wing Commanders were David Bywater and Clive Rustin and the flight lieutenant was Colin Cruickshanks. It transpired that the three were together because Wing Commander Bywater was leading a Board of Inquiry into the loss of the two-seat Jaguar that the other two had been flying. It had entered an unrecoverable manoeuvre during a handling and performance flight test involving hard turns in a new configuration. The pilots had had to resort to 'Martin Baker let-downs', using their ejection seats. This sort of incident was rare, but not unknown, in the world of flight testing and was, in this instance, not attributable to any lack of ability on the part of these two test pilots, both of whom would become holders of the Air Force Cross, not once but twice each.

These three men would eventually play different but important roles in my test flying life. About a year later I would graduate from the ETPS course and go to the Weapons Flight of the Experimental Flying Squadron at the Royal Aircraft Establishment at Farnborough where Wg Cdr David Bywater was OC Flying. He would therefore be my second reporting officer, that is my Boss's Boss, and we would go on to build up a good working and personal relationship. In the small world of military test flying he would be my Boss's Boss twice more, always staying two ranks ahead of me as I progressed up the ladder. I had then and still have a great respect for David and we remain friends to this day.

Wg Cdr Clive Rustin was OC A Squadron at Boscombe Down, which was the unit that tested all military fighters and trainers. But it wasn't until some years later that I got to know Clive much better and we also remain in touch to this day. Colin Cruickshanks was one of the A Squadron Jaguar Project Test Pilots at the time I was at ETPS so I used to see him in passing. Later, however, he and I worked together briefly at HQ RAF Strike Command at High Wycombe and then Colin was my boss during the last part of my final RAF test-flying tour, eighteen years later! Little did I know watching those three having a drink together what the future would bring and how they would become such a part of the tapestry of the rest of my life.

My very last sortie at No 231 OCU was with Paddy Thompson, who renewed both my Instrument Rating and my A2 Instructional Category before I entered the new and esoteric world of the Test Pilot. A world in which I would stay for the majority of the rest of my flying career, both in and out of the RAF. That part of my story, dear reader, is yet to come!

NOTES

1 For the full story please see my book *A Bucket of Sunshine* published by The History Press in 2012.

2 A hiring was an off-base house rented by the RAF and occupied by an officer and his family who paid the same charges as if he occupied a married quarter. Before a change to the rules that came later, 25 years of age was deemed by the armed forces to be the minimum age at which officers should marry. Thus any entitlement to subsidised service accommodation was reckoned to be inappropriate!

3 The Westland Wapiti was a lumbering 1930s biplane that saw most of its service in the Middle East.

4 The Hawker Tempest was a high performance 1940s single-seat fighter and fighter-bomber with a large radial engine of over 2,000hp.

5 The first person to build a working four-stroke engine, a stationary engine using a coal gas-air mixture for fuel (a gas engine), was German engineer Nikolaus Otto. This is why the four-stroke principle today is commonly known as the Otto cycle and four-stroke engines using spark plugs often are called Otto engines.

6 The metal propeller, rotating at nearly 2,000rpm, acts like a gyroscope. So when a force is applied to the disc, in this case trying to rotate it forwards, then that force is transposed through 90° in the direction of rotation, so trying to twist the aeroplane sideways – what's known as yaw. The rudder is then needed to stop the yaw and keep the aircraft going in a straight line down the runway.

7 The mnemonic stood for: **M**ixture – fully rich, **F**uel – selected on and check contents, **F**laps – up, **H**ood – closed and locked, **H**arness – tight, **B**rakes – set.

8 The White IR added specific extra heights above the minima allowed for instrument approaches to the zero additions conferred by the Green IR. This reflected one's lack of experience on the aircraft type and the test could still be passed with broader limits of accuracy.

9 'Standard NATO' was RAF shorthand for 'coffee, white with two sugars'.

10 These days this manoeuvre is known as the Avalanche.

11 The RAF Regiment is an arm of the service for people who wanted to join the army but prefer blue to khaki and dislike getting too dirty. The

Regiment's war role is the ground and air defence of airbases. They are also good at doing drill properly, unlike most RAF personnel.

12   I believe that Roy Cope-Lewis later became an All England Tennis Club umpire and did duty at several Wimbledon Championships.

13   The 'Quiet Frequency' was one that all CFS aircraft could use. It was monitored by the air traffic controllers but not used for direction by them; so it was what it said on the label: quiet.

14   Holding posts were allocated for personnel having to wait appreciable periods for their next posting. These were most commonly used for students waiting between flying courses.

15   *Ab initio* students were those that had not flown previously under instruction and had yet to go solo.

16   About a year later I was making an identical approach down the side of this hill when there was a bang. On inspection after landing it was discovered that we had been hit by a golf ball!

17   A common and somewhat derogatory term for light, usually privately operated, aircraft.

18   The Air Navigation Order (ANO) is a collection of all the laws, enacted by Parliament, to regulate all aviation activity over the UK.

19   This exam was abolished just a few years later.

20   In those days there were no student loans. The students received a small grant.

21   The 'Bingo' call was made when a pre-agreed fuel level had been reached. This gave the formation leader a feel for how the fuel plan for each aircraft in the formation was actually working out.

22   Run-in-and-break is RAF terminology for the arrival of a single or formation of aircraft by flying level down the runway and then making a very sharp roll and turn to then fly parallel with runway and slow down to landing speed. In a formation break a two or three second pause is observed between each aircraft's 'break' turn.

23   See *A Bucket of Sunshine* by this author, published by The History Press, 2012.

24   IFR means Instrument Flight Rules and is the published procedure for leaving the airfield and its airspace if you were in cloud.

25   For our younger readers a 'bob' was a shilling. Post decimalisation in February 1971 a shilling became worth 5 pence.

26   See *A Bucket of Sunshine* by this author, published by The History Press in 2012.

27   Safety Altitude is calculated as 1,500ft above the highest obstacle within the area that the flight is passing through. There's a bit more to it than that, but it will suffice to say that if you fly at the correctly calculated Safety Altitude you will not bump into any solid bits.

28 A ceilidh (pronounced caylie) is an often rather wild Scottish musical gathering with lots of songs in Gaelic.

29 The ailerons are small hinged flaps at the back of the outer part of the wings. They move up and down when the control stick is moved left or right and roll the aircraft around its longitudinal axis.

30 In a 1970s episode of *The Morecambe and Wise Show* the main guest was the world famous musician and conductor André Previn. During one sketch, when Eric's appalling piano playing was criticised by Mr Previn, Eric responded with: 'I am playing all the right notes, but not necessarily in the right order.'

31 There are always two diversions; one in case the weather deteriorates below limits for recovery to base and one in case the runway gets blocked; the latter is usually the closest.

32 Precision Approach Radar – two radar beams give the controller the ability to guide the aircraft down the ideal approach path in azimuth and 3° glidepath simultaneously. It is the most precise of all radar guided approach aids.

33 Safety altitude was 1,500ft above the highest ground or obstacle within a given area which were marked on our maps.

34 As related in Chapter 27 of my book *A Bucket of Sunshine* published by The History Press, 2012.

35 Service speak for Unserviceable.

36 Birdland is, as its name suggests, a collection of many bird species in the grounds of an old manor in the village. It is open to the public and a very popular visitor attraction.

37 Canberra crews often referred to the MRCA as 'Must Refurbish the Canberra Again'.

38 'Three greens' indicates that the wheels are down and locked and the 'roll' call indicates that we were going to land and then take off again without stopping; these days often known as a touch-and-go.

39 Just as applied to alcohol consumption, we were not supposed to fly after taking analgesics.

40 The HP Cock controls the fuel at its entry to the engine fuel system. Closing this stops the fuel going to the engine and the engine runs down rapidly; thrust ceases within a second.

41 A 'Jolly' was a term given to anything that might be seen as a non-essential event and which may have been loosely termed as 'fun'.

42 Yogi Bear was a very popular cartoon character of the day.

43 I think that the 'Night Flying Supper' of bacon, sausage, egg and chips was a relic from the Second World War. It was free and only available if you

had flown in the dark. It always made me think of the old Bomber Boys' line 'You can have my egg if I don't come back.' However, we usually washed it down with beer rather than steaming mugs of tea!

44   Aide-de-Camp means a very senior officer's Man Friday or, as more frequently referred to, Dogsbody.

45   This is covered in much more detail by Bill Larkworthy in his autobiography *Doctor Lark*, published by Mosaïque Press, 2010.

46   The letters indicate the three main occupational areas for aircrew: A – Airborne duties, G – Ground duties, and Z – Geographical Zone. The numbers run from one to four, one being unlimited, and four being severely limited. The exact restrictions are given in the rubric that accompanies this rating system.

47   Largest by surface area. Kielder Reservoir in Northumberland is England's largest by volume.

48   The pilot's ejection seats in the Canberra B2 had two operating handles. One, known as the top handle or face blind, was above the pilot's head. The other was on the top edge of the seat pan, between the pilot's thighs. Later seats deleted the top handle.

49   Lightning T5 XS 422 would re-enter my life the following year when it arrived at ETPS. I would fly it on the course and, a few years later, as an ETPS Fixed Wing Tutor. XS 422 is now in the USA where some brave soul is refurbishing it to fly. I'm not sure what the FAA will have to say about that!

50   Crab is Navy-speak for an RAF person.

51   Blue Circle was (and still is) a well-known Portland cement brand.

52   'March In' was the quaint military term used for the formal take-over of service-provided housing. 'March Out' was the term for the handover, back to the Station.

APPENDIX
COCKPIT ILLUSTRATIONS

The following images of three of the aircraft described in this book are taken from the now unclassified RAF Pilot's Notes that were issued to all pilots who would fly the aircraft, along with the Flight Reference Cards (FRCs) that gave all the normal and emergency procedures for the correct and safe operation of the aeroplane.

Each image is accompanied by numbered keys to identify all the instruments, switches and levers in the cockpit.

The three cockpits illustrated are:

- The De Havilland Chipmunk T Mk 10
- The English Electric Canberra T Mk 4
- The English Electric Canberra PR Mk 9

All images reproduced by kind permission of Mach One Manuals.

CHIPMUNK T10 – FRONT COCKPIT

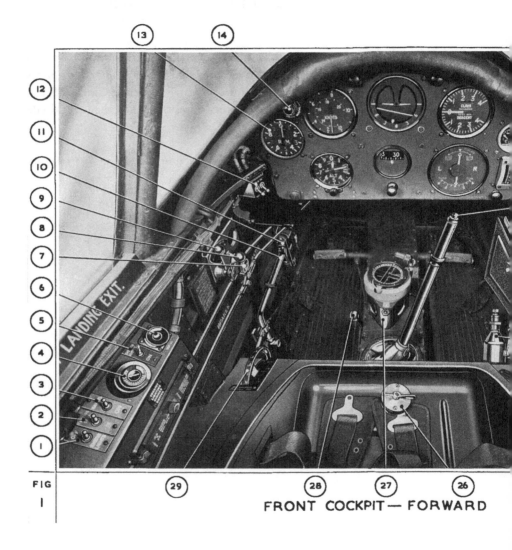

FRONT COCKPIT — FORWARD

FIG
1

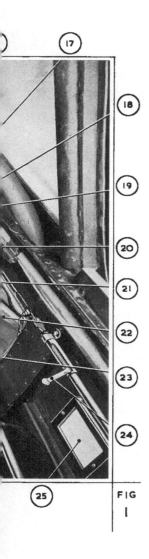

1. Emergency lamp switch.
2. Taxying lamp switch.
3. Navigation lights switch.
4. Cockpit lamps OFF and dimmer switch.
5. Identification light switch.
6. Identification light morsing pushbutton.
7. Throttle and mixture controls friction nut.
8. Mixture control lever.
9. Throttle control lever.
10. Brake lever.
11. Ground/flight switch.
12. Ignition switches.
13. R.p.m. indicator.
14. Generator failure warning light.
15. Oil temperature gauge.
16. Oil pressure gauge.
17. Cartridge starter control.
18. V.H.F. radio controller.
19. Press-to-transmit pushbutton.
20. Flap lever.
21. Amber screens stowage.
22. Goggles stowage.
23. Hand fire-extinguisher.
24. Carburettor air-intake control.
25. Compass deviation card holder.
26. Harness release box.
27. Compass lamp switch.
28. Fuel cock control.
29. Elevator trimmer wheel.
30. Harness release box.
31. Elevator trimmer wheel.
32. Cockpit lamps OFF and dimmer switch.
33. Front cockpit lamps override switch.
34. Emergency lamp switch.
35. Ignition switches.
36. Throttle control.
37. Mixture control.
38. Throttle and mixture controls friction nut.
39. Brakes control.
40. R.p.m. indicator.
41. Press-to-transmit pushbutton.
42. Compass lamp switch.
43. Fuel cock control.
44. Maps case.
45. Oil temperature gauge.
46. Oil pressure gauge.
47. Air-intake heat control.
48. Flaps control.
49. V.H.F. change-over switch.
50. V.H.F. radio controller.
51. V.H.F. muting switch.
52. Compass deviation card holder.
53. Mic-tel socket.

NOTE.—(i) In the front cockpit the following items are hidden by the seat: Maps case, Pilot's Notes stowage and Tel-mic socket.

(ii) The following items are not shown: Pressure head heater switch, generator test switch, safety flap over cartridge starter control.

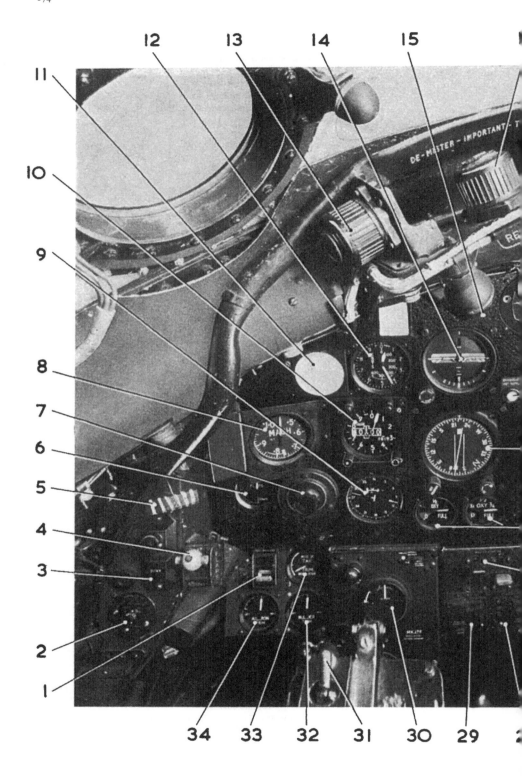

CANBERRA T4 – STUDENT'S INSTRUMENT PANELS

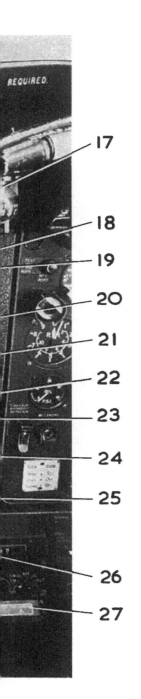

1 Undercarriage master switch
2 Undercarriage position indicator (pupil)
3 Undercarriage selector switch unit
4 Flaps selector switch (pupil)
5 Undercarriage emergency lowering control
6 Flaps position indicator
7 Ventilation louvre
8 Machmeter
9 Tacan indicator
10 Altimeter
11 Direct vision panel (pupil)
12 Airspeed indicator (pupil)
13 Dimmer switch (port U/V lamps)
14 Horizon gyro unit
15 Marker light (on panel behind U/V lamp)
16 Dimmer switch (port red lamps)
17 Standby compass
18 ILS indicator
19 ILS control switch
20 Zero reader indicator
21 Emergency instrument supply MI
22 Vertical speed indicator
23 Mk 4B compass
24 Turn and slip indicator
25 Oxygen contents gauges
26 No 1 and No 2 engine master starting switches
27 V/UHF control unit
28 No 2 engine ignition switch and starter pushbutton
29 No 1 engine ignition switch and starter pushbutton
30 Oxygen regulator (pupil)
31 Airbrakes control switch (pupil)
32 Rudder trim indicator
33 Tail trim indicator
34 Aileron trim indicator

CANBERRA T4 – LEFT-HAND SIDE

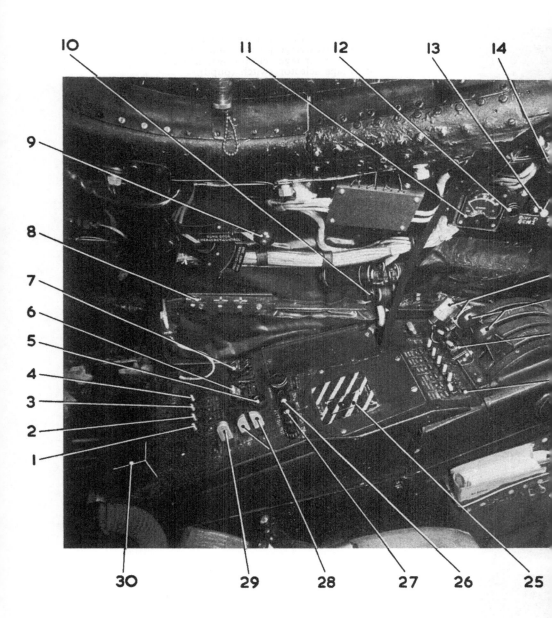

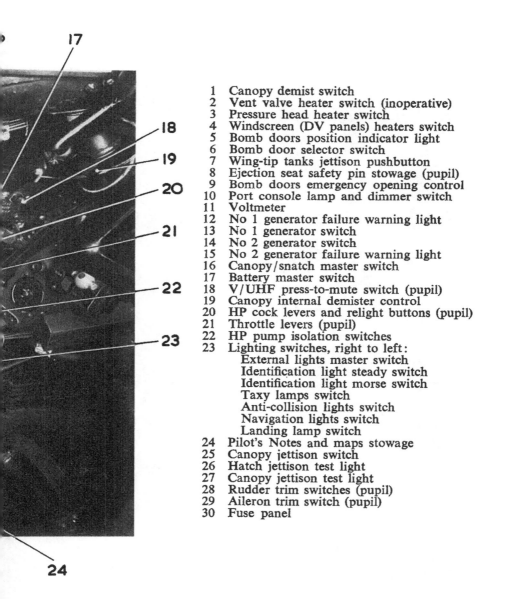

1 Canopy demist switch
2 Vent valve heater switch (inoperative)
3 Pressure head heater switch
4 Windscreen (DV panels) heaters switch
5 Bomb doors position indicator light
6 Bomb door selector switch
7 Wing-tip tanks jettison pushbutton
8 Ejection seat safety pin stowage (pupil)
9 Bomb doors emergency opening control
10 Port console lamp and dimmer switch
11 Voltmeter
12 No 1 generator failure warning light
13 No 1 generator switch
14 No 2 generator switch
15 No 2 generator failure warning light
16 Canopy/snatch master switch
17 Battery master switch
18 V/UHF press-to-mute switch (pupil)
19 Canopy internal demister control
20 HP cock levers and relight buttons (pupil)
21 Throttle levers (pupil)
22 HP pump isolation switches
23 Lighting switches, right to left:
    External lights master switch
    Identification light steady switch
    Identification light morse switch
    Taxy lamps switch
    Anti-collision lights switch
    Navigation lights switch
    Landing lamp switch
24 Pilot's Notes and maps stowage
25 Canopy jettison switch
26 Hatch jettison test light
27 Canopy jettison test light
28 Rudder trim switches (pupil)
29 Aileron trim switch (pupil)
30 Fuse panel

CANBERRA T4 – INSTRUCTOR'S INSTRUMENT PANELS

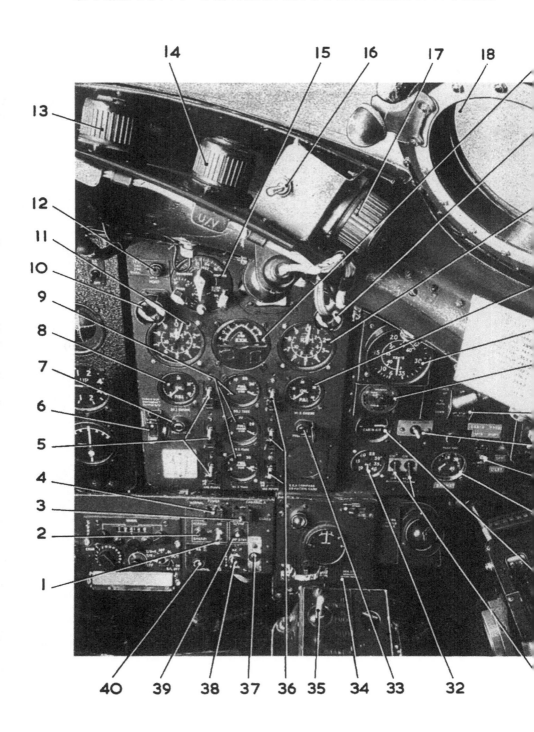

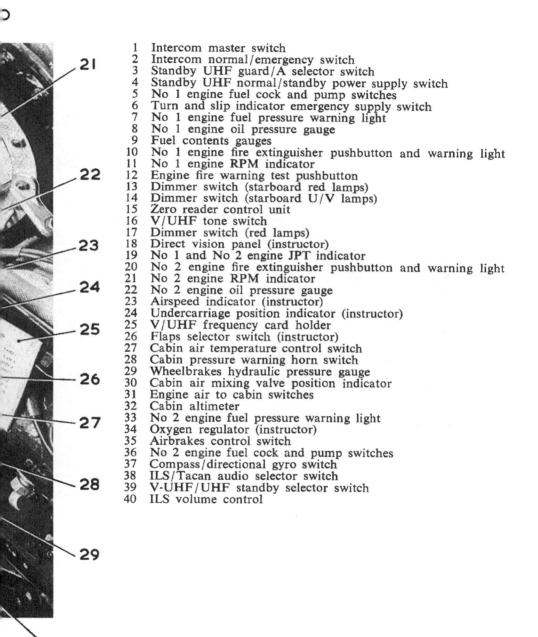

1 Intercom master switch
2 Intercom normal/emergency switch
3 Standby UHF guard/A selector switch
4 Standby UHF normal/standby power supply switch
5 No 1 engine fuel cock and pump switches
6 Turn and slip indicator emergency supply switch
7 No 1 engine fuel pressure warning light
8 No 1 engine oil pressure gauge
9 Fuel contents gauges
10 No 1 engine fire extinguisher pushbutton and warning light
11 No 1 engine RPM indicator
12 Engine fire warning test pushbutton
13 Dimmer switch (starboard red lamps)
14 Dimmer switch (starboard U/V lamps)
15 Zero reader control unit
16 V/UHF tone switch
17 Dimmer switch (red lamps)
18 Direct vision panel (instructor)
19 No 1 and No 2 engine JPT indicator
20 No 2 engine fire extinguisher pushbutton and warning light
21 No 2 engine RPM indicator
22 No 2 engine oil pressure gauge
23 Airspeed indicator (instructor)
24 Undercarriage position indicator (instructor)
25 V/UHF frequency card holder
26 Flaps selector switch (instructor)
27 Cabin air temperature control switch
28 Cabin pressure warning horn switch
29 Wheelbrakes hydraulic pressure gauge
30 Cabin air mixing valve position indicator
31 Engine air to cabin switches
32 Cabin altimeter
33 No 2 engine fuel pressure warning light
34 Oxygen regulator (instructor)
35 Airbrakes control switch
36 No 2 engine fuel cock and pump switches
37 Compass/directional gyro switch
38 ILS/Tacan audio selector switch
39 V-UHF/UHF standby selector switch
40 ILS volume control

CANBERRA PR9 COCKPIT – MAIN INSTRUMENT PANELS

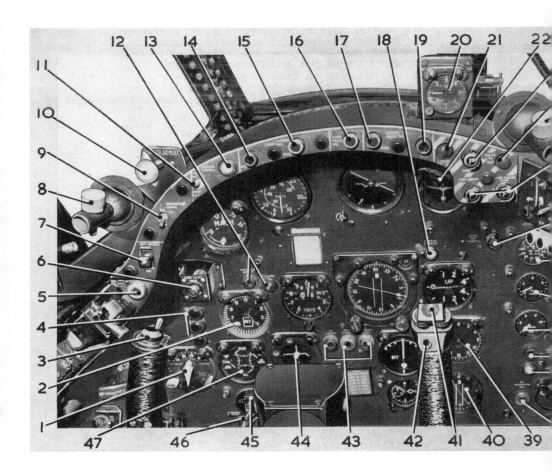

A&AEE   Aeroplane and Armaments Experimental Establishment
AEO   Air Electronics Officer
ACR   Annual Confidential Report
ADC   Aide de Camp
agl   Above Ground Level
amsl   Above mean sea level
AH   Artificial Horizon

1. Zero reader combined heading selector and control unit
2. Radio altimeter
3. F.95 camera button
4. Radio altimeter limit light
5. Crew call light
6. Dump valve "open" light
7. Anti-dazzle lights BRIGHT/DIM switch
8. Cabin heating louvre control
9. Emergency lights ON/OFF switch
10. Windscreen demisting control handle
11. Aileron gear change LOW/HIGH altitude switch
12. Oxygen remote flow indicators
13. Aileron gear change indicator
14. Rudder 50% hydraulic failure light (amber)
15. Rudder 100% hydraulic failure light (red)
16. Cabin pressure failure light
17. Aileron 100% failure light
18. Standby inverter indicator
19. Aileron 50% hydraulic failure light (amber)
20. Accelerometer
21. Fuselage fire warning light press-to-test pushbutton
22. Zero reader indicator
23. Fuselage and photoflash bay fire warning light
24. Engine fire warning lights press-to-test pushbutton
25. Cabin heating louvre control
26. Engine fire warning lights
27. Standby UHF control panel
28. Reset No. 2 inverter pushbutton
29. F.95 camera indicator lights
30. Port engine RPM indicator
31. Oxygen contents gauge
32. JPT indicators
33. Fuel flowmeters
34. Fuel pressure failure lights
35. Oil pressure failure indicators
36. Starboard generator failure light
37. DC voltmeter
38. Port generator failure light
39. Radio compass bearing indicator
40. Auto pilot heading selector
41. Tailplane trim switches
42. Press-to-transmit switch
43. Left to right:
    ILS marker light
    F.49 camera pre-exposure light
    Flashes going indicator
44. ILS indicator
45. Auto pilot remote trim indicator
46. Auto pilot READY and ENGAGED indicators
47. Combined trim indicator

CANBERRA PR9 – LEFT-HAND SIDE

1. Oxygen line valve
2. Switches from outboard to inboard:
   Anti-collision lights ON/OFF
   Navigation lights ON/OFF
   Taxying lamps ON/OFF
   Landing lamps HIGH (forward)/LOW/OFF
   Identification lights STEADY (forward)/OFF/MORSE
   External lights master ON/OFF
3. Photoflash bay doors emergency open selector lever
4. Canopy port aft locking pin indicator
5. Switches, from outboard to inboard:
   PHOTOFLASH JETTISON/off/DOORS DELAY OVER-
   RIDE
   PHOTOFLASH DOORS OPEN/CLOSED (door position
   indicators forward of switches)
   Engine ANTI-ICING PORT and STARBOARD ON/OFF
   (indicators forward of switches)
6. Canopy port forward locking pin indicator
7. ABANDON/NORMAL and DUMP/NORMAL switches
8. Airbrakes IN/MID/OUT switch
9. Wing drop tanks jettison button (Guarded)
10. Undercarriage position indicator
11. Rudder auto stabiliser control switch
12. Undercarriage emergency lowering handle
13. Undercarriage UP/DOWN pushbuttons
14. Flap position indicator
15. Flap selector lever
16. Canopy unlocking switch (guarded)
17. Throttle/HP cock levers friction adjuster
18. JPT control master switches. Forward pair ON/OFF, rear
    pair CRUISE/MAX
19. Combined throttle and HP cock levers
20. Tailplane incident control switch
21. Rudder trim control switch
22. Aileron trim control switch
23. Canopy independent jettison handle (under flap)

CANBERRA PR9 – RIGHT-HAND SIDE

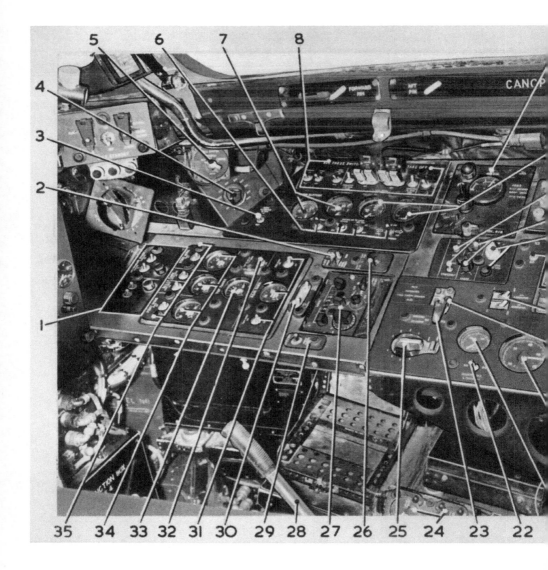

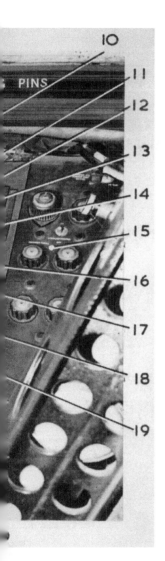

1. Engine starter panel:
   Port and starboard engine master start and ignition switches
   Port and starboard engine starter pushbuttons
2. UHF LOWER/UPPER aerial switch
   UHF TONE switch
3. Radio altimeter ON/OFF switch
4. Radio altimeter height band selector
5. Roll damper OFF/STANDBY/ENGAGE switch
6. Switches left to right:
   COMPASS/D.GYRO
   Port engine air switch
   Starboard engine air switch
   Cabin air temperature COLD/HOT switch
7. Cabin altimeter
   Services system hydraulic pressure gauge
8. Take-off panel, switches, left to right:
   Canopy demist
   Pitot head heater
   Vent valve heater
   Port integral tank LP cock/transfer cock
   Port engine master LP cock
   Starboard engine master LP cock
   Starboard integral tank LP cock/transfer cock
   Battery master switch
9. Pilot's oxygen regulator
10. Brakes hydraulic pressure gauge
    Air conditioning mixing valve position indicator
11. Intercomm. ON/OFF switch
    Intercomm. NORMAL/EMERGENCY switch
12. Auto pilot control panel
13. ILS volume control (top)
    V/UHF volume control
14. RC/MIX RT-HF selector
    Press-to-call navigator button
15. Cockpit lighting control panel
16. ILS ON/OFF switch
17. ILS channel selector
18. Generator ON/OFF switches
19. Generator field circuit breakers
20. AC frequency meter
21. AC voltmeter
22. No. 1/No. 2 INVERTER VOLTAGE and FREQ selector switch
23. No. 1/No. 2 inverter selector switch
24. Rudder feel simulator primary and secondary pressure gauges
25. Auto pilot controller
26. UHF STBY/HF/UHF-VHF selector
27. V/UHF controller
28. Hydraulic handpump handle
29. UHF-VHF press-to-mute switch
30. HF master ON/OFF switch
    HF LOW/HIGH output switch
31. Rear fuel tank port LP pump ON/OFF switch
    Rear fuel tank contents gauge
    Rear fuel tank starboard LP pump ON/OFF switch
32. Top tanks to belly tank fuel transfer cock
33. Top tanks fuel contents gauge
34. Port integral tank fuel contents gauge
    Belly tank fuel contents gauge
    Starboard integral tank fuel contents gauge
35. Port integral tank LP pump switch
    Belly tank port LP pump switch
    Belly tank starboard LP pump switch
    Starboard integral tank LP pump switch

GLOSSARY OF ABBREVIATIONS

APO	Acting Pilot Officer
ATC	Air Traffic Control
BAC	British Aircraft Corporation
CFI	Chief Flying Instructor
CFS	The Central Flying School of the Royal Air Force
CGI	Chief Ground Instructor
DH	De Havilland Aircraft
DI	Direction Indicator
EFATO	Engine Failure After Take-Off
EOKA	A Cypriot terrorist group active in the 1950s and '60s
ETPS	The Empire Test Pilots' School
Flt Lt	Flight Lieutenant
fpm	Feet per minute
FRADU	Fleet Requirements Aircraft Direction Unit
FSO	Flight Safety Officer
ft	Feet
Gp Capt.	Group Captain
hp	Horsepower
HQ	Headquarters
IR	Instrument Rating
IRT	Instrument Rating Test
IRE	Instrument Rating Examiner
JCSS	Junior Command and Staff School
JP	Jet Provost
kts	Knots
kW	Kilowatts
MAFF	Ministry of Agriculture, Food and Fishery
MOD	Ministry of Defence
NATO	North Atlantic Treaty Organisation
NCO	Non-Commissioned Officer
OC	Officer Commanding
OCU	Operational Conversion Unit
OMQ	Officers' Married Quarters
PAR	Precision Approach Radar

PC	Permanent Commission
PR	Photographic Reconnaissance
QFI	Qualified Flying Instructor
QHI	Qualified Helicopter Instructor
RAF	Royal Air Force
RAFVR	Royal Air Force Volunteer Reserve
RNAS	Royal Naval Air Station
rpm	Revolutions per minute
SATCO	Senior Air Traffic Controller
SBAC	Society of British Aircraft Companies
SFSO	Station Flight Safety Officer
Sqn Ldr	Squadron Leader
SWO	Station Warrant Officer
UAS	University Air Squadron
UGSAS	The Universities of Glasgow and Strathclyde Air Squadron
U/S	Unserviceable
USAF	United States Air Force
Wg Cdr	Wing Commander

INDEX

If you enjoyed this book, you may also be interested in …

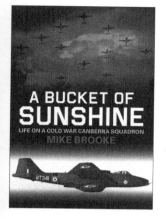

A Bucket of Sunshine
MIKE BROOKE

A Bucket of Sunshine – a term used for the use of a nuclear bomb – is a first-hand insight into life in the mid-1960s on an RAF Canberra nuclear-armed squadron in West Germany on the frontline in the Cold War. Mike Brookes describes not only the technical aspect of the aircraft and its nuclear and conventional roles and weapons, but also majors on the low-level flying that went with the job of being ready to go to war at less than three minutes notice. Brooke tells his story warts and all, with many amusing overtones, in what was an extremely serious business when the world was standing on the brink of nuclear conflict.

978 0 7524 7021 4

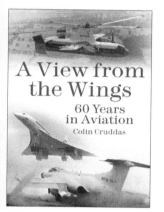

A View from the Wings
COLIN CRUDDAS

A View from the Wings is unique, recalling a wartime boyhood in which aircraft flying constantly overhead played a large part. This experience led to a lifetime career in the aviation industry both in the UK and overseas. Mixed with events of a more personal nature, often coated with whimsical humour, the author has evocatively captured the rise and demise of Britain's aircraft industry in the post-war period. In setting out to be non-technical, this book will appeal to those whose memories embrace the sound barrier-breaking years and the leap of faith and technology that saw Concorde defeat the Americans in the race to produce a practical supersonic airliner.

978 0 7524 7748 0

Spitfire's Forgotten Designer
MIKE ROUSSEL

Whenever the Spitfire is mentioned, the name of its designer R.J. Mitchell comes to mind. However, Mitchell died in June 1937 and never saw his prototype design progress into becoming one of the most famous fighter aircraft of the Second World War. Working under Mitchell as chief draughtsman was Joe Smith. After Mitchell's death, Smith first became manager of the design department, and then chief designer. This illustrated book celebrates the inspirational and innovative work of Mitchell, Smith and their successful design team. Including first-hand accounts of members of the design team and apprentices, it reveals a little-known but pivotal figure.

978 0 7524 8759 5

Visit our website and discover thousands of other History Press books.

www.thehistorypress.co.uk

Lightning Source UK Ltd.
Milton Keynes UK
UKOW07f0412201114

241871UK00001B/7/P